Contents

Plates

Acknowledgement

The publishers are grateful to the Folger Library, Washington, DC for permission to reproduce the stage-plan of *The Castle of Perseverance* (V.a.354, f. 191v).

STRATFORD-UPON-AVON STUDIES 16

General Editors

MALCOLM BRADBURY
& DAVID PALMER

Already published in this series

* *Under the general editorship of John Russell Brown and Bernard Harris*

STRATFORD-UPON-AVON STUDIES 16

MEDIEVAL DRAMA

ASSOCIATE EDITOR
NEVILLE DENNY

EDWARD ARNOLD

© EDWARD ARNOLD (PUBLISHERS) LTD 1973

First published 1973 by
Edward Arnold (Publishers) Ltd
25 Hill Street, London W1X 8LL

Cloth edition ISBN: 0 7131 5688 0
Paper edition ISBN: 0 7131 5689 9

Printed in Great Britain by
Butler & Tanner Ltd, Frome and London

Preface

RECENT YEARS have seen a marked shift of interest where drama studies are concerned from the private encounter with the printed play-text (essentially a literary interest) to the total theatrical experience for which the text exists as a properly dramatic blueprint. As a direct consequence of this, and stimulated by the remarkable theatrical success of a number of important medieval plays in recent revelatory revivals, more and more attention has come to be given to the native dramatic inheritance of the Elizabethan and Jacobean play-makers. The essays in this volume offer a collective survey of a few important aspects of that tradition.

Richard Axton looks at the earlier medieval English drama, concentrating on the popular elements in it that have had less attention than they deserve and which he shows to be considerably more important than has generally been supposed. David Bevington is in part concerned with much the same theme in his study of the distinct but complementary traditions affecting the evolution of Tudor staging forms. Like Richard Axton, he gives some attention to the morality play *Mankind*, in many ways a crucial play in any consideration of the theatrical principles informing early English drama.

Paula Neuss offers a close analysis of the metaphorical strategy, in properly theatrical terms, operating in the same play to precise homiletic ends. (She has the advantage of having been associated with a notable Canadian revival of the work.) Similar homiletic considerations are involved in the dramatic genre David Jeffrey goes on to discuss, that of the English Saints' play, a badly neglected area of medieval drama studies, and one in which popular elements can be seen uniting with homiletic and romantic ones in the shaping of a unique dramatic form.

The great Corpus Christi cycles attract special attention. Arnold Williams concerns himself with the nature of comedy in the cycles; while T. W. Craik treats the parallel subject of violence. The importance of both these elements to our understanding of medieval drama is being increasingly recognized, expressive as they are of a radical feature of the gothic imagination at work in these plays. With the sublime and the terrible they lie close to the heart of the religious apprehension of reality, and provide both the psychological and the philosophical means for coming to terms with the presence of evil in human experience.

I myself offer an analysis of staging issues in the Cornish Passion play (part two of the cycle that stands as one of the chief landmarks of celtic culture in these islands), while at the same time trying to demonstrate something of its extraordinary dramatic quality. Martial Rose attempts much the same with his detailed analysis of the staging and presentation of the Hegge cycle, a work that possesses suggestive affinities with the Cornish cycle in its presentation and internal dynamics.

Kevin Roddy discusses the epic character of the miracle cycles, breaking important new ground in his approach and inviting research into the evolutionary processes linking this strain of early English drama with the chronicle plays of the Elizabethan period. John Elliott, in a thought-provoking consideration of 'epic' and spectacular staging in the early Elizabethan theatre, is concerned with organic connections of a parallel order.

Between them the essays confirm the importance of a deeper appreciation of the medieval dramatic tradition to our fuller understanding of the dynamics of the Elizabethan stage.

NEVILLE DENNY
February 1973

Bibliographical Note

The following works are referred to widely in this volume. The abbreviations indicated (in Sections A and B) are used throughout in reference to them.

A. Texts:

BM   *Beunans Meriasek:* the Life of St. Meriasek, ed. and tr. Whitley Stokes (Bristol, 1872).

CP   *The Chester Plays,* ed. Hermann Deimling and J. Matthews (EETS, Oxford, 1892, 1916).

CPD   *Chief Pre-Shakespearean Drama,* ed. J. Q. Adams (Boston, 1924).

CC   *The Ancient Cornish Drama,* ed. Edwin Norris (Oxford, 1859, 2 vols.).

DP   *The Digby Plays,* ed. F. J. Furnivall (EETS, Oxford, 1896).

DMC   *The Drama of the Medieval Church,* ed. Karl Young (Oxford, 1933, 2 vols.).

GB   *Gwreans an Bys: the Creation of the World,* ed. and tr. Whitley Stokes (Berlin, 1863).

LC   *Ludus Coventriae,* ed. K. S. Block (EETS, Oxford, 1922).

MP   *The Macro Plays,* ed. Mark Eccles (EETS, Oxford, 1969).

MSR   Malone Society Reprints.

NCP   *Non-Cycle Plays and Fragments,* ed. N. Davis (EETS, Oxford, 1970).

OEP   *A Select Collection of Old English Plays,* ed. R. Dodsley and W. Carew Haxlitt (London, 1874-6, 15 vols.).

TFT   Tudor Facsimile Texts.

TP   *The Towneley Plays,* ed. George England and Alfred W. Pollard (EETS, Oxford, 1897).

CCP   *Two Coventry Corpus Christi Plays,* ed. Hardin Craig (EETS, Oxford, 1902).

YP   *York Mystery Plays,* ed. Lucy Toulmin Smith (Oxford, 1885; reprinted New York, 1963).

B. Scholarship:

Imagery   M. D. Anderson, *Drama and Imagery in English Medieval Churches* (Cambridge, 1963).

Mimesis   Erich Auerbach, *Mimesis,* tr. Willard Trask (New York, 1946; reprinted Princeton, 1968).

M–M   D. M. Bevington, *From Mankind to Marlowe* (London, 1962).

ES   E. K. Chambers, *The Elizabethan Stage* (Oxford, 1923, 4 vols.).

MS   E. K. Chambers, *The Medieval Stage* (Oxford, 1903, 2 vols.).

ERD   Hardin Craig, *English Religious Drama of the Middle Ages* (Oxford, 1955).

TI   T. W. Craik, *The Tudor Interlude* (Leicester, 1958).

ME   H. C. Gardiner, *Mysteries End* (New Haven, 1946).

Annals A. Harbage and S. Schoenbaum, *Annals of English Drama* (London, 1964).

CRCD O. B. Hardison, *Christian Rite and Christian Drama* (Baltimore, 1965).

PCC   V. A. Kolve, *The Play Called Corpus Christi* (London, 1966).

L–P   G. R. Owst, *Literature and Pulpit in Medieval England* (Oxford, 1961, 2nd edn.).

DR   E. Prosser, *Drama and Religion in the English Mystery Plays* (Stanford, 1961).

HLEL *History of Literature in the English Language*, Vol. III: *English Drama to 1710*, ed. Christopher Ricks (London, 1971).

EDET A. P. Rossiter, *English Drama from Early Times to the Elizabethans* (London, 1950).

MTR   Richard Southern, *Medieval Theatre in the Round* (London, 1957).

SAE   Bernard Spivack, *Shakespeare and the Allegory of Evil* (London, 1958).

EES   Glynne Wickham, *Early English Stages* (London, 1959, 3 vols. projected).

DME   Arnold Williams, *The Drama of Medieval England* (East Lansing, 1961).

ED   F. P. Wilson and G. K. Hunter, *The English Drama, 1485–1585* (OHEL, Oxford, 1969).

EMP   Rosemary Woolf, *The English Mystery Plays* (London, 1972).

C. *Additional Texts:*

Medieval French Plays, ed. and tr. Richard Axton and John Stevens (Oxford, 1971).

Everyman and Medieval Miracle Plays, ed. A. C. Cawley (London, 1956).

The Wakefield Pageants in the Towneley Cycle, ed. A. C. Cawley (Manchester, 1958).

Medieval Interludes, ed. Neville Denny (London, 1972).

The Cornish Ordinalia, ed. and tr. Markham Harris (Washington, 1969).

Specimens of the Pre-Shaksperean Drama, ed. J. M. Manly (Boston, 1897, 2 vols.).

English Miracle Plays, Moralities and Interludes, ed. Alfred W. Pollard (Oxford, 1890).

The York Cycle of Mystery Plays, ed. and modernized J. S. Purvis (London, 1962).

The Wakefield Mystery Plays, ed. and modernized Martial Rose (London, 1961).

English Morality Plays and Moral Interludes, ed. Edgar T. Schell and J. D. Shuchter (New York, 1969).

Ten Miracle Plays, ed. R. G. Thomas (London, 1966).

Note

Texts.
The *Interludium de Clerico et Puella* and *Dame Sirith* are printed in *Early Middle English Verse and Prose*, ed. J. A. W. Bennett and G. V. Smithers (Oxford, 1968, 2nd edn.). The Winchester *Visitatio Sepulchri* is printed by Young, *DMC* and Adams, *CPD*. See also *Le Mystère d'Adam*, ed. P. Aebischer (Paris, 1963); *La Seinte Resureccion*, ed. T. A. Jenkins, *et al.* (Oxford, 1943); Davis, *NCP*; Deimling and Matthews, *CP*; and Eccles *MP*. Translations of the *Adam* and *Resurrection* plays and of *Le Garçon et l'Aveugle* are contained in Axton and Stevens, *Medieval French Plays*.

Scholarship and Criticism.
Survey of dramatic records: Chambers, *MS*, especially Appendices to Vol. II; Young, *DMC*, Appendix D; Harbage, *Annals*.
Interpretations of early dramatic developments: Craig, *ERD*; Wickham, *EES*, Vol. I; Kolve, *PCC*, Chs. 1, 2; Hardison, *CRCD*; Woolf *EMP*. Chs. 3, 4.
Evidence for a secular tradition: Dino Bigongiari, 'Were there Theaters in the Twelfth and Thirteenth Centuries?', *Romanic Review* XXXVII (1946), pp. 201–224; Mary H. Marshall, 'Theatre in the Middle Ages: Evidence from Dictionaries and Glosses', *Symposium* IV (1950), pp. 1–39, 366–89; J. D. A. Ogilvy, '*Mimi, Scurrae, Histriones:* Entertainers in the Middle Ages', *Speculum* XXXVIII (1963), pp. 603–19.
'*Folk*' tradition: E. K. Chambers, *The English Folk Play* (Oxford, 1933); Alan Brody, *The English Mummers and Their Plays* (London, 1971).
Dance-plays: J. Bédier, 'Les plus anciennes danses françaises', *Revue des Deux Mondes* XXXI (1901) i, pp. 398–424; R. L. Greene, *The Early English Carols* (Oxford, 1935).
Preaching and plays: Owst, *L–P.*
The Anglo-Norman Plays: Auerbach, *Mimesis*, Ch. VII; Omer Jodogne, 'Recherche sur les débuts du théâtre religieux en France', *Cahiers de Civilisation Médiévale, Xe–XIIe siècles* (Université de Poitiers) VIII (1965), pp. 1–24, 179–189; Hardison, *CRCD*, pp. 253–83.
Staging: Grace Frank, 'Genesis and Staging of the Jeu d'Adam', *PMLA* LIX (1944), pp. 7–17; John Stevens, 'Music in Some Early Medieval Plays'; *Studies in the Arts*, ed. Francis Warner (Oxford, 1958); Southern *MTR*.

Abbreviation.
PL—Patrologia Latina.

I

Popular Modes in the Earliest Plays

RICHARD AXTON

I

KNOWLEDGE of the early drama in England is very incomplete.
Between about A.D. 965, the earliest date for the *Visitatio Sepulchri* play
of St. Ethelwold's *Regularis Concordia*, and the first years of Richard II's
reign, when records begin for Corpus Christi plays at Beverley and
York, texts are few and fragmentary. Two more liturgical Latin Easter
plays (from Barking and Dublin) survive from the second half of the
fourteenth century, but otherwise the extant texts of the twelfth,
thirteenth and fourteenth centuries are either Anglo-Norman French
or English. The miscellaneous fragments and records of plays will
scarcely support any single interpretation of this period, although they
have often been cited in general terms as evidence of the 'evolution'
of English drama from a liturgical 'seed' towards more complex and
secular forms.[1] The Darwinian notions implicit in standard accounts
of the medieval drama have recently been perceptively analysed and
their truth challenged as inconsistent both with chronology and with
dramatic practice.[2] A full assessment of this period would have to
reckon with the existence and apparent decline of highly-developed
conventions of stagecraft in the twelfth-century Anglo-Norman plays
(*Adam, La Seinte Resureccion*) as well as with the notable paucity of
liturgical plays in England which could have served as 'models' for
the cycle plays. The traditional idea that the early Middle Ages saw a
'gradual secularization' of liturgical drama, in preparation, as it were,
for the coming of the cycle plays, is clearly inadequate. It is the sense
of this inadequacy that prompts the present study of the dramatic
traditions which pre-date the cycle plays in England.

In approaching this material it may be useful to keep in mind the
clerical bias of dramatic, and of all medieval, records. Our knowledge

---

[1] See Craig, *ERD*, pp. 88ff.
[2] Hardison, *CRCD*, pp. 1–34.

of even such secular activities as the performance of mimetic round-dances (*caroles*) during the twelfth and thirteenth centuries is largely dependent on clerical prohibitions of them in churchyards.[3] Drama is not always a written form, but scholars quite properly give priority to written evidence. This very preference for documentary evidence ought to have prevented some of the falsifications of fact and chronology that have been perpetrated on the early medieval drama in the name of evolutionary theory. For instance, the uniqueness of dramatic form and method in the Anglo-Norman *Mystère d'Adam* (c. 1150) and its difference from known liturgical drama are obscured by a scholar's reference to its 'liturgical source', implying a Latin play where none is known to have existed, and to the author's technique as 'translation'. A saint's play (*ludus de Sancta Katherina*) of about 1100 is stated to have been 'of course, in Latin' on grounds of its earliness. Yet the auspices of the play, arranged at Dunstable by the schoolmaster, were secular and very likely courtly.[4] The circumstantial account of a churchyard play at Beverley in about 1220 (discussed below) has often been misrepresented so as to avoid description of its distinctly 'popular' nature. It is always assumed, without evidence, that the first recorded cycle plays (at Cividale in 1298 and 1303) were in Latin, despite the fact that a cycle of vernacular dramatic *laude* dated some thirty years earlier has survived from Perugia.[5] So it appears that the 'secular' aspects of the early religious plays have often been played down for the sake of the larger 'development'. 'Secular' drama has fared worse. The *Interludium de Clerico et Puella*, a wooing farce of the late thirteenth century, was thought by one authority to be 'unpromising' as a miracle play and consequently denied the status of a play altogether.[6]

It is easy enough to find fault with those courageous enough to try to establish the larger patterns of continuity and change in the drama, but the fact remains that the relationship between the surviving plays of the twelfth and thirteenth centuries and the later Corpus Christi

---

[3] Chambers, *MS*, Vol. I, pp. 161ff.; Greene, *The Early English Carols*, pp. cxiii ff.

[4] Craig, *ERD*, pp. 97–9, 321. See Catherine B.C. Thomas, 'The Miracle Play at Dunstable', *MLN* XXXII (1917), pp. 337–44.

[5] See Kolve, *PCC*, p. 33. For the Perugia plays see Vicenzo de Bartholomaeis, *Laude drammatiche e rappresentazioni sacre* (Florence, 1943, 3 vols.).

[6] Craig, *ERD*, pp. 329–30.

drama is oddly discontinuous. My purpose in re-examining some aspects of these scattered texts and records is to assess the 'popular' element in this early drama.

The word 'popular' is commonly used in this context in two senses: 'by the people' and 'for the people'. Drama invented 'by the people' or 'folk-drama' is thought to be an oral tradition (in contrast to the written playbook tradition of the monastic church or crafts guilds). 'Folk-drama' is usually only committed to written form by a collector. This is true of the early Scots 'pleugh play' (*c.* 1500?), preserved as a three-part song in a seventeenth-century printed collection, and of the first texts of the true mummers' drama, written down by eighteenth- and nineteenth-century antiquarians.[7] The remarkable persistence of formal elements and character-types in the folk-plays (fool, champions, quack-doctor, man-woman, comic devil; presentation, vaunting, combat, death, 'cure' and *quête* or collection) argues for the antiquity of these plays. Structural motifs in the folk-drama from the Middle Ages have sometimes been preserved by being incorporated into a 'clerical' drama, written with a sense of distance 'for the people'. The German ring-dance of Mary Magdalene in the *Carmina Burana* Passion Play (*c.* 1200), the quack-doctor episode in the fifteenth-century Croxton *Play of the Sacrament* or the Fool's wooing in Lyndsay's *Satyre of the Thrie Estatis* (1542) are examples of clerical provision of 'popular' diversion in didactic contexts.

The search for *verbal* evidence of 'borrowings' from folk tradition in the clerical drama is not likely to be conclusive; and it is anyway of secondary importance. In drama the primary element is the actor and what he does for an audience. Whilst the story element may easily be borrowed, it is arguable that the basis of any performance is a mode of acting; such modes are generated slowly as the result of experiment and collaboration between performer and audience in different social contexts. They are never invented entirely. By looking at the role of the actor and the conventions governing his relationship with the audience, it may be possible to distinguish the use of popular modes in the earliest plays.

[7] H. M. Shire and K. Elliott, 'Pleugh song and Plough play', *Saltire Review* II: 6 (1955), pp. 39–44, and *Musica Britannica* XV, No. 30. For a recent discussion of the formal elements in the Mummers' plays see Brody, *The English Mummers and their Plays.*

II

The frankly secular *Interludium de Clerico et Puella* already mentioned will make a convenient starting point. The text, written on a small parchment roll, appears to be the sort of entertainment offered by professionals, perhaps at a feast. At least, in *Sir Gawain and the Green Knight* King Arthur asserts that 'laykyng [playing] of enterludez' is appropriate to Christmas. Moreover, the Green Knight's appearance between the first and second courses of the banquet at Camelot, and later Tudor practice all suggest such a context. The fragmentary *Interludium* shares a plot with the Middle English fabliau *Dame Sirith*. The clerk's wooing of a reluctant girl is brought to a successful end through the trickery of a bawd, Mome Elwis or Dame Sirith. The wooing of a girl by a clerical seducer is one of the commonest themes of medieval poetry and of the Middle English dancing songs in particular. While it is likely that clerks cultivated this romantic image, it is also true that anticlerical satire was the stock in trade of mimic performers in England from the time of Charlemagne. An episcopal *capitulum* of 789 prescribes corporal punishment and exile for any actor who apes priestly garb or the habit of a monk or nun. King Edgar, writing in 967 (contemporary with the introduction of the *Visitatio Sepulchri* into English Benedictine monasteries), complains that the scandals of monastic life are often the subject of mimes' singing and dancing shows in the market-places.[8]

The *Interludium* and *Dame Sirith* can hardly be the first entertainments of their kind. Both are skilfully versified, full of salty, proverbial expressions, exclamations of greeting and farewell, colloquial ejaculations. The characters in the *Interludium* are patently and pointedly conventional. The Clerk's love-sickness, with its extravagant declarations and pious asseverations, echoed in contemporary love-lyrics, is a transparent pose. His speech is learned by rote. 'For þe Hy sorw nicht and day— / Y may say "Hay, wayleuay!"' The Girl recognizes the convention of the 'clerc fayllard' (drop-out) and scolds him in general and satirical terms:

> Puella　By Crist of heuene and Sant Ione,
> 　　　　　Clerc of scole ne kep I non,　　　　　　　*care for*
> 　　　　　For many god wymman haf þai don scam,
> 　　　　　By Crist, þu michtis haf ben at hame!
>
> (27–30)

[8] Ogilvy, '*Mimi, Scurrae, Histriones*', p. 614.

Mome Elwis's pretence that she is a 'holy woman' and not a bawd
is presented satirically, by means of a string of pious formulae:

Mome Elwis A, son! vat saystu? Benedicite!
Lift hup þi hand and blis þe . . .
Can I do non oþir dede
Bot my pater noster and my crede
To say Crist for missedede,
And myn Auy Mary
(For my scynnes Hic am sory),
And my *De profundis* . . .

(63–75)

Performance of this spirited dialogue necessitates that the speakers
imitate stock characters who are themselves feigning, adopting conventional postures; and these stock poses are undercut by the satirical
mimicry of the performers. Such verbal and facial subtlety are precisely the points on which the mime Vitalis, writing his own epitaph
probably in Carolingian times, prides himself.[9] It is possible that
a skilled mimic might play all the parts, but in the case of the *Interludium* there is no evidence for this: the text consists entirely of dialogue
rubricated with the speakers' names. Proof that such wooing plays
were acted by several performers is found in a Cornish text (*c.* 1340)
of the part of the bawd in a play involving a similar trio.[10]

Dame Sirith, however, has a first person narrator. He rapidly dis-
appears, leaving the characters to speak for themselves, and solo mimic
performance may have been the case here. Of course, many Middle
English dialogue poems may have received a partially dramatic performance by a ventriloquist mime. But a solo performer of *Dame Sirith*,
however skilful, could not have worked quite alone. He needed to act
as well as to change voice and, in order to demonstrate the trick by
which the bawd wins round the reluctant Margeri, he needs the collaboration of a dog. Dame Sirith demonstrates the trick of feeding
mustard to her bitch. This is the 'wicchecrafft' that will turn Margeri's
heart to Wilekin. The following sequence, in which nine lines pass
before the dialogue reveals whom, or rather what, Dame Sirith is
addressing, would be meaningless unless accompanied by mimetic
action.

[9] Georges Gougenheim, 'Le Mime Vitalis', *Mélanges d'histoire du théâtre du
Moyen-Age et de la Renaissance offerts à Gustave Cohen* (Paris, 1950), pp. 29–33.
[10] 'W.S.', 'The Fragments of a Drama', *Revue Celtique* IV (1880), pp. 258–62.

(*Dame Sirith*) So Ich euere brouke hous oþer flet,   *As I enjoy house or hearth*

Neren neuer pones beter biset   *pence were never better spent*

þen þes shulen ben!
For I shal don a juperti   *stratagem*
And a ferli maistri,   *remarkable feat*
Þat þou shalt ful wel sen.

Pepir nou shalt þou eten;
Þis mustart shal ben þi mete,
   And gar þin eien to rene.   *make your eyes run*
I shal make a lesing   *pretence*
Of þin heie renning—   *eyes running*
   Ich wot wel wer and wenne.

(*Wilekin*) Wat! nou const þou no god!   *have you no sense*
Me þinkeþ þat þou art wod—   *mad*
Ʒeuest þou þe welpe mustard?

(*Dame Sirith*) Be stille, boinard!   *fool*
I shal mit þis ilke gin   *with this very device*
Gar hir loue to ben al þin.   *make thine*

(273–90)

Performing dogs scarcely figure in a modern notion of legitimate theatre, but they were a standard feature of medieval entertainments and the 'gleeman's bitch' was a proverbial phrase to Langland. An improvised diversion caused by a weeping dog is described in the eleventh-century Latin romance *Ruodlieb*, a work liberally sprinkled with set-pieces culled from the repertoire of the Spielleute or play-folk.[11] Such a gleeman's act is apparently the structural high point of the fabliau plays *Dame Sirith* and the *Interludium*. (That the tradition survived into Shakespeare's time is suggested by the character of Launce in *The Two Gentlemen of Verona*, with a name that suggests something of his bawdy humour as go-between as he woos for his master Proteus, equipped with an 'understanding staff' and a dog that will not weep.)

The conclusion of *Dame Sirith* introduces a fresh motif which smacks of professional performance. Having won over the girl by demonstrating to her in the shape of the weeping bitch the misfortune of girls

---

[11] *Ruodlieb*, ed. Edwin H. Zeydel (Chapel Hill, 1959), Fragment X, pp. 92ff.

who reject the advances of magic-working clerks, Dame Sirith gives the lovers some bawdy advice. She then turns to the audience and offers her services to any who need them—for a price:

And wose is onwis	*whoever is inexperienced*
And for non pris	
Ne con geten his leuemon,	*lover*
I shal, for mi mede,	*reward*
Garen him to spede,	*make thrive*
For ful wel I con.	

(445–50)

In folk-play tradition the 'dame' or 'witch' is always played by a man, as 'she' is here. As in the folk-play's concluding *quête*, and in the earliest Northern French farce, *Le Garçon et l'Aveugle*, the performer speaks to the audience from the play world and begs in character. The offer of aid to the audience is an invitation to join in the game and show appreciation.

If the *Interludium* and *Dame Sirith* may be taken as examples of professional dramatic activity, then the mode of this entertainment is distinctly 'low-mimetic'. The basis of performance is a concept of drama as impersonation or mimicry. The plot proceeds by a series of humorous tricks or deceptions whose make-believe nature is plain to a knowing audience.

III

The role required of the actors in the first ecclesiastical play offers a striking contrast in almost every way: they sing, in Latin, and within the confines of a church service. The play, a *Visitatio Sepulchri* set down in St. Ethelwold's *Regularis Concordia* (A.D. 965–75) for use in English Benedictine monasteries, is to be performed just before the conclusion of Easter Matins. It is acted by four clerics, representing the three Marys and the angel at the empty sepulchre. Directions are given for costumes, movements and gestures, manner and pitch of singing. The action of seeking, the text says, is done in imitation (*ad imitationem*) of the events of the Gospel narrative. Yet the degree of historical impersonation is severely limited. In the most recent discussion of the *Visitatio*, Glynne Wickham suggests that the action is in the nature of 'office' rather than 'play' and points to the 'double image' which it presents: it is both historical scene and contemporary cere-mony.[12] The 'Marys' wear clerical vestments not women's clothes, they carry thuribles not spices, and some of their gestures are necessitated by the context of ceremonial worship rather than by the aim of repre-senting historical action. Thus they turn away from the Angel at the sepulchre in order to announce the resurrection to the choir, and then again to display the empty grave-clothes to the clergy. As impersonation the action is very incomplete, but this is not its primary aim. The last gesture directly recalls the priest offering tokens of the risen Christ to the Easter congregation in the ancient liturgical ceremony of the *Elevatio Crucis*. One could go further in this analysis and point out that the very act of seeking, of approaching the Easter Sepulchre is not directly mimetic of the historical scene, but is modelled on a liturgical practice previously performed by the congregation itself during Easter night. In several of the Easter and Christmas (*Pastores*) plays the congregation is invited by the Marys or Shepherds to come and see the place where Christ has lain. The actor here is partly an officiant; his job is merely to point, offering the congregation visible proof of the holy mysteries by means of traditional ceremonial objects.

Such a filtering of historical action through the prism of liturgical ceremony and gesture as well as language is characteristic of the litur-gical drama. Various generic terms are used to describe the plays; they are most commonly known as *officium* or *ordo*, the same words as describe non-dramatic liturgical offices. Other terms are used: *repre-sentatio* and cognate forms denote a sense of the dramatic nature of proceedings, and are found to describe several plays concerning Herod; a few clerical authors use *ludus* (e.g. the *ludus de Sancta Katherina*, men-tioned already, and the Beauvais *Danielis Ludus*), thus connecting the festive drama of the Church with the traditions of popular revelling.[13]

The 'double image' of ecclesiastical drama, noted in discussion of the *Visitatio Sepulchri*, is suggested again by the manuscript title of the Anglo-Norman *Adam*, *Ordo representacionis Ade*. A Janus-like quality appears also in the visual effect of the play, performed out of doors, in a public place (*platea*) adjoining a church. A choir sings litur-

[12] Glynne Wickham, 'Stage and Drama till 1660', in *English Drama to 1710* (*HLEL* Vol. III), ed. Christopher Ricks (London, 1971), p. 31.

[13] See the discussions in Young, *DMC*, Vol. II, pp. 407ff., and Kolve, *PCC*, pp. 11ff.

gical reponsories and lessons; God wears a priest's dalmatic and later dons a stole for the expulsion; He goes to and from the church. Yet much in the play is representational: the stage Paradise is adorned with branches, flowers and fruit, and contains a mechanical Serpent; God speaks to Eve as a priest to a young bride, and Satan wins her confidence by means of courtly flattery.

The basic premise of the play's three 'acts' is provided by two liturgical texts: the outline of the Adam and Cain sections is contained in the responsories sung by the choir and belonging at that time to Matins of Sexagesima. The model for the concluding Procession of Prophets is a pseudo-Augustinian sermon normally used at Christmas. Each half of the play begins with a Latin *lectio* whose substance is then freely expanded by the use of mimetic action and vernacular dialogue. *Ordo* is extended into *repraesentatio*.

The roles of the performers are more varied and more distinct than in the liturgical play of the sepulchre. They fall into three broad categories: singers, speakers, and mimes. The first, the choir, have no precise part in the historical drama. They may, in a sense, represent the heavenly host at the threshold of heaven (the church porch) singing the praises and instructions of God. But there are no directions for their costuming (presumably choir-robes), their placing or movements. The role of the choir is familiar and ecclesiastical; whether they are singing responsories or intoning the lessons, both Latin words and plainchant 'melodies' are those of traditional worship. As singers they do not speak or take part in the *action*. This fact distinguishes the technique of the play from that of the liturgical drama proper (as in the *Visitatio Sepulchri*).

The second class of actors speak and do not sing. They are the historical persons of the Old Testament drama. They might be further divided into those, like Adam and Eve, Cain and Abel, God, Satan, who interact with one another; and the prophets, who are dislocated from history, existing simply as isolated figures in a procession and having no dramatic relationships one with another. There are extensive instructions regarding the costuming, speaking and gestures of these central agents in the drama:

Adam shall wear a red tunic, but Eve a woman's garment in white with a white silk scarf; and they shall both stand in front of God— Adam, however, nearer to God with a calm countenance, Eve with face lowered. Adam shall be well trained not to answer too quickly nor too slowly, when he has to answer. Not only Adam but all the persons shall be instructed to control their speech and to make their actions appropriate to the matter they speak of; and, in speaking the verse, not to add a syllable, nor to take one away, but to enunciate everything in the order laid down. Whenever anyone shall speak of Paradise, he shall look towards it and point it out with his hand.

The last sentence suggests that the gestures required are formalized and literal. Adam and Eve must 'stoop a little, because of the shame of their sin', and after the expulsion their greater grief is shown by their weeping, looking back towards Paradise, striking their breasts and thighs and prostrating themselves on the ground.

These directions, detailed throughout, show a keen concern for decorum in the matters of style and timing. The explicitness cannot be taken as the sign of an art newly born, any more than can Hamlet's strictures to the players at Elsinore. The warning to 'stick to the text' strikes one as the thought of a man who has at least envisaged the possibility of improvisation, as well as neglect or incompetence on the part of his actors. At a time when priests and clergy were sometimes rebuked for 'histrionic' gestures and pulling faces in the performance of divine service as well as in social life, the caution may have been particularly apposite.[14] But the caveat makes sense in view of the relative freedom enjoyed by the third class of performers—the silent *demones*.

The rubrics do not specify costumes for the devils or for Satan. It seems the rubricator assumed the producer knew what was appropriate; either iconography or eschatological poetry would have suggested to him quasi-human figures with animal parts, claws, hair and wings, and smoke and fire coming from various parts of their anatomy. A twelfth-century Latin *Dialogue of Body and Soul* describes them thus, manhandling souls with pitchforks and chains into cauldrons.[15] The *demones* of the play inhabit an *infernum* provided with cauldrons and kettles, which they bang together and brew smoke in. The devils' activities are governed by a distinct set of conventions. They are not 'historical', but participate in the action throughout, from the first mimic temptings of Eve to the removal of the last of the prophets to

[14] See Marshall, 'Theatre in the Middle Ages', p. 377.
[15] *The Latin Poems Commonly Attributed to Walter Mapes*, ed. Thomas Wright (London, 1841), Appendix E.

hell. They have no set lines, but convey their meaning by dumb show. They enjoy a special relationship with the audience, a freedom to roam through the open spaces (*plateae*) between Paradise and Hell and in amongst the audience. Their characteristic mode is running: they either 'run' or 'make a discursus' through the place or *per populum*, always retiring to Hell before the dialogue continues. After disposing of Adam and Eve, some of the devils return from Hell to make diversion in the 'place' before the introduction of Cain and Abel. They have energy and hilarity. The loquacious Satan, who shares their demonic mode of playing, appears 'glad and gay' to tempt Adam and presents a smiling face to Eve. The imprisonment of Adam and Eve is greeted with diabolical rejoicing and a 'great dance'. The association of the devil with dancing dates from early Christian times and was an important clerical weapon against the obstinate survival (often under the auspices of church festivals or vigils) of folk-dancing.[16] The devils then, are purveyors of entertainment as well as objects of doctrinal terror. They possess a patently theatrical function in keeping the mechanics of the action going. Satan plants thorns and thistles in Adam's plot of digging; he does it when Adam's back is turned so that the audience perceives the 'trick' nature of the symbolic action. The whole crew of devils perform as stage hands, removing the bodies (fifteen in all) to Hell at the end of each 'scene'—an economic histrionic and doctrinal device found also in the later Cornish drama. Finally, though the devils' entries are 'scored', it is clear that the actors are required to improvise both gestures and words:

> From hell they shall make a great smoke to arise, and shall shout to each other in their joy . . .

This brief consideration of the basic conventions governing the roles of the actors suggest that the story of Genesis is refracted through several kinds of convention: some of the liturgy, some of liturgical drama; others (in particular the devils, and also perhaps the Jews' mocking of Isaiah as a palm-reading quack-doctor) touched by popular modes of dramatic entertainment. The existence of these modes apparently invited the ecclesiastical dramatist to expand his material in accordance with expectation for a certain kind of show. After all, there is only a serpent in Genesis, and *Adam* gives us a mechanical

---

[16] Greene, *The Early English Carols*, pp. xci ff.

serpent, a highly articulate Satan, and a pack of mimic devils into the bargain.

If the devils in *Adam* form part of a conventional expectation of the audience, what dramatic tradition do they belong to? Erich Auerbach has written in this context:

> The subliterary survival of the tradition of the antique mime and the more forceful observation of life, which, beginning in the twelfth century, seems to have set in among the lower classes, too, led at that time to a flourishing development of the popular farce, whose spirit may well be assumed to have soon found its way into the religious drama as well. (*Mimesis*, pp. 138–9)

That such a mimic tradition existed in Anglo-Saxon England has already been noted. Indeed, study of Latin/Anglo-Saxon glosses has shown that when native authors were required to interpret Roman theatrical terms they usually did so in terms of gleemen's performances on raised and canopied platforms in the open air; and they repeat the view, originating in Isidore of Seville, that mimes set out the fable spoken by the poet.[17] Several continental authors of the twelfth century give details of the *scena* as a shaded place enclosed by curtains, similar to a merchant's curtained stall, in which are hidden masked figures (*personae larvatae*) who express by gestures the substance narrated by the poet.[18] Even allowing for 'the curious confusion of actuality, archæology and fiction' found in these sources, it seems that mimes in the early Middle Ages regularly used masks and performed in curtained stalls on raised stages.[19] Whether the *Adam* poet modelled his Paradise (set up 'in rather a high place' and 'surrounded by curtains and silk cloths') on such a gleeman's platform, familiar in Anglo-Saxon secular life, is mere speculation. After all, he had good iconographic reasons for giving Paradise a wall. Still, the appearance of mimic devils and the relative freedom of their part in the play, their running, dancing, improvising, their rapport with the audience, all point to such a tradition enriching the ecclesiastical drama in England by the mid-twelfth century.

The tradition of *diablerie* seems to thrive in the thirteenth century,

[17] See Marshall, 'Theatre in the Middle Ages', pp. 10ff.

[18] See Bigongiari, 'Were There Theaters in the Twelfth and Thirteenth Centuries?', p. 211.

[19] Ogilvy, '*Mime, Scurrae, Histriones*', p. 614; Marshall, 'Theatre in the Middle Ages', p. 13.

despite paucity of texts. An anglo-Norman rhymed sermon of the mid-century, apparently relying heavily on the dialogue of a play of the Fall, gives us a self-explaining *deable*, who described how he climbs into the body of a dragon so that nothing of his own form shows; he admires its shining green head and the mouth through which he will speak and sing, 'moltz doucement . . . Come lui clerks fount en sainte eglise'.[20] Two centuries later the Chester devil's mode of adopting disguise is very similar (*CP*, II, 189–208), while the devil-minstrel's parody of church music reappears in the Cornish *Origo Mundi* (213ff.). An English poem of about 1250, described as 'A strif . . . of Jesu and of Satan', introduces dramatic dialogue of the Harrowing of Hell, with speeches assigned to Christ, Satan, six prophets and a Janitor of Hell. The form as well as several details suggest the adaptation of a play with lively dialogue and action. David prays to Christ to 'Bring ous fram þis dredful *hous*' (a stage building?) and Satan taunts Christ to 'ben oure fere (companion), And fonden hou we *pleien* here'. At Christ's command to undo Hell-gate, the Janitor runs away in a comic fright.[21]

In contrast with the evident fusion of literary and acting traditions in the *Adam*, the dramatic method in *La Seinte Resureccion* (originally composed *c.* 1180) is uniform, though distinctive. The two versions of the prologue suggest two ways of regarding the production—as a recitation and as a representation:

> En ceste manere recitom
> La seinte resureccion . . .
>
> (Paris MS 1–2)
>
> Si vus avez devociun
> De la sainte resurrectiun
> En l'onur Deu representer
> Et devant le puple representer . . .
>
> (Canterbury MS 1–4)

The apparent contradiction between recitation and representation is resolved by the mediation of a narrator. Although the precise nature of the 'stage directions' is obscured by the fact that both texts are intended for private reading rather than performance, the evidence for such a narrative persona seems conclusive. [22] He speaks the prologue

[20] See *Symposium* VI (1952), pp. 88–99.
[21] Pollard, *English Miracle Plays,Moralities and Interludes*, pp. 166–72.
[22] On the 'narrator', see W. Noomen, 'Passages narratifs dans les drames médiévaux français', *Revue Belge de Philologie et d'Histoire* (1958), pp. 761–85.

which, in both versions, introduces the audience to a very extensive set consisting of structures and marked areas within a large outdoor space, and to the characters who inhabit these. The narrator also provides an explanatory gloss, anticipating and describing almost every move the actors make between stations. In addition, at two points he calls attention to the introduction into the play of a new character. The story of the resurrection from deposition through to ascension can thus be told as a continuous narrative acted out.

Hardison's fine study of the staging has revealed the poet's principle of stagecraft. It is based on a concept of the acting area as a number of territories in which each character or group is geographically distinct in an 'estal', 'liu' or 'maisun'. The actors can speak to one another only by travelling through common land (where nothing can happen) to one another's 'islands'. Hardison observes that

> The principle of creating episodes on the basis of movement between stations is so regularly observed in *La Seinte Resureccion* that it must have been a well-established convention at the time the play was written. (*CRCD*, p. 270)

Much of the 'action', then, consists of journeys whose significance is made clear by the narrator. This concept of dramatic action, though stiff and formalized, enables the story to be presented as a continuous historical process in time and space. The use of the narrator guarantees the independence of the actors from the audience, so that *Unus in via*, the curious figure who pops into the action to overhear the soldiers talking at the tomb and convey this information to Joseph of Arimathia, has no need to explain his role. The narrator does that for him, so that tight control is exercised over a large cast (upwards of forty-two) occupying a large space (fourteen 'houses' or 'stalls'). In the section of the play which remains, a single representational mode is used for all the characters (it does not, however, contain speeches for any of the heavenly or diabolical persons). The characters similarly share a linguistic style, Anglo-Norman couplets, rather stiff and uncoloured.

This delightful play is extremely prodigal in the use of actors and of space, and must have been very lengthy. It is a fascinating example of an attempt at literal representation of history in time and space. In this respect, as Hardison has shown, its dramatic method is completely different from that of the liturgical plays of the resurrection.

It is a vast spectacle, so complex in its ramification of a simple principle, that a running explanation is required, 'devant le puple'.

A play of this scope clearly requires 'asez large place'. The manuscript tradition suggests that it was clerically organized. Anglo-Norman was the language of the court and of many of the middle class in Southern England. One of the manuscripts was copied at Christ's Church, Canterbury, c. 1275, where Edward I and his court sometimes visited. The Wardrobe Books record payments to Canterbury minstrels for performing before the King in the crypt there in 1297, and to court minstrels for 'playing a miracle and minstrelsies' (*ludentibus miraculum & facientibus menestralcias suas*) in the Queen's presence in 1307.[23] Perhaps there was some collaboration here between clerical and court performers. Much earlier than this, from about 1220, there survives a well-known account of a *repraesentatio Dominicae resurrectionis* in St. John's churchyard, Beverley. On this occasion a boy watching the play outside through a window in the tower dislodged some masonry and fell on the church floor, yet neither he nor any bystanders were hurt. The real life miracle occasioned the record of the play. The account has often been translated and discussed, yet the most interesting aspects of it have been overlooked or falsified.[24]

The play was of the resurrection and it was played in summer; it was therefore unconnected with its appropriate liturgical feast. Yet such is the power of evolutionary thought that A. F. Leach translated *Dominicae resurrectionis* as 'the Lord's Ascension'—a suitable liturgical subject for summer. For Waterhouse[25] this became *proof* that at this time the drama was 'still associated with some particular office of the church, celebrated on a certain fixed day'! The performance in St. John's churchyard was attended by a great crowd of people, drawn together by various impulses, the chronicler says: delight, curiosity, and devotion (in that order). The play was apparently 'in the round' since the crowd formed a *corona*. Some that could not see, including the boys, went into the church; and the costumes (*habitus*), action (*gestus*) and dialogue (*dialogus*) were sufficiently distinct from those of 'some

[23] British Museum Add. MS 7965 (25 Ed. I), f. 55v., and P.R.O. 101/370/16 (35 Ed. I), f. 13v.

[24] The account is printed in Young, *DMC*, Vol. II, pp. 539-40, tr. A. F. Leach, 'Some English Plays and Players', *Furnivall Miscellany* (Oxford, 1901), pp. 206ff.

[25] O. Waterhouse, *Non-Cycle Mystery Plays* (Oxford, 1909), p. xvii.

particular office of the church' to make a dangerous climb worth the view. Not only was the play performed in summer, the traditional time for folk *ludi*, but it took place in the churchyard on the north side of the church (*ex parte aquillonari*). The chronicler would scarcely have mentioned this fact unless he wished to connect the occasion with those folk-dances and practices that the medieval Church dedicated to the devil by allowing on the north side of the church building.[26] Further, the Beverley play was performed 'by masked actors, as usual' (*larvatorum ut assolet*). Whether it is the masked actors or the performance itself that is 'as usual', the passage is striking. Masks are mentioned in clerical writings with almost invariable condemnation, are forbidden to clergy by the Council of Nantes in 890, and forbidden, William of Wadington reminds English clerks in about 1300, by a series of later decretals.[27]

Several aspects then—the outdoor summer performance, in the round, in a place associated with folk *ludi*, and by masked actors, though the play is of the resurrection—provide some helpful indications of the way in which clerical drama of the church co-operated with a popular tradition in the early thirteenth century.

IV

La Seinte Resureccion and the Beverley *repraesentatio* appear clearly outside the office of the Church's set worship, as do the *miracula* of saints' lives performed publicly in the London streets according to William Fitzstephen, writing about 1170–82.[28] This religious drama for the people did not replace the Latin drama which continued under liturgical auspices. According to William of Malmesbury, his abbey had a Peregrinus play in about 1125.[29] In the thirteenth century York Minster had properties for plays of the Three Kings and Shepherds, and a Norwich Ordinal, dated 1265–78, refers to a *Visitatio*. Lichfield statutes of the thirteenth or fourteenth century made provision for a *Pastores*, a *Resurrexio* and a *Peregrinus*, and the same three traditional plays were up-

---

[26] See Bertha Phillpotts, *The Elder Edda and Ancient Scandinavian Drama* (Cambridge, 1920), p. 209.

[27] See Chambers, *MS*, Vol. I, pp. 279ff.; Ogilvy, '*Mimi, Scurrae, Histriones*', p. 613; Young, *DMC*, Vol. II, pp. 417–18.

[28] Cited in Young, *DMC*, Vol. II, p. 542.

[29] *De Gestis Pontificum Anglorum* V (*PL*, Vol. CLXXIX, col. 1679).

dated in the early fifteenth century by provision of some English text to form the so-called 'Shrewsbury Fragments'.[30] From very early on, the 'popular' religious plays established separate traditions. Who then organized and acted them?

G. R. Owst[31] suggested long ago the important function of preaching friars in adapting and developing entertaining forms of instruction. The recurrent association of sermons and plays during the thirteenth and fourteenth centuries suggests how crucial this role was.

A sermon might function in relation to a play in three ways. First, it could sterilize or consecrate a popular 'play' form by giving it a religious significance. The twelfth- and thirteenth-century *caroles* often contained a mimetic element in the dance; many of these were concerned with wooing or cuckolding, perpetrated by a girl soloist and a young man on an old 'jealous' husband.[32] One of these, known as *La bele Aelis*, was a craze in England in the early thirteenth century, to the infuriation of preachers. A sermon in a famous Dominican manuscript (Trinity College, Cambridge, MS 323) allegorizes the significance of the dance as a union between Jesus and his disciples, where the seductress Bele Aelis represents the Virgin Mary, plucking the flowers of charity, chastity and so forth.[33] Other preachers introduced a macabre note. Jacques de Vitry told his congregation in parodic French couplets how 'when Aelis had risen and adorned and admired herself, Mass had already been sung so the devils carried her off'. The introduction of the devil into the wooing dance provides a homiletic model for the Dances of Death, a play form curiously close to the 'stolen bride' *caroles* and performed, in some of the earliest instances, by Franciscans.[34]

Secondly, a sermon might form an expository prelude to a play; this function continued in the cycle plays of the Hegge manuscript ('*Ludus Coventriae*'), Chester and Coventry. The Dominican manuscript mentioned above contains a homily for the anniversary of St. Nicholas in which the preacher tells his mixed audience ('boþe þis lewede ant

---

[30] Davis, *NCP*, pp. 1–7, xiv–xx. For this interpretation of the Shrewsbury Fragments see my review of *NCP* in *Medium Aevum* XLI (1972), pp. 159–60.

[31] *L–P*, Ch. 8.

[32] Bédier, 'Les plus anciennes danses françaises', pp. 406ff.

[33] Printed in Greene, *The Early English Carols*, p. cxiv.

[34] Chambers, *MS*, Vol. II, p. 153; Hellmut Rosenfeld, *Der Mittelalterliche Totentanz* (Münster/Köln, 1954).

þis clerkes') that

> yf ye wollet stille ben
> in þis pleye ye mowen isen . . .

and he promises them a story similar in outline to that of Wace's *Vie de Saint Nicolas* found in the same manuscript.[35]

Thirdly, the sermon itself could function as a play. In a lively verse sermon from about 1300 the preacher impersonates Caiaphas.[36] The role is conceived as in the later cycle plays, as that of a Jewish bishop who spoke his prophecy (*Expedit unum hominem mori*) in ignorance. 'Bẏsschop Caẏface' addresses a large crowd on Palm Sunday procession, expounding his 'prophetic' text, singing and inviting them to join in. He excuses the apparent frivolity of his device with reference to the minstrelsy of God:

> A welsoþe sawe soþlich ẏs seyd
> Ech god game ẏs god ẏ-pleẏd
> Louelych & lẏȝt ẏs leue   (31-3)

It is a true saying that belief is a matter of joy, so the 'game' is appropriate. The punning assurance that he has obtained 'leue of þe grete' and his request to the Dean for permission to sing, suggest the uneasy position of a preaching friar at, or rather outside, a large secular cathedral. The purpose of his preaching, when he has explained his historical role and the meaning of the palms, is to bring his audience to a sense of sin and to shrift. The economic motive is not explicit, but it appears to be his purpose in recommending the 'schrewen vnschrẏve' to his partner, one 'Symon Cumpayngnoun' who has 'power of disciplyne' and who gives shrift and administers penances. As in the folk-play tradition, the performance ends in a *quête*.

The performance has a double aspect, of sermon and game: the audience are invited to participate as Jews bearing palms and singing to welcome Jesus, but they are also plainly the sinful objects of Caiaphas's preaching address. This curious hybrid mode of acting, the solo 'Spiel' of audience address, forms a basic type in the folk tradition and it is also found, of course, as a means of characterizing a range of cycle-play figures from Noah to Pilate.

[35] Carleton Brown, 'An Early Mention of a St. Nicholas Play in England', *Studies in Philology* XXVIII (1931), pp. 594–601.

[36] Printed in Carleton Brown, 'Caiaphas as a Palm Sunday Prophet', in *Kittredge Anniversary Papers* (Boston, 1913), pp. 105–17.

Caiaphas is an equivocal figure, offering a new style of instruction and playing his sermon game by special permission of the cathedral authorities. Such caution seems to have been well placed in view of a developing hostility in thirteenth-century ecclesiastical pronouncements towards 'unlicensed' performance of religious plays by clerics. Bishop Grosseteste's decretals of 1236–44 forbade clerical participation in 'folk' pastimes (ales, ram-raisings, etc.) and in 'miracles'.[37] William of Wadington, writing c. 1300, cites the decretals as condemning 'miracles' as a 'folie apert' contrived by 'fols clercs' who disguise their faces with masks.[38] It is not absolutely certain that William intends 'miracles' to mean religious plays, but it seems likely in view of the popular nature of the tradition we have been following. Moreover, he goes on to contrast miracles with 'representement . . . en office de seint eglise quant hom fet la Deu seruise'—he instances the sepulchre—which are allowable to clerks. Again, he maintains that one should not believe the clerks who claim that their shows performed 'en cymiters apres mangers' and in city streets are done to the honour of God, when they are in fact done for the devil. Robert of Brunne, adapting William for his *Handlyng Synne* (1303) makes the same distinction:

> And he may pleye withoutyn plyght   *peril*
> Howe God was bore yn ȝole nyght,   *Yule*
> To make men to beleue stedfastly
> þat he lyght yn þe vyrgyne Mary.   *descended*
> Ȝif þou do hyt yn weyys or grenys,
> A syght of synne truly hyt semys.

Whilst the disputed 'hyt' of the penultimate line could simply mean acting of any sort, a more natural interpretation of the context (and of its source) is simply that miracle plays of religious subjects performed in secular auspices have become notoriously secular occasions.[39]

Two verse prologues of the late thirteenth century give a hint of what these miracles may have been like (*NCP*, IX and X). The two fragments are bilingual, having both Anglo-Norman and English verses. The existence of bilingual texts suggests that the plays are not occasional community drama, but portable commodities, which were

[37] Chambers, *MS*, Vol. I, p. 91.

[38] The relevant parts of *Manuel des Pechiez* and *Handlyng Synne* are printed in Young, *DMC*, Vol. II, pp. 417–18.

[39] I disagree with the interpretation of F. M. Salter, *Medieval Drama at Chester* (Toronto, 1955), p. 120.

to appeal to audiences made up of French-speaking gentry and common people (the Cambridge herald bullies the 'hardi man' but requests silence of 'tes lordes'). Or the two languages are possibly alternatives for use in different parts of the country, since English or French speaking seems to have been determined by geography as well as by class.[40] Both pieces are boisterous and popular in tone and call for silence in minstrels' formulae. The Cambridge prologue is spoken by the messenger of 'þ'amperur', who commands silence in the name of his lord and of Mahomet. The Rickinghall fragment is spoken by a 'rey coronné' who makes a similar gesture on his own behalf. The gesture itself is apparently an established convention and it is one that we find made in the cycle plays (for instance by Herod or his Nuncius in *Towneley* XIV and XVI, and by Pilate himself in *Towneley* XX).

The Cambridge messengers orders the audience not to venture into the acting area or disturb the play, on penalty of imprisonment:

S'il i a nul que noyse face,	*If anyone makes a noise*
V que entre en cet(e) place	*or enters into the 'place'*
Pur nostre iu ren desturber	*to disturb our play for any reason,*
Prendre le frun saunz demorrer	*we shall have him taken without delay*
E jucer (juter?) ley(n)s la prisun.	*and thrown into the prison.*

(*NCP*, IX, 9–13)

Penalty for escape from prison will be hanging or beating at least, he swears by Mahound. The English text is more explicit about the physical proximity of actors and audience which forms the basis of performance here. They must sit well spaced and allow the actors to pass among them 'And sittet rume and well atwo / þat men moзt among ev go.'

Their idle chatter ('lude tale') must not 'lette hure game' (impede the play). The messenger promises hanging, though more lenient tortures for children and simple folk ('vitles man þat nones mannes wit ne can'). This curious touch is hardly explicable as Mahoundish humanitarianism, but it makes good sense as a hint of things to follow in the play itself. Indeed, the whole dramatic function of the conventional exhortation to silence and good order seems to be a positive invitation to frolic—a challenge to a 'game' in which actors and audience provoke one another and the audience's misdemeanours are punished 'in play'

[40] R. M. Wilson, 'English and French in England, 1100–1300', *History* XXVIII (1943), pp. 37–60.

by the lackeys of a pagan emperor using a stage prison. The mingling of actors and audience necessitated by the playing place, and the evident scope for improvisation, first noted as strictly controlled within the *Ordo representacionis Ade*, here forms the basic principle of a boisterous 'game' drama, in which both actors and audience have a physical part.

This particular mode seems to have been developed from the exigencies of performance where the audience surrounds the playing place and the actors need to make their entrances and exits through them. It is one which thrives in the later non-cyclic drama. The Prologue to the mid-fourteenth-century *Pride of Life* ends his exposition with a similar request:

> Nou beith in pes and beith hende   *well behaved*
> And distourbith noȝt oure place,
> For þis oure game schal gin and ende
>   Through Jhesu Cristis swete grace. (*NCP*, VII, 109–12)

while Dux Moraud (in early fifteenth-century manuscript) commands all estates of men,

> No yangelyngys ȝe mak in þis folde   *chatter/quarrelling*
> To-day;   (*NCP*, VIII, 8–9)

and threatens to punish inattention with blows. Like the emperor of the earlier fragment, Dux Moraud commands the audience within a play-world whose boundary is the enclosure (*folde*) where the performance takes place. The use of play enclosures is attested in the manuscript of *Castle of Perseverance* (c. 1405) which includes the sketch of a playing-place surrounded by circular ditch with bank and fence. Other later plays such as the Digby manuscript *Mary Magdalene* (which too has an emperor prologue) may also have been performed in the round. The purpose of the elaborate *Castle* enclosure may have been to keep out non-paying audience but the arrangement is much too cumbersome to serve as a model for performances on a smaller scale.

The performance of even the simplest miracle play would be costly. Professionals would need to devise some method of obtaining money from the audience. Friars who produced plays would be likely to take a collection, since 'profit' was a licensed goal of their preaching. How could this best be managed?

In the mummers' play tradition, as already noted, the performance usually concludes with a collection; this *quête* is an integral part of the form and is the justification for introducing a string of bizarre characters unconnected with the previous action. The fifteenth-century play *Mankind* adapts this device; in the middle of the play the vices make the audience pay for the privilege of seeing the 'abhominable presense' of the devil Titivillus. Again, the collection is integral, and generates a fresh rapport with the audience and satirical comment. It seems to me quite possible that the early miracle plays sometimes did the same. It has been conjectured that the play king of the Rickinghall Fragment is Augustus Caesar.[41] In this case the action on which he sends his messenger at the conclusion of the fragmentary text would be the taxing of 'all the world' (as in *Chester* VI and *Towneley* IX). The perplexing rapidity of action and the 'secular' nature of the Chester *Octavian* play with its 'miracles of midwyves' has often been noted.[42] Without offering an 'explanation' of the curious nature of this play, it may be relevant to point out correspondences with both the earlier fragments and with folk tradition.

Coming after a typically restrained treatment of Joseph's troubles, the voice of the Chester play Nuncius introducing Octavian has the clearest ring of the mummers' play presenter heard anywhere in the cycle-play drama:

> Make rowme, lordinges, and geve us waie,
> and let octavian come and plaie.
>
> (VI, 177–8)

The emperor Octavian introduces himself, parading and boasting of his might, commanding homage. He speaks first in Anglo-French and then in English, warning the audience not to come too close with evil intent. He will prove his might by counting the heads of his subjects. He sends his 'bedill' among them to collect a penny from each:

> Each man one peny shall paye,
> therefore, my bedill, do as I saie;
> in mydds the world by any waie
> this gamon shall begin.
>
> (VI, 257–60)

The emperor's subjects are his medieval audience, according to the vaunting mode as old as the Cambridge and Rickinghall fragments. Would they not also be included in the 'taxing'? Is is possible that this episode, of negligible liturgical significance, was chosen for dramatiza-

[41] J. P. Gilson's letter in *The Times Literary Supplement* 21 May 1921, p. 340.
[42] Craig, *ERD*, p. 187.

tion by the early makers of 'miracles' of the nativity because it provides the opportunity for a *quête* within the play? If this was so, then once again the 'game' of the drama ('this gamon shall begin') refers to the physical movement of actors in among the audience, using the play disguise to beg 'in earnest'. The anomalous nature of *Chester* VI in the cycle may possibly be due to its reliance on the material and dramatic modes of a popular play whose 'myracles' are expounded by an Expositor who refers his audience to the authority of one 'fryer Bartholomew'.

V

The use of the expository prologue with a plea not to disturb 'oure place' has already been noted in *Pride of Life*. The most recent editor of the play concludes from a study of its language that *Pride of Life* is 'likely to have been composed as early as the middle of the fourteenth century'.[43] This means it is not only much earlier than any other vernacular morality play but also earlier by more than half a century than any of the cycle-play texts. *Pride of Life*, then, demands consideration in relation to the early, pre-cycle traditions. It is clerical: the few stage directions are Latin; affinities with the Kildare Poems suggest that the play is the work of an Anglo-Irish religious order.[44] Performance is outdoors, since the audience is asked, 'Teryith [possibly *prayith*] al for þe weþer'. Its theme is homiletic, *memento mori*, inviting comparison with the Dance of Death in the pungent generalization of the satiric verses. But there is more to it than a dramatized sermon.

The 'place' of the play is apparently at ground level and is flanked by the audience. When the King of Life's messenger goes through the 'place' to ask if any man will fight with his master, he delivers the challenge to the audience: 'Pes and listenith to my sawe . . .' The King himself uses the same vaunting form of address, commanding silence and threatening violence. Both the King and the Bishop are saluted by the messenger as they sit upon thrones ('þou sittis on þi se', 296, 323). The King's throne is a curtained tent which is closed to let him sleep (303ff.). The acting place may also be divided or bounded by a ditch or stream (as in the *Castle of Perseverance*), for, as the messenger comes running, the King praises his ability to 'lepe oure the lake'. A more usual meaning for *lake* in the Middle English drama, however, is pit or

[43] Davis, *NCP*, p.c.　　　　　　　　　　　　　　[44] *Ibid.*, p. xcix.

prison of hell (*e.g. LC*, p. 288, l. 497; p. 324, l. 1556; *C of P*, l. 99).
So perhaps one should imagine the Nuncius skipping over a hole in
the ground (similar to the Devil's Spoon in the medieval Cornish
'rounds' or to the *prisun* of the Cambridge Fragment. Such a focal
'lake' of hell would be appropriate to the needs of a play on the certainty of death.

The dramatic method makes much of posting to and fro between
thrones and of direct audience address. Dialogue is rarely an exchange,
usually a monologue: a sermon prologue, a vaunt, a proclamation of
challenge, a satirical homiletic 'complaint', or simply a command. The
messenger Mirth is the principal agent of action. He is described as a
Nuntius, but he is also apparently a tumbler (his leaping 'over the
lake') and a minstrel: sent by the Queen to the Bishop, he sings on his
way. The vaunting mode is similar to that of the mummers' plays.
Indeed, the whole play promises to be a battle in which Death will
fight against the King of Life. The King's first 'wonschild' (champion,
or defender of his household) is called Strength and boasts:

> Ic am Strent, ṣtif and strong,
>> Neuar is suc non,   *none such*
> In al þis world brod and long,
>> Imad of blod and bon.
>>>>>   (147-50)

Strength brandishes a 'bronde' and hails the King as one who 'florres-
schist with þi briȝt bronde' (277). 'Flourishing' in the technical term
for the sword display in the earliest sword-dance text. The champions
present themselves in the manner of the heroes of the mumming
plays:

> *I Miles* I wol withstonde him with strife
>> And make his sidis blede,
> And tel him þat þou are King of Life
>> And lorde of londe and lede.   *people*
>>>>>   (251-4)

The King of Life, like the worldly dancers of Franciscan exemplary
tradition, is determined to defy the voice of the Bishop with its
memento mori until the hand of Death strikes him:

> *Rex* I wool let car away,
>> And go on mi pleying.
> To hontyng and to oþir play
>> For al þi long prechyng.
>>>>>   (427-30)

The concepts of 'prechyng' and of 'playing', upon which the structure of the drama depends, are here separated for us. Playing is the not-real. The modes of playing used in *Pride of Life* show marked similarities with those established in the thirteenth-century drama: the vaunt, intimidation of the audience, running about the 'place'. The modes survive most simply and purely in the stylized combat of the mummers' plays.

The conjunction and opposition of sermon and 'game' or play appears to constitute a distinct concept of popular drama (drama for the people) long before the Corpus Christi plays. There is some evidence for thinking of this as a 'professional' tradition rather than community drama. Moreover, to judge from *Mankind* (*c.* 1465–70) the tradition continued alongside the civic cycle plays. *Mankind* has been described as 'the most indisputably popular play of the fifteenth century'.[45] Whether performed indoors or out (there is textual evidence to suggest both), by strolling players or by Cambridge clerks as a Shrovetide *jeu d'esprit*, the actors certainly took money from the audience. The elements of mummers' plays have long been recognized in the play: there is a 'beheading' combined with a mock-castration; a collection before the entry of Titivillus; this figure, 'a man wyth a hede þat ys of grett omnipotens', is himself a Big-head-and-little-wit or Beelzebub character and introduces himself with the folk-play formula: 'I com wyth my leggys wnder me'. He is also 'presented' by means of a 'make space and be ware' formula.[46] The vices jostle close to the audience, tumbling in the 'narow space', now pulling Mercy into a dance to a 'Walsyngham wystyll', now calling for a football, now instructing the audience in the singing of a scatological song.

More remarkable than the element of 'game' in *Mankind*, the endlessly resourceful improvising and role-playing of the vices, is the way these elements are controlled in the dramatic structure. Viewed in the context of the early traditions of popular drama in England, *Mankind* appears as a fruitful conjunction and opposition of sermon and game: a preached text and a series of histrionic 'improvisations' based upon it. The characters are conceived in two opposing modes: Mercy and Mankind sermonize, pray and speak in 'Englysch Laten'; Mischief, Nought, New Guise, Nowadays and Titivillus play games, run amongst

45 Bevington, *M–M*, p. 48.
46 W. K. Smart, '*Mankind* and the Mumming Plays', *MLN* XXXII (1917), pp. 21–5.

the audience and 'speak foul'. On a linguistic level the conflict is generated between the language of the soul, Mercy's 'mellyfluose doctryne' on the one hand and the obscene punning chant of 'Holyke' ('holy', 'hole-lick', etc.), the reminders 'Aryse and avent þe nature compellys!' on the other. But the play is much more than a 'flyting', a *reductio ad fundamentum* of scholastic rhetoric and Church doctrine. The action appears as a conflict between two casts of characters, conceived in different modes of behaviour and language, for possession of the acting space. Each team must hustle the other off in order to gain the audience's attention.

The text that Mercy preaches at the beginning of the play simply states the condition of Mankind. It provides no plot, no plan of action, nothing for Mankind as an actor to *do*. It is up to the vices to instigate action. They thus have a double function as agents of action and as moral values in the conflict they generate. Entertainment is equivalent to vice. The vices of the play make capital out of this, for, as Mischief and Mercy try to shoo each other off stage, Mischief tells the audience, 'I am cumme hedyr to make yow game'. Nowadays later tells Mercy:

> Men have lytyll deynte of yowre pley   *delight*
> Because ʒe make no sporte.
>
> (267–8)

Mankind's single physical activity, apart from prayer, is digging, a role he has inherited from Adam of the old play referred to by Nowadays (83–4). The digging and planting of corn are ludicrously mocked by the vices, who pretend to admire Mankind's spade-work, but point out that the play-garden is far too small to provide his year's grain, and end up by suggesting what he do in case rain fails or he cannot get manure. Mankind is forced to use his spade to beat away the impudent vices, while his digging is finally thwarted by the 'invisible' Titivillus placing a plank under his earth. The audience is explicitly invited to abet Titivillus' 'praty game' and not to wake Mankind by giving the alarm.

In conclusion, when Mankind has been reclaimed for the church, Mercy prays that the audience 'may be pleyferys with þe angellys abowe'. The angels as 'play-mates' suggests a sanctified concept of game as a state of spiritual delight which the play is singularly unable to convey. In *Mankind* play the game are exclusively the domain of the world and the devil:

Farwell, euerychon! for I haue don my game,
For I haue brought Mankynde to myscheff and to schame.

(605–6)

This farewell to the audience, spoken by Titivillus, the 'invisible'
shape-shifter who appears to the audience as a folk-play devil, emphasizes the functionality of 'game-players' in a clerical drama. These
virtuoso performers, from the scurrying diabolical stage-hands of the
Mystère d'Adam down to these sophisticated parodists, come from a
secular tradition. In the Corpus Christi plays, although game-playing
is indulged in occasionally by some of the 'good' characters (the
Towneley Noah and the Shepherds in the *Prima Pastorum*), the only
true counterpart to these actors of popular tradition is Mak.

In his authoritative study of the Corpus Christi drama, V. A. Kolve
develops the argument that the English words 'play' and 'game' became 'the ubiquitous generic term for the vernacular drama'.[47] His
concern is with the genre of the cycle plays and his book does not discuss
in any detail the dramatic nature of the early texts in which these terms
are established. The present examination of these texts and records in
the English tradition before the cycle plays has identified some precise
elements of 'game' and 'play' and some of the recurrent popular modes
of acting that were used in them. It appears that in the process of assimi-
lating these modes the clerical composers of the earliest religious plays
often turned the secularity of them to advantage in the presentation of
secular or diabolical characters, and by the pointed juxtaposition of
'game' and sermon.

The earliest plays and records cannot be said to support a notion of
'gradual secularization' of the Latin drama. Nor do they attest to much
strength or variety of liturgical traditions in England. Indeed, it is
striking that the most 'popular' modes of acting (and those closest to
the traditions of folk-drama) found in the fifteenth-century cycle plays
are the ones that dominate the thirteenth- and fourteenth-century
fragments. Granted the incompleteness as well as the bias of the records,
is it not possible that the Corpus Christi plays (far from being the
culmination of a secularizing tendency) were in some ways a *reaction* on
the part of orthodoxy to a long and flourishing tradition of miracle
plays performed for popular audiences by preaching friars and enterprising worldly clerks?

[47] Kolve, *PCC*, p. 12.

Note

Texts.

The edition used for this chapter is Eccles, *MP*, the notes of which are very helpful. The play may also be found in Manly, *Specimens of the Pre-Shaksperean Drama*, Volume I, and in Adams, *CPD*, though here it appears in a rather severely expurgated form.

Quotations from medieval religious manuals are from A. Brandeis, *Jacob's Well* (EETS, London, 1890), and M. B. Salu's translation of the *Ancrene Riwle* (London, 1955).

Scholarship and Criticism.

Sister M.P. Coogan, *An Interpretation of the Moral Play, Mankind* (Washington, 1947) deals helpfully with the play's theological aspects. Hers is the only full-length study of the play, but there are useful accounts of *Mankind* in Spivack, *SAE*, and Bevington, *M–M*. Glynne Wickham deals with the morality play in more general terms in Chapter II of *Shakespeare's Dramatic Heritage* (London, 1969).

Owst, *L–P* is invaluable on the medieval sermon, as is L. Réau, *Iconographie de l'Art Chrétien* (Paris, 1955–9), Volume II i of which covers the iconography of the Old Testament.

Abbreviation.

PL—*Patrologia Latina*.

II

Active and Idle Language:
Dramatic Images in Mankind

I

WHILE the popularity of the miracle play increases all the time, the morality is still regarded with a suspicious eye. It is considered essentially 'pre-Shakespearian': something one may be obliged to dig up in order to see what kind of 'roots' underlay the drama that 'blossomed' with the Elizabethans, but really rather brown and grubby and of no intrinsic interest. The author of one of the few readily available books covering morality plays describes the genre as a 'field of reading for the most part admittedly and unrelievedly dull', a view that's hardly an encouragement to the uninitiated to venture further. As with most plays, one would naturally take more pleasure in seeing a morality play than in reading it (though this is not Rossiter's point), but unfortunately performances of morality plays are extremely rare. Everyone has seen *Everyman*, of course, but that is neither a very typical nor a very exciting morality. It is no coincidence that *Everyman* is the only play of the genre that appears in an inexpensive and easily obtainable edition. Any enterprising director who might leaf through the learned editions of moralities in search of new material would soon be discouraged by the introductory remarks of their editors. *Mankind* has suffered especially in this way. One editor, J. Quincy Adams, wrote that

> The moral element is reduced to a minimum, and even the sole representative of good, Mercy, is deliberately made fun of with his ponderous Latinistic diction and his saccharine talk; the humour becomes at times exceedingly vulgar; and the literary skill of the writer is unusually poor. (*CPD*, p. 304)

[1] Rossiter, *EDET*, p. 86.

Admittedly this attack was made in 1924, when some of the 'exceedingly vulgar' humour was even felt to be unprintable, but the play's latest editor is hardly enthusiastic—

> the speeches of Mercy are tedious, but moralizing must be expected in a moral play. . . . The play is amusing to read and would probably be even funnier when acted. (*MP*, p. xlv)

—faint praise that would not lead a director to expect full houses. Yet when the play was performed in Toronto (in 1966) it was received with enormous enthusiasm. It seems that we have yet to come to a proper appreciation of the dramatic potential of the morality genre, at least as it is exemplified in *Mankind*.

The lack of immediate enthusiasm for the morality play is also partly accounted for by the allegorical nature of its action. Allegory is alien to our modern way of thinking, or at least it is not now conventional to think in allegorical terms, even though (according to C. S. Lewis)

> it is of the very nature of thought and language to represent what is immaterial in picturable terms.[2]

The allegorical nature of the morality play has a great deal to do with its success as drama, however, for 'the picturable', the visual qualities of allegorical imagery seem to obtain their best effect when presented dramatically. The use of a concrete metaphor to convey an abstract idea presupposes some kind of audience to whom that idea is to be conveyed. The medieval preachers realized that they could reach *their* audience—their congregation—by using allegory. They enlivened their messages by appealing to the visual imagination of their congregation through concrete images, so making their subject both more interesting and easier to grasp. The feeling of guilt, for example, would be allegorized as

> the worm of conscience, that is grutching in her conscience, [that] shal gnawe the soule[3]

for the imaginations of their hearers could seize upon the picture of a worm gnawing more easily than they could visualize guilt. From such a visual image it would be a short step to dramatic presentation,

[2] *The Allegory of Love* (New York, 1958), p. 44.
[3] Quoted in Owst, *L–P*, p. 522.

and one finds in the Coventry Leet Book, among the items listing the payment to 'players' by the Drapers Company, the item

> payd to ij wormes of conscience xvjd.[4]

Although that scene would not have been directly connected with a sermon, many of the preachers began to give their *exempla* (the illustrations to the themes of their sermons) in dramatic form (see Richard Axton's chapter above, pp. 29–31). They would include dialogues between such allegorical personages as Mercy, Truth, Righteousness and Justice, or would demonstrate a point by a piece of symbolic action, like one preacher who

> suddenly displayed the skull of a dead man which he had been carrying under his cloak,[5]

thereby reminding the audience of the nearness of Death. The preachers made abstract ideas come to life by using concrete images, and they began to convert these verbal images into visible actions, turning to good account what the allegory already naturally demanded. So they would make words flesh.

Whether or not the morality play had its origins in these dramatic sermon illustrations (as Owst and others believe), it does employ the preacher's technique of conveying meaning to an audience through visual metaphors that occur first in the spoken word and then in the action. The similarity between sermon and drama here is due perhaps not so much to kinship as to their sharing the needs of a common mode, allegory; but the use of metaphor in *Mankind* at least has further parallels with that in the sermon. The *artes praedicandi* (the medieval preaching manuals) advocated various forms of repetition among their ornaments of style, including the sustained repetition of a key-word over a long passage, which was called *traductio*. Preachers could drive home an important word to their audience through this device. Key images in *Mankind* are also emphasized by frequent repetition either in the spoken word or in the action, and several images are repeated and linked together in different patterns throughout the play. In its interweaving of a number of images into its structure, *Mankind* rather resembles the 'modern' or 'university' sermon. In this kind of sermon, the preacher did not expound a text, but took a single

---

[4] Craig, *CCP*, p. 100.
[5] G. R. Owst, *Preaching in Medieval England* (Cambridge, 1926), p. 351.

theme and explored it from various different angles, elaborating as he went along, and introducing other topics all in some way connected with the main theme. The whole was held together by a pattern of words and images that frequently reappeared. Elizabeth Salter and A. C. Spearing have shown how the art of these sermons influenced *Piers Plowman*,[6] a work that has much in common with the moralities (not only its allegorical mode). But in a sermon or a poem, such a pattern of images can only be a verbal one: in drama the pattern emerges visually as well as through words.

In *Mankind*, as in the medieval sermon, verbal images become visual as the ideas are developed, so that something spoken becomes something seen, and different images are repeated and interrelated in varying patterns. Both these aspects of the imagery give a density and unity to the events of the play.

II

The main theme of *Mankind*, of which all the ideas expressed in the play are amplifications, is concerned with *Accidia*, or Sloth (as the *Castle of Perseverance* is concerned with Covetousness, or the *Pride of Life* with Pride). The events of the play may be seen as a dramatization of the proverb:

> Satan finds some mischief still
> For idle hands to do

which Chaucer, in the *Tale of Melibee*, attributes to St. Jerome:

> therefore seith Seint Jerome, 'Dooth somme goode dedes that the devel, which is oure enemy, ne fynde yow nat unocupied.'

The play opens with a long speech from Mercy, the gist of whose message is that his hearers must persevere in good works and avoid the temptations of earthly pleasure, if they wish to be saved at the Last Judgment:

> In goode workys, I awyse yow, souerence, to be perseuerante
> To puryfye your sowlys, þat þei be nat corupte;

6 Elizabeth Salter, *Piers Plowman: An Introduction* (Oxford, 1962), pp. 24–58; A. C. Spearing, *Criticism and Medieval Poetry* (2nd edn., London, 1972), pp. 107–34.

For yowr gostly enmy wyll make hys avaunte,
Your goode condycyons yf he may interrupte.
O ȝe souerens þat sytt and ȝe brothern þat stonde ryght wppe,
Pryke not your felycytes in thyngys transytorye.
Beholde not þe erth, but lyfte your ey wppe.　　　(25–31)

For sekyrly þer xall be a streyt examynacyon,
The corn xall be sauyde, þe chaffe xall be brente.　　　(42–3)

—he does not yet specifically mention idleness, merely its opposite: hard work. The moralizing and hectoring tone of Mercy's speech resembles that of a sermon, and one can imagine an audience being annoyed and rather puzzled by it. They have come to be entertained, and now Mercy tells them that they ought not to take pleasure in any-thing transitory. If they are supposed to be actively engaged in good works they should not be sitting (or standing) about idly like this, and Mercy is virtually telling them not to look at the play ('Beholde not þe erth') but to turn their attention to God ('lyfte your ey wppe'). If Mercy is speaking from a raised station, or a 'pulpit' as used in some medieval plays, he might be telling the audience to look up at himself, but, either way, he is directing their attention away from the 'place' of playing. When he goes on to mention Christ and the Saints with still no sign of action, the audience might well wonder whether they have come on the right day, or have been tricked into hearing a sermon instead. Some critics argue that Mercy would actually have been dressed as a priest, and this would have added further to the be-wilderment of the audience.[7] Their attention would begin to wander, they might whisper to each other, possibly even fall asleep, thus exemplifying in themselves the sin of Sloth against which Mercy, with his emphasis on good works, is implicitly speaking. Gossiping and not attending to the sermon was a very serious form of Sloth, as the author of *Jacob's Well*, a fifteenth-century religious manual, tells his readers, when he condemns

. . . ȝoure ydell woordys, þat ȝe iangelyn in cherche in slowethe
(p. 115)

However, the audience are soon rudely awakened by the abrupt entry of Mischief, who bursts in while Mercy is still in rhetorical flight.

[7] Coogan, *An Interpretation of the Moral Play, Mankind*, pp. 1–7; Eccles, *MP*, p. xliii.

Mischief's appearance provides a concrete example of the point that Mercy had been at pains to make, that, given the opportunity, their 'gostly enmy' will do his best to interrupt and interfere with their good behaviour. Mischief (the word had then a much stronger meaning, something closer to 'harm' or 'evil') is a personification of evil—here specifically the bad tendencies that distract people from the good work of listening to a sermon. He 'makes his avaunt', fulfilling Mercy's prophecy, and in case anyone in the audience has missed the point, Mercy tells Mischief:

> Ʒe ben culpable
> To interrupte thus my talkyng delectable.   (64–5)

The transition from sermon to dramatic allegory is skilfully created. The dramatist satisfies the audience's desire to end Mercy's harangue with an interruption just at the right moment. Also, if, as is probable, Mischief enters by pushing his way through the audience (as the Vices do, when they ask the audience to 'make room' in l. 331) the impression given would be that it is actually a member of the audience who has thus burst in. (Pretending to be a member of the audience was not an unusual procedure for actors in the early theatre; compare the behaviour of the characters 'A' and 'B' in Medwall's *Fulgens and Lucrece* (1497), who comment on the play as if they were members of the public.) With Mischief's appearance, the audience is given a visual example, or personification, of the kind of evil interference of which Mercy had been speaking, and which they themselves had helped cause, their impatience being objectified in the character Mischief. The audience's feelings are thus immediately and intimately connected with the action of the play, for Mischief tells Mercy:

> I am cumme hedyr to make yow game   (69)

and Mischief's 'game' is to tempt the protagonist, Mankind, to sin. The audience are given a personal foretaste, in this episode, of what is going to happen to Mankind himself later on, when the devil is able to interrupt and distract him from his work because he too is impatient. This parallel is appropriate, for Mankind, as his name shows, represents all mankind, including the audience who are watching him.

Impatience (unwillingness to persevere with doing good works) was one of the forms of Sloth that led man towards an evil ending in despair, as the author of *Jacob's Well* explains:

for þat makyth a man þat he wyl noȝt blethely here what he is
worthy for his synne. Þis vyce putteth a man fro resoun, to suffre
ony-þing þat is aȝens his wyll. (p. 112)

A warning against impatience has so far only been implicit in the
theme of Mercy's sermon, but it soon becomes explicit in the advice
Mercy offers to Mankind. He tells him:

> The temptacyon of þe flesch ye must resyst lyke a man,
> For þer ys euer a batell betwyxt þe soull and þe body:
> '*Vita hominis est milicia super terram*' (226–8)

—quoting from the book of *Job* (7, 1), and before he goes away he
warns Mankind of the coming danger in words that echo those he has
previously used to the audience:

> Yuwr enmys wyll be here anon, þei make þer avaunte (278)

and exhorts Mankind to be patient like Job:

> Ȝe may not haue your intent at your fyrst dysyere.
> Se þe grett pacyence of Job in tribulacyon;
> Lyke as þe smyth trieth ern in þe feere, *iron*
> So was he triede by Godys vysytacyon.
>
> He was of your nature and your fragylyte;
> Folow þe steppys of hym, my own swete son. (285–90)

The story related in the Book of Job would have been well known to
the audience. Job was a devout and virtuous man, one of the most
important men in the land, until the devil boasted to God that he could
easily cause him to sin. When God (trusting in Job's strength) agreed
to allow Satan to try, Job was deprived of all his fortune, and then,
when this had no effect, attacked with physical diseases. He sat on a
dunghill, according to the Vulgate rendering (although the form in
the original Hebrew, and now in the Authorized Version, was 'a heap
of ashes'), where he was visited by his three well-meaning friends,
who, in trying to comfort him, tempted him to blame God. Through
all his trials, although he did complain, he never actually accused God
of wronging him, and never technically sinned, so that eventually
he was rewarded, while his friends were rebuked. The story was the
subject of a long commentary by Gregory the Great (*In expositionem
Beati Job Moralia*, PL 75), who saw Job in his sufferings as a type
of Christ especially during his trial, and said that Job chose to sit on

a dunghill as a reminder of man's origin, and the corruption of his flesh:

> In sterquilinio ponebat corpus ut ex terra sumpta quæ esset carnis substantia, bene proficiens perpenderet animus. In sterquilinio ponebat corpus ut etiam ex loci fetore caperet, quod festine corpus ad fetorem rediret. (*PL* 75, 603)

The story was frequently cited by the medieval preachers, as by Mercy here, to prove that it was humanly possible to have patience in any kind of adversity, and Job became a recognized symbol of patience.

When Mercy exhorts Mankind to follow the steps of Job, the audience would notice the similarity between the situations of the two characters, for the behaviour of Mercy and Mischief is comparable to that of God and Satan in the Book of Job. Some of the exchange between Mercy and Mischief after Mischief's entry has been lost with a missing leaf of the manuscript, but it is possible to reconstruct their conversation from subsequent remarks, and it seems that they have a 'bet' (if such an undignified word may be used in connection with Mercy and God) similar to that of God and Satan. Mischief 'makes his avaunt' that he will easily be able to tempt Mankind into sin, with the help of the Vices New Guise, Nowadays and Nought (who say later that they have heard themselves spoken about), while Mercy, trusting to Mankind's goodness (or perhaps believing that it will be a lesson to him to experience temptation), agrees to go away and leave him open to the wiles of his enemies. (This does explain why Mercy deliberately abandons Mankind to the Vices, a desertion that otherwise seems out of character, although of course his exit would be essential if, as Bevington suggests, the same actor doubled Mercy and Titivillus!)[8] Mankind makes his first appearance with the words:

> Of þe erth and of þe cley we haue owr propagacyon.
> By þe prouydens of Gode þus be we deryvatt,   (186–7)

and he goes on to speak of the need for mortifying 'owr carnall condycyon, ande owr voluntarye dysyres, þat euer be pervercyonatt'

---

[8] R. L. Ramsay, following Pollard, states in his introduction to *Magnificence* (London, 1908, p. cxxxii) that the parts of Mischief and Titivillus were the ones doubled. Titivillus' line: 'Myschyff hat informyde [me] of all þe matere thorow [*through*]' (500) might then be amusingly ironic.

(191–2), both which thoughts Job had borne in mind in his temptation. And as Mankind continues:

> O thou my soull, so sotyll in thy substance,
> Alasse, what was þi fortune and þi chaunce,
> To be assocyat wyth my flesch, þat stynkyng dungehyll?
>
> (202–4)

the associations of the word dunghill call to mind the image of patient
Job, seated on his dunghill in commemoration of man's carnal nature.
So when Mercy's overt reference to Job comes, it is only making
explicit an image of which the audience had already been made half-
aware. There is seen to be a similarity in the situations of the Biblical
character and the allegorical one, as the image of Job is presented in
opposition to the idea of Sloth condemned by Mercy. The similarity
becomes less than superficial, too, in the kind of temptation to which
Mankind is exposed. Job's most difficult temptations came from the
mocking words of his wife and the well-meaning, but wrong-headed,
speeches of his friends, and similarly it is through *words* that Mankind
is to be tempted. Immediately after his reference to Job, Mercy warns
Mankind specifically against the excessive language of the Vices:

> Moreouer, in specyall I gyue yow in charge,
> Be ware of New Gyse, Nowadays and Nought.
> Nyce in þer aray, in language þei be large;
> To perverte yowr condycyons all þe menys xall be sowte.
>
> (293–6)

> Gyff þem non audyence; þei wyll tell yow many a lye.
> Do truly yowr labure and kepe yowr halyday.   (299–300)

Mankind is to work hard and pay no attention to idle gossip, for,
Mercy tells him, it is through the excessiveness of their language that
the Vices will attempt to corrupt Mankind, to bring him to the sin
of Sloth.

The 'large' language and lies of Mischief and the Vices are familiar
to the audience by the time of this warning, but they were startling at
the time of Mischief's opening words. He had interrupted Mercy in
a low style of speech that contrasted sharply with Mercy's dignified
and aureate language:

> *Mercy:* The corn xall be sauyde, þe chaffe xall be brente.
> I besech yow hertyly, haue þis premedytacyon.

> *Mischief:* I beseche *yow* hertyly, leue yowr calcacyon   *threshing*
> Leue yowr chaff, leue yowr corn, leue yowr dalyacyon
> Yowr wytt ys lytyle, yowr hede ys mekyll, ȝe are full of
> predycacyon.   (43–7)

The play's rhyme-scheme allows Mischief to employ Latinate words in mocking echo of Mercy's aureate style. He goes on to use short common words in meaningless (or riddling) sentences, and further to mock Mercy's Latinate language with some dog-Latin of his own invention which he says prove Mercy's words untrue:

> For a wynter corn-threscher, ser, I haue hyryde,
> Ande ȝe sayde þe corn xulde be sauyde, and þe chaff xulde be feryde,
> Ande he prouyth nay, as yt schewth be þis werse:
> 'Corn seruit bredibus, chaffe horsibus, straw fyrybusque.'   (54–7)

The words 'corn' and 'chaff' in Mercy's speech were a reference to the remarks of John the Baptist (*Matthew* 3, 12; *Luke* 3, 17) about the Last Judgment, which Mischief had failed to recognize. In parodying Mercy's words, he creates the character of a corn-thresher who has different views to express on the fate of corn and chaff, but he has therby reinforced Mercy's message by reminding us of the thresher implicit in the original imagery, 'whose fan is in his hand' thoroughly to cleanse his threshing-floor (*Luke* 3, 17), bringing firmly home the reference to the Last Judgment. The words 'corn' and 'chaff' are repeated frequently in this exchange between Mercy and Mischief, in a manner that emphasizes the imagery for the benefit of the audience. Most of the Vices' 'nonsense' has this function.

III

The Vices, as agents of Mischief, use the same mocking style of conversation. New Guise cries to Mercy:

> Ey, ey! ȝour body ys full of Englysch Laten   (124)

and challenges him to turn a couple of scurrilous sentences into Latin:

> 'I haue etun a dyschfull of curdys,
> Ande I haue schetun your mowth full of turdys.'
> Now opyn yowr sachell wyth Laten wordys
> Ande sey me þis in clerycall manere.   (131–4)

As well as introducing an image (of excrement) that will function later in the action, he is neatly parodying one of the grammarians' arguments about classical languages, that you cannot use them for ordinary everyday conversation. (As Skelton later complains, in *Speke Parrot*:

> But our Grekis theyr Greke so well haue applyed
> That they cannot say in Greke, rydynge by the way,
> How, hosteler, fetche my hors a botell of hay!   (148–50)

The argument is a clever one, because no virtuous person should use the kind of language that New Guise has been speaking, and Mercy is therefore unable to produce the words that would prove the Vice wrong, and remains silent. For the proper use of language is an essential aspect of virtuous behaviour, as Stephen Hawes explains in his didactic poem *The Pastime of Pleasure*, written (in 1506), only a little later than *Mankind*.

> And thus the gentyll rethorycyan
> Through the labour of his ryall clergy
> The famous nurture orygynally began,
> Oppressynge our rudenes and our foly,
> And for to gouerne vs ryght prudently
> The good maner encreaseth dygnyte,
> And the rudenesse also inyquyte   (1219–25)

The lady Rhetoric explains that rude people (by which she means those who are idle and ignorant) will laugh at language that is beautifully aureate and uses images, because they are unable to understand it (which would be a suitable comment on Mischief's quibbling about corn). The inability to use language properly was another consequence of Sloth: young men who were too lazy to attend in rhetoric classes would come to a bad end:

> Fy upon slouth, the nouryssher of vyce
> Whiche vnto youthe doothe often preiudyce   (1147–8)

Thus the 'large', the 'idle' language of the Vices (though it may be entertaining to the audience) is a dangerous form of temptation to Mankind, and when Mercy tells the Vices

> Thys ydyll language ȝe xall repent   (147)

he is not speaking lightly, for the Vices will be sorry when the Day
of Judgment comes—as he goes on to explain to the audience:

> Thys condycyon of leuyng, yt ys prejudycyall;
> Be ware þerof, yt ys wers þan ony felony or treson.
> How may yt be excusyde befor þe Justyce of all
> When for euery ydyll worde we must ȝelde a reson?
>
> They haue grett ease, þerfor þei wyll take no thought.
> But how þen when þe angell of hewyn xall blow þe trumpe
> Ande sey to þe transgressors þat wykkydly have wrought
> 'Cum forth onto your Juge and ȝelde yowr acownte'?
>
> Then xall I, Mercy, begyn sore to wepe;
> Noþer comfort nor cownsell þer xall non be hade;
> But such as þei haue sowyn, such xall þei repe.   (170–180)

Every idle word spoken will have to be accounted for before God at
the final Judgment: whatever is sown must be reaped. Mercy is speaking on good authority here, for he is recalling the words of Christ:

> But I say unto you that every idle word that men shall speak, they
> shall give account therof in the Day of Judgment. For by thy
> words thou shalt be justified, and by thy words thou shalt be con-
> demned. (*Matthew* 12, 36–7)

Mercy had warned the audience to prepare for the Last Judgment in
his first speech, with his use of John the Baptist's corn and chaff
imagery. Here he uses similar imagery (also from a scriptural source,
Galatians 6, 7) of sowing and reaping, and the images are seen to refer
not, as might be expected, to actions, but to words. Words themselves,
if they are idle ones, are sins that will have to be accounted for; speaking an 'idle word' is doing a bad action, is committing the sin of Sloth.
Mischief had parodied Mercy's earlier reference to the Judgment,
because he did not understand it, with his 'leave your chaff, leave your
chaff'.[9] Ironically, his use of idle language meant that he would be
condemned by the very thing he was making the subject of mockery.
The joke he meant to have at Mercy's expense turns on himself.

Caxton uses this same imagery for language when he praises
Chaucer for 'castyng away the chaf of superfluyte and shewyng the

---

[9] There may well be a play upon words here—with 'chaff' as light or idle
language, banter, flippancy—although *NED* is uncertain of the earliest recorded
usage.

pyked grayn of sentence utteryd by crafty and sugred eloquence'.[10]
Wordiness and chatter were thought to be actually sinful: 'good'
language consisted of few words properly arranged ('fewe wordes
swete and sententencyous / Depaynted with golde harde in con-
struccyon', as Hawes had it—911-12). Mercy tells the Vices to use
'Few wordys, few, and well sett' (102), only to be contradicted by
New Guise:

> Ser, yt ys þe new gyse and þe new jett:
> Many wordys and schortely sett,
> Thys ys þe new gyse, euery-dele.   (103-5)

After Mercy has explained to the audience how bad language will need
accounting for at the Last Judgment, he speaks particularly against this
'new guise' that New Guise has been extolling:

> I dyscomende þe vycyouse gyse; I prey haue me excusyde,
> I nede not to speke of yt, your reson wyll tell it yow.   (183-4)

Mercy sounds like a rather embarrassed headmaster ('I don't need to
go into details, boys; you all know the kind of thing I mean') but he
is in a difficult position because to explain further would mean using
the kind of bad language he is condemning. He is in the same position
as when New Guise asked him to translate 'turds' into Latin. But also,
by refusing to be more explicit, he is following his own injunction to
use few words.

This is a good moment for the dramatist to choose for Mankind's
first entry, when he appears using language as dignified and rhetorical
as Mercy's own (thereby showing the audience that he is in a state of
grace); and speaking words that are reminiscent of Job.

Mercy had gone on to emphasize to Mankind that the way to avoid
hearing idle language was to keep too busy to listen, and he leaves
Mankind with a last warning against Sloth:

> Do truly your labure and be neuer ydyll.   (308)

Once he is left alone, Mankind protects himself by pinning to his breast
the text for Ash Wednesday:

> *Memento, homo, quod cinis est, et in cinerem reverteris*

which, it is important to know, is taken from the words of Job whose
example Mercy had suggested Mankind should follow. When Man-

10 *The Prologues and Epilogues of William Caxton*, ed. W. Crotch (EETS,
London, 1928), p. 90.

kind sits down actually wearing the Ash Wednesday text, a strong visual association is made with Job sitting on his dunghill, lamenting the state of man. What was expressed in words is now seen on the stage, and it is to be further developed. It is as well that Mankind has taken some precautions to protect himself, for immediately we hear the 'idle language' of New Guise, who is taking the opportunity to indulge in some anti-clerical satire by adding some words to the opening of Psalm 67:

'Ecce quam bonum et quam jocundum', quod þe Deull to þe frerys, 'Habitare fratres in unum' (325–6)

implying that the friars will have a jolly brotherly time living with the devil in Hell.[11] Mankind, however, remembers Mercy's advice to 'give them none audience':

I her a felow speke; wyth hym I wyll not mell.
Thys erth wyth my spade I xall assay to delffe,
To eschew ydullnes   (327–9)

and he sets to work (thus ignoring, like Job, the chattering of his idle visitors).

Mankind's digging is important because it shows that he is working (not being slothful), but it also has a symbolic significance. He is digging to plant corn, and this action again recalls the earlier corn and chaff imagery. The corn symbolizes the good words and deeds that Mankind is intending to sow, and the action shows that at this point he is worthy of being saved. The Vices set about trying to distract him from his work and prevent him from sowing anything worth reaping, and, as by this time is to be expected, their distracting takes the form of 'many wordys and schortely sett'. They invite the audience to join them in a 'Christmas song' which again employs excremental imagery, and used to participation, the audience will probably begin to do so before realizing what kind of language they are singing. So Mankind is surrounded by people singing a dirty (and no doubt tuneless) song—very difficult for him to work under such circumstances.

This piece of action further develops the visual association with Job, for a popular element in the iconography of Job, occurring in many illustrations (though it does not appear in the Biblical account), was the episode in which Job's three 'friends' try to rouse him by playing

[11] There must have been some quite literate people among the audience, if they were meant to understand this joke.

a discordant tune with drums and tabours.[12] Here Mankind is similarly assailed with a discordant tune from the three Vices.

He is—at least outwardly—unimpressed by the Christmas song, and defends the necessity to work:

> Leue yowr derysyon and your japyng.
> I must nedys labure, yt ys my lyvynge.   (349–50)

and so the Vices turn their attention to his corn (playing on the word to emphasize it for the benefit of the audience, as Mischief had done earlier). They joke about the amount of corn he is planting, offer to buy the corn from him, and finally make lewd suggestions about how he might water and manure it (suggestions involving bodily functions which at this point seem merely provoking for Mankind, but which are later seen to have a more serious significance). Incensed, Mankind beats the Vices with his spade, and they flee. Thus he is the victor in the first round of temptation, putting to flight the personifications of idleness with the symbol of his work. He goes away to fetch corn, promising to 'live ever with labour'.

IV

But his pride in his own achievement has come a little too soon, for he has forgotten the remainder of Mercy's warning. He announces proudly:

> Thre of myn enmys I haue putt to flyght   (395)

but seems not to have remembered that there is another. Mercy had told him also to

> Be ware of Tytivillus, for he lesyth no wey,
> Þat goth invysybull and wyll not be sen.
> He wyll ronde in your ere, and cast a nett befor yowr ey.
> He ys worse of þem all . . .   (301–4)

Given the particular type of sin in which the Vices are going to try to interest Mankind, their employment of Titivillus to assist them is particularly appropriate. The tricks of this demon were well known from sermons and church carvings. He appears to have been invented by the medieval preachers especially to deal with those who used 'idle language' in church, either by repeating parts of the

---

[12] See Réau, *Iconographie de l'Art Chrétien*, II i, pp. 317–18.

liturgy in a careless and irreverent fashion or by whispering and gossiping instead of paying attention. The story is told in *Jacob's Well*, after
its author has finished listing the various parts of Sloth, of how

> an holy man stood in cherch . . . and seyʒ a feend beryng a gret
> sacchell full of thyng[s] . . . as þe man askyd þe feend what he bare,
> þe feend seyde: 'I bere in my sacche sylablys and woordys, ouer-
> skypped and synkopyd, and verse and psalms þe whiche þese clerkys
> han stolyn in þe qweere, and haue fayled in here seruyse.'

And he continues:

> Forsothe, þanne I trowe þe feend hath a gret sacche full of ʒoure
> ydell woordys, þat ʒe iangelyn in cherche in slowthe. For þis same
> clerk seyth þat þe deuyl in a cherche wrote þe woordys of þe peple,
> whiche þei iangleden and rownedyn in cherch . . . An holy man
> seyʒ þis, and askyd þe feend why he dyde so. Þe feend seyde: 'I wryte
> þise talys of þe peple in þis cherche, to recordyn hem a-fore god at
> þe doom for here dampnacyon.' (pp. 114–15)

In this story the fiend is not named, but that it was Titivillus who took
this role can be seen from a fifteenth-century lyric which begins:

> Tutivillus, þe deuyl of hell,
> He wryteþ har names soþe to tel,
> *Ad missam garulantes*[13]

and Titivillus appears performing these duties in the Last Judgment
play of the Towneley cycle, where he rounds up the damned having
explained to the audience:

> Fragmina verborum Tutivillus colligit horum (251)

In fact this demon may well have been a personification created to
illustrate just that Biblical text to which Mercy has referred ('for every
idle word that men shall speak, they shall give account thereof at the
Day of Judgment'). A preacher could have brought that text vividly
to life by creating a picture of this devil, lying in wait to catch every
dropped word; certainly the author of *Mankind* does so here. The
earlier warnings about the Day of Judgment are linked with the

---

[13] *Religious Lyrics of the XVth Century*, ed. Carleton Brown (Oxford, 1939),
p. 277.

dangers of 'idle language' by the character of Titivillus. Those of the audience who were inattentive during Mercy's opening harangue might well feel uncomfortable at the arrival of Titivillus (not to mention all who had joined in the Christmas song), while it is fortunate for the Vices that they are already beyond redemption, considering the way they misuse psalms. New Guise's opening gambit, one recalls, was to try to get Mankind to take part in perverting Psalm 67, and thereby to use words that would qualify for Titivillus' sack. Could the Vices succeed in getting Mankind to use 'idle language', Titivillus would be there ready to gather up the words and present them at the Last Judgment.

Although Mercy tells Mankind at the end of the play that Titivillus 'syngnyfyth the Fend of helle', all we know at this stage, like Mankind himself, is that:

> He wyll ronde in yowr ere and cast a nett befor yowr ey *whisper*
> (303)

but the whispering should identify Titivillus as the Devil (even though the use of a net or veil is unusual) for it was a well-known activity of his, and again was a common theme among the preachers, this extract from the *Ancrene Riwle* (a manual of instruction for anchoresses) being a good example.

> The man who is slothful lies sleeping in the devil's bosom, his dear darling, and the devil puts his mouth to his ear and whispers to him all he wants to. Thus it is, assuredly, with anyone who is idle, neglecting to do good. The devil is very ready to talk to him, and the idle man welcomes this teaching of his. Lazy and heedless is this sleep of the child of the devil, but at the Day of Judgment he will be fiercely awakened by the terrible sound of the angels' trumpets. (p. 95)

The passage shows that the whispering devil has a close connection with the events of the Day of Judgment, and points out the importance of Titivillus' activities in the play in relation to Mercy's warning about the Judgment Day. The image of the devil as whispering tempter (the 'soft voice of the serpent') was of course ultimately derived from the story of the Fall, where the devil waits 'close at the ear of Eve' and murmurs to her how she can become a goddess. The scene would be familiar from the miracle-play dramatizations of that episode, as well as other episodes relating to it, like that in which the Devil whispers to Pilate's wife while she is asleep that she ought to try to stop the Crucifixion (an episode that is visually, because of the sleeping, closer to the one in *Mankind*), which occurs in the York, Hegge, and Cornish cycles. It was generally believed that the devil found women more willing than men to listen. The Serpent had used Eve as a way of getting at Adam, and thereby caused the Fall of Man. (Milton actually shows Satan attempting to approach Eve when she is asleep, *before* the Fall:

> Squat like a Toad, close at the ear of Eve;
> Assaying by his Devilish art to reach
> The Organs of her Fancie, and with them forge
> Illusions as he list, Fantasms and Dreams
> *Paradise Lost* IV, 800–03)

Gregory pointed out that the Devil attempted to do the same thing with Job—tempt him through his wife—but that he was in this case unsuccessful:

> Quaerit mulierem quasi scalam, qua in cor Job ascendat: sed frustra . . .
> Nam antiquae artis insidias repetit; et quia scit quomodo Adam decipi solleat, ad Evam recurrit.[14]

So in the scene in which Titivillus whispers in Mankind's ear, there would be a visual association made with the whispering of the devil that caused the fall of man.

There would already have been an unavoidable association of Mankind with Adam, partly because of his name, but more especially through his digging with a spade, for this action was commonly used to symbolize fallen man and the spade was the iconographical attribute of Adam as the key was of Peter and the cockle-shell of James. When Adam and Eve were expelled from Paradise they were made to work for their living: God told them, 'In the sweat of thy face shalt thou eat bread' (*Genesis* 3, 19), and in the iconography of this episode Adam and Eve are shown holding the tools of their labour, a spade and a distaff. There is a good example of this scene in the *Holkham Bible Picture Book* (fol. 4v) and an excellent representation of Adam digging may be found in the west window of Canterbury Cathedral. The imposition of work was originally a punishment, but it was also useful in demonstrating God's desire for man henceforth:

> For this ye may understonde that hit ys the wyll of Gode that every man and woman schuld labour besyly. For yf Adam and Eve had ben occupyed wyth labour, the serpent had not overcum them: for ydulnesse ys the devylles dyssyre. Wherfor ye may know well yt ys the wylle of Gode that we schuld labour and put our body to penaunce for to fle synne. Thus dyd Adam and Eve, to example of all tho that schuld come after them.[15]

Thus the image of Mankind with a spade is a somewhat ambiguous one. As explained earlier, it showed that Mankind was working and so avoiding Sloth, but it also had less pleasant associations.

As long as the main parallel with Mankind is that of Job, the image of Adam is only latent (additionally because Job's mortifying of his flesh was done in commemoration of fallen man). But as Mankind goes away, to fetch his corn, he says:

> Wyth my spade I wyll departe, my worschyppull souerence,
> Ande lyve euer wyth labure to corecte my insolence   (409–10)

words which are an unconscious recalling of the punishment for the Fall; and the audience remembers, even if Mankind does not, the dangers of Titivillus.

However, before the Vices bring in Titivillus, they insist on a collection. The audience pay up, because they want to see Titivillus, and in this way they again become accomplices in Mankind's temptation, as they did if they joined in the ribald 'Christmas' song. When Titivillus does appear, he seems to be following Mischief's habit of riddling, for instead of referring to his usual function (as he does in the Towneley play), he makes the enigmatic remark:

> 3e þat haue goode hors, to yow I sey caueatis!   (476)

One meaning of his remark soon becomes clear when it is discovered that the Vices claim to have no money to pay Titivillus (they have stolen what they collected from the audience), and they are sent to steal horses and other property as payment instead. But Titivillus' reference to horses also has a more ominous significance, for it continues a line of imagery used earlier in the play.

[15] Quoted in Owst, L–P, p. 555.

Mercy had warned Mankind:

> Yf ȝe dysples Gode, aske Mercy anon,
> Ellys Myscheff wyll be redy to brace yow in hys brydyll
>
> (305–6)

using the image of Mankind as a horse of which Mischief will be waiting to take control. Mischief had said earlier to Mercy that he could not ride (go away) because he had no horse. It had seemed then to be one of Mischief's enigmatic remarks, perhaps suggested by his dictum that chaff was for horses. Subsequently though, Mercy, discussing the battle between the soul and the body in quoting the text from Job, used the image of an unruly horse to show what happens when the body takes charge of the soul:

> Yf a man haue an hors, and kepe hym not to hye, *too proud*
> He may then reull hym at hys own dysyere.
> Yf he be fede ouerwell he wyll dysobey
> Ande in happe cast his master in þe myre. (241–4)

The horse is the body ('my flesch, þat stynkyng dungehyll') which should be ruled by the soul, as would happen as long as Mankind remained 'Crystys own knyght' (229). But Mischief, who is lacking a horse, will try to find one in Mankind's flesh. And he will do this by feeding him 'ouerwell': on excessive 'chaff' (or 'idle language'), chaff being the food for horses, as Mischief had already pointed out. So when Titivillus tells the audience to beware lest their horses are stolen he is speaking metaphorically: the Vices' idle language is the chaff that will feed the horses (their flesh) too well (with many words) and thereby gain control of their souls. Titivillus, in fact, is going to help the Vices find Mischief a horse in Mankind: 'brace' Mankind in Mischief's 'bridle'. And this metaphor too, is made concrete in the action later, when we see Mischief's 'bridle' in the shape of the halter or noose with which Mankind tries to hang himself. Titivillus is right to tell the audience 'caveatis'.

V

When the Vices have gone off to steal all the horses they can find, Titivillus remains, ominously

> To *speke* wyth Mankynde (525)

He has a more subtle approach than the Vices; not to try to speak to Mankind while he is working, but to use devices to distract him from work, and so obtain his full attention. Mankind will be more vulnerable when idle (as Mercy has pointed out). Titivillus' first actions are to put a board under the earth to make it the harder for Mankind to dig, and then to mix weeds and tares among his corn, so that when it does grow, it will be worthless. That is, he does not simply talk to distract Mankind from his corn-sowing (symbol of his goodness) but takes active measures to prevent his growing any.

These actions would also have provided further visual associations with fallen man, making the image of Adam now stronger than that of Job, and strengthening our sense of Mankind's (and all mankind's) propensity to sin. For in Genesis God curses the ground and makes weeds spring up instead of corn:

> And unto Adam he said, Because thou hast hearkened unto the voice of thy wife, and hast eaten of the tree of which I commanded thee, saying, Thou shalt not eat of it: Cursed is the ground for thy sake; in toil shalt thou eat of it all the days of thy life; Thorns also and thistles shall it bring forth to thee. (*Genesis* 3, 17–18)

In the iconography of this episode, devils are shown sowing the tares among the corn, and there is a counterpart in drama. In the *Mystère d'Adam*, there is a stage direction:

> Meanwhile the devil shall come and shall plant thorns and thistles in their plot and go away. When Adam and Eve come to their plot and see the thorns and thistles growing, they shall be seized with violent grief and prostrate themselves on the ground.[16]

while in a later Breton Creation play, *several* devils are shown sowing bad seeds among the corn.[17] The result of the devil's work in these Creation plays is to bring Adam and Eve to a state of despair, and Mankind is near to such a state after Titivillus' actions, for he exclaims (somewhat petulantly)

> Here I gyff wppe my spade for now and for euer. (549)

[16] Axton and Stevens, *Medieval French Plays*, p. 33.

[17] God's curse is dramatized in an unusual way in the Cornish *Origo Mundi*. The earth cries out in pain when Adam tries to dig it, and Adam has to wheedle God into making the ground soft enough for him to dig. Titivillus' use of a plank to prevent Mankind digging seems analogous to this episode, but the similarity is perhaps coincidental.

He has not yet fallen completely into idleness, for he says he is going to say his prayers. But now Titivillus attacks in precisely the way Mercy had warned:

> I xall go to hys ere and tytyll þerin   (557)

and encourages him to abbreviate his prayers:

> A schorte preyere thyrlyth hewyn   'thrills'—pierces
> (558)

hoping, no doubt, that Mankind will now produce some suitable words for his sack.

Unfortunately Mercy did not warn Mankind of what exactly Titivillus would say. Perhaps he did not know, but more probably he was unable to use the kind of language necessary to express it, for Titivillus makes a palpable hit:

> Aryse and avent þe. Nature compellys.   (560)

It shows the power of Titivillus that Mankind, who in his opening speech thought we ought to

> mortyfye owr carnall condycyon
> Ande owr voluntarye dysyres, þat euer be pervercyonatt.   (191–2)

should now submit so easily to a bodily need.[18] From our modern point of view, Mankind's temporary (as he thought) abandoning of his devotions to such a necessary end seems not unreasonable, but strict medieval morality held differently. One medieval sermon, for instance, tells the story of a man who was tempted by the devil to leave Mass. The devil took the form of one of his servants, and came to tell him that his wife was dying. But the man refused to go home until Mass was over, when he returned to find that his wife was perfectly well, and he realized that he had been tempted by the devil.[19] Titivillus emphasizes for the audience that Mankind was wrong to leave his prayers, by the kind of imagery he employs: 'I haue sent hym forth to schyte lesyngs [lies]' (568).

Here, then, lies (another form—the most perverted form—of idle language) are overtly associated with excrement. Up to this point the

---

[18] This is probably another reminder of man's fallen state, for it seems unlikely that pre-lapsarian man would have needed to perform such an action.

[19] *Middle English Sermons*, ed. W. O. Ross (EETS, London, 1960), pp. 184–5.

speeches of the Vices have been full of 'Billingsgate language', such as New Guise's query about whether Mercy can translate 'turds' into Latin, the words of the Christmas song, the teasing of Mankind by suggesting he might personally manure his corn, even the reference to Nought's purse ('as clean as a bird's arse'). Mankind had resisted that first suggestion of the Vices and suppressed the promptings of the flesh, 'that stinking dunghill', in a way that associated him with Job. But now he associates himself with the Vices, for he obeys Titivillus, and goes out to

go do þat nedys must be don.   (563)

At least he does go out: later, Nought indulges (or says he is indulging) in this physical act actually in the presence of the audience (783–6), thus outdoing in 'realism' anything that has yet occurred (so far as I know) on our contemporary stage. Here is the most striking example in the play of a verbal image being made visual (word becoming not flesh, in this case, but faeces).

Once Mankind has reached this stage of degradation, it is easy for Titivillus and the Vices to engineer his complete collapse. When Mankind has fallen asleep, Titivillus whispers to him that Mercy has been hanged for horse-stealing, and then the Vices run in, New Guise with the remains of a noose still about his neck, having just escaped hanging for that very act. The word 'neck' is repeated several times in this section—'I herd esey he brake hys neke' (597); 'Mercy hath brokyn hys neke-kycher' (607); 'he hangyth by þe neke' (608); 'I was twychyde by þe neke' (615); 'halffe ys abowte my neke' (617); 'Myscheff is a convicte, for he coude hys neke-verse' (618). Through all these remarks, which work just like a *traductio* in a sermon, an ironic point is being made in the emphasizing of references to necks and hanging. The neck-verse was the verse that had to be repeated by a defendant claiming benefit of clergy to escape hanging. It was the opening of Psalm 51:

> Have mercy upon me, O lord, after thy great goodness. According to the multitude of thy mercies, do away mine offences.

As 'goodness' is a translation of *misericordiam* in the Vulgate version, a form of the word 'Mercy' appeared three times in the verse as the medieval clergy would have spoken it. Yet Mankind is willing to believe that *Mercy* (the personification of such a text) has been hanged,

while Mischief is saved *because he knew his neck-verse*. It dramatizes the
state of degeneracy Mankind has now reached. He is even willing
to believe New Guises's story that the thing round his neck (the
remains of the noose) is the mark of ring worm.

He now submits himself completely to the Vices, and asks for
their Mercy:

> I aske mercy of New Gyse Nowadays and Nought,
> Onys wyth my spade I remember þat I faught.   (650–1)

thus completely reversing the earlier scene (of which he reminds
the audience), when he had beaten the Vices with the instrument
of his labour. His action also recalls the scene where he had knelt
to be blessed by Mercy, for here he kneels to the Vices, who tell him
to 'stonde wppe on yowr feet' (661) exactly as Mercy had done (218).
The audience now sees Mankind in exactly the position he had been
lamenting on his first entry, with

> þe flesch prosperouse, and þe soull trodyn wnder fote   (206)

The parody of proper order is reinforced in the powerful 'court'
scene. New Guise cries out:

> Master Myscheff, we wyll yow exort
> Mankyndys name in yowr bok for to report   (662–3)

—lines that unpleasantly recall Titivillus' scroll of Sinners and their idle
words collected for the Last Judgment, so that when Mischief replies:

> I wyll not so; I wyll sett a corte   (664)

the words seem to imply a decision not to wait for the Last Judgment,
but to hold the Judgment now. The proceedings of Mischief's court
(as well as providing an entertaining parody of the proceedings of a
manorial court of justice) parody the scenes of the Last Judgment
plays, when Christ asks those who fed the hungry, clothed the naked
and performed other good deeds to come into Heaven with him, and
casts the wicked into Hell. Mankind now mechanically agrees to a
whole series of acts, any of which would serve to damn him:

> *New Guise:* Ʒe xall goo robbe, stell, and kyll, as fast as ye may gone.
> 'I wyll', sey Ʒe.
>
> *Mankind:*   I wyll, ser.   (708–9)

and this 'examination' continues for some time, until the Vices see Mercy coming in the distance.

Mercy had warned at the beginning that there would be a 'streyt examynacyon' and all the verbal references to the Last Judgment were leading up to this visual representation of a 'judgment'. This episode is both a parody and a warning, for Mankind falls into despair exactly as if it *had* been the *Last* Judgment and he could not possibly be saved.

The audience would have a distinctly uncomfortable feeling at this point. They had been at least partly responsible for bringing on Mischief; had joined in the Vices' 'Christmas Song', thus taking their side; and had paid up for the appearance of Titivillus, so finally helping to make Mankind sin. They now find they have been playing a 'game' in which someone has actually been hurt: a soul is in danger of being lost.

The entry of Mercy at this point is of great importance dramatically. The moment seems to be the exact opposite of that in which Mischief had entered. The impatience of the audience with Mercy had brought Mischief on; now, suddenly sobered by the goal they have reached, the path they have come, they wish once more for Mercy. Mischief sees Mercy coming from some way off (722) and he should come in from beyond the audience and make his way through them, as Mischief did, so seeming to come with the audience's support. The powerfully dramatic quality of Mercy's entry—as borne out in the Toronto and the Bristol revivals—contradicts the common view that it is the Vices who really hold our attention: 'the virtues . . . are reduced to solemn, lifeless homilists whereas the vices monopolize the theatrical life of the play'.[20] Mercy's aureate language is dignified and moving after what we have been hearing:

I dyscomende and dysalow þin oftyn mutabylyte.
To euery creature þou art dyspectuouse and odyble.
> *despicable and hateful*
Why art þou so oncurtess, so inconsyderatt?
> Alasse, who ys me!
As þe fane that turnyth wyth þe wynde, so þou art conuertyble.
> (746-9)

This was the style that Mankind had originally been using. He has just gone out shouting for a tavern wench, with New Guise, who is

[20] Spivack, *SAE*, pp. 125-6.

c

calling for a football, and Mischief, who threatened: 'I shall beshit you all.' We had become so accustomed to the 'vicious guise' that we had almost forgotten how Mankind's language had changed. The contrast in style and mood well demonstrates the superiority of virtue. As Mercy, weeping, seeks Mankind, the Vices' mocking of his Latin is no longer funny. Also, the audience could hardly fail to compare Mercy's weeping (at Mankind's fall from grace) with the childish crying of the Vices after they had been hurt by Mankind—physically beaten by his spade. Here, Mischief mocks Mercy as he had 'his babes' the Vices, and, as he made them whole again, so Mercy will make Mankind whole by forgiving him. The earlier scene showed the deceptive nature of Mischief's actions: he did not actually do anything to the Vices to make them better (his action was really rather a parody of a mother's 'let me kiss it better, dear'), whereas we see Mankind kneeling and receiving forgiveness from Mercy.

But before this final forgiveness, we are made to witness the state of despair into which Mankind has been brought, so that he is ready to hang himself. The author of *Jacob's Well* had shown how the ultimate end of Sloth was despair:

> Wanhope, þat makyth a man noȝt to trusten in goddys mercy; for hym thynketh his synne is so myche, þat he may neuere haue forȝevenesse, and so peradventure, he may sle hym-self thruȝ þe feendys combryng . . . for þise fyve ferste [degrees of sloth] wyll bryngen a man to þe sexte, þat is, wanhope, and wanhope wyll makyn a man to holdyn himself so synfull and cursed, þat hym thynketh þat he may noȝt ben amendyd, and þat he is so feble, þat he may withstonde no temptacyon, but sufferyth þe feend, þe world, and þe flesch, to haue here wylle, and he folwyth all here lust in every temptacyon, noȝt crying to god of helpe, but demyth him-self to be dampnyd. he wyll noȝt repentyn hym, ne cryin god mercy. he thynketh þat god were unryȝtfull, ȝyf he ȝaf hym mercy (pp. 112–13).

This is the state of mind to which Mankind is brought when he learns that Mercy is not dead, in fact is seeking him. He calls for a rope to hang himself: 'A roppe, a roppe, a rope! I am not worthy' (800). All the earlier references to necks and hanging have been leading up to this: the noose is 'Mischiefs bridle' which had been the subject of Mercy's warning. Mischief's 'game' was not really as entertaining as the audience thought. What he was doing was trying to ensnare an immortal soul, by bringing it through all the stages of Sloth to the final one of Despair. If the Vices had succeeded in getting Mankind to hang himself he could not have been saved, because, as Mercy later explains, you cannot ask for mercy after Death. The noose provides a concrete image of the dangers of submitting to Mischief.[21] Mankind believes (in his despair) that he is unworthy of mercy:

> What, ask mercy ȝet onys agayn? Alas yt were a wyle petycyun.
> Ewyr to offend and euer to aske mercy, yt ys a puerilite.
> Yt ys so abhominabyll to rehers my iterat transgrescion,
> I am not worthy to hawe mercy be no possibilite.   (819–22)

(Notice the change in his language now that the Vices have gone.) But Mercy insists that God will forgive, if he is asked for mercy.

> God wyll not make ȝow preuy onto hys Last Jugement   *privy*
>   (839)

and he emphasizes that mercy is available right up until a man's deat h as long as he asks for it. After that, however, he will get his reward, whatever that may be. Mankind kneels and receives forgiveness from Mercy, and when Mercy tells him to rise (811, 877), a visual parallel is made with the former occasions when Mankind was seen kneeling, first to Virtue (218) and then to Vice (661). Now he kneels to Virtue again, and the action symbolizes his vacillating nature, which seems

> Ewyr to offend and euer to aske mercy   (820)

It also emphasizes that mercy is always available, as long as it is *wanted*. The character Mercy, we realize, was present in the play as long as he was wanted. The audience's slothful impatience had brought on Mischief and started Mischief's game, thus dismissing Mercy; later, tired of the Vices and chastened by the Devil's work, they longed for Mercy again, and he returned. This final action symbolizing Mankind's own changeability, his weathervane character, makes us realize the central image implicit throughout the play, or rather, of what the play itself has been an image. Mankind stands for mankind, and the action the audience has been watching has really been about themselves. Their inner feelings have been externalized, personified in the play's action: the play has reflected, like a mirror, their own state of mind.

[21] Coogan (*An Interpretation of the Moral Play, Mankind*, pp. 58–61), comparing Mischief with his counterpart in *Magnificence* (the only other play in which such a personification appears), suggests that Mischief represents suicide.

Note

Texts.

Plays referred to in this chapter can be found in Stokes, *BM*, and Furnivall, *DP*. A more recent but unpublished edition of *St. Meriasek*, by R. Morton Nance, is contained in the Nance Bequest, Royal Institution of Cornwall, Truro.

Non-dramatic texts referred to are the *Early South England Legendary*, ed. C. Horstmann (EETS, No. 87, London, 1887), and *Monumenta Franciscana* (Rolls Series, 1858).

Scholarship and Criticism.

Chambers, *MS*, and Wickham, *EES*, are basic works of reference. Gardiner, *ME*, is helpful on the demise of early religious drama; and Auerbach, *Mimesis*, is a useful touchstone on the nature of dramatic experience. Wickham has also written illuminatingly on the staging of East Midland saints' plays in 'The Staging of Saint Plays in England' (*The Medieval Drama*, ed. Sandro Sticca, Albany, 1972).

III

English Saints' Plays

DAVID L. JEFFREY

I

CARLYLE'S suggestion that religion and human history have for their basic measure the biographies of great men was probably never better appreciated than by our medieval forefathers. Yet their own sense of history, less linear and with a much more comprehensive scope of 'present' than Carlyle's, found its most attractive margin in spiritual biography—the lives of the saints. It is difficult for us to imagine how large and important a body of medieval literature was devoted to this subject. Stories of martyrs such as Katherine, Laurence, or Thomas à Becket were as popular in their own day as tales of Sigfried, Roland or Arthur, and whether as conventionalized portrayals of a high romantic ideal or as a recurrent token of God's power in the world of men, they were much prized and faithfully preserved until the time of Henry VIII. The dramatic form of the saint's life, no less than its now more familiar versified counterpart of the legendary, very much participated in this general popularity. Between the mid-thirteenth-century play of St. Nicholas and the last play of Thomas the Apostle at York in 1535, extant records attest to the performance of English plays on a veritable host of saints: Christiana, Clara, Feliciana, Margaret, Sabina, Susanna, Andrew, James, John, George, Placidus, Swithin, Sylvester, Martin, Eustace, Dionysius, Robert King of Sicily and others.[1] The dramatic quality of some of these plays, many of whose protagonists we now scarcely recognize, must have been superior; for their performance span of three centuries is much longer than that generally reported for cycles and moralities. It is unfortunate, then, that (aside from the Cornish *St. Meriasek*) we are now left with but two late fifteenth-century texts from a once-great repertoire of English saints' drama.

[1] See Harbage and Schoenbaum, *Annals, passim*; Stokes, *BM*. The plays, including *Herod's Slaughter of the Innocents*, and an imperfect fragment of the morality *Wisdom, Who is Christ*, have been edited by F. J. Furnivall (*DP*).

The *Conversion of St. Paul* and *Mary Magdalene* both occur in the same manuscript, MS Digby 133. Happily, they are not only in good condition, but are complete, well-wrought plays, capable of offering a splendid theatrical experience to the student of English drama. *Mary Magdalene* particularly has an enormous potential for modern production. And while it would be unfair to expect either play to be fully typical of its genre, with certain allowances they can stand very well as representatives of the tradition to which some criticism has made them seem but dusky shadows.

Our most important allowance must be that suggested by the textual history of the saints' plays. They have not always been universally popular. Following Henry VIII's break with Rome, even references to saints' plays very rapidly disappear, and—as in the case of saints in sculpture and stained glass—it is more than likely that at this or in Cromwell's time their texts suffered a similar fate.[2] It is not difficult to imagine why this should have happened. As with other romantic literature, the engagement of the saints' life is in identification and, as in all good drama, its proper experience a kind of participation. That at least some of the English saints' plays were powerful in this way is made more than clear by Henry's damning bans and proclamations, which unwittingly commend the plays' effectiveness in so insistently regarding them as seditious. (The last York play of Thomas the Apostle, for example, was held to be directly responsible for a general uprising against the new order.[3]) But Henry was not the first opponent of the plays—even particularly of the saints' plays—and many of his theologically orientated anti-thespians were simply following a prejudice already established among their philosophical predecessors of the fourteenth century. These men must have been aware that the roots of their opposition struck at a deeper level than mere political tactic or expediency.

Some of the earliest objections to the plays give us a fair apprehension of what was to become their insurmountable opposition. One Wyclifite, after viewing some performances by the Franciscans, wrote a critical review in verse. Following his description of one sequence, he says:

> Went I forther on my way in that same tyde,
> Ther I sawe a frere blede in myddes of his syde,

[2] Gardiner, *ME*, pp. 54-7.
[3] Documents reproduced by Wickham, *EES*, Vol. II (i), pp. 62-3.

Bothe in hondes and in fete had he woundes wyde,
To serve to that same frere the Pope mot abyde.

With an O and an I, I wonder of thes dedes
To se a Pope holde a dishe whyl the frer bledes.
A cart was made al of fyre as it shuld be,
A Gray frere I saw ther inne that best lyked me.
Wele I wote thai shal be brent by my leaute,
God graunte me that grace that I may it se.[4]

What he seems to have observed is a play on the life of St. Francis, involving the stigmatization and the saint's vision at Rivo Torto, besides other visionary material from the early spiritual biographies. Clearly he didn't like what he saw, partly for personal reasons perhaps (apparently he was an ex-Franciscan), but ostensibly because he objected to the untruthfulness of what he considered to be blasphemous representation. This becomes even clearer in his critique of the cruci-fixion staging, probably part of the same objectionable play about St. Francis:

With an O and an I, thai praysen not Seynt Poule,
Thai lyen on seyn Fraunceys by my fader soule;
First thai gabben on God that alle men may se
When thai hangen him on hegh on a grene tre,
With leues and wit blossemes that bright are of ble,
That was neuer Goddes Son by my leute.

(5-10)

Our critic has a fundamentally historical bias: what he sees is an un-faithful representation. Having read the text he knows that Christ wasn't really crucified that way, and he seems pretty much unconvinced that the Pope was handy enough to catch the blood dripping from Francis's stigmatic wounds. Even the later Protestant criticism of the bare fact of representation seems to be anticipated in his virulence: since the figure on the Cross could not be God's son, surely it cannot avoid being blasphemous pretence. The attack accords with others which survive: as, for example, one by another Wyclifite, which finds the plays composed of 'lies', 'distortions of Scripture' and 'abominations',[5] and this general sort of criticism seems to have gradually built up the

[4] Ed. J. S. Brewer, *Monumenta Franciscana*, Vol. I, pp. 606ff.
[5] Ed. Thomas Wright and J. O. Halliwell in *Reliquae Antiquae* (London, 1841), Vol. II, pp. 42-57.

position from which the saints' plays came under insurmountable fire in the early sixteenth century.

Together, these criticisms help to illustrate a point of major importance in the study of drama at the end of the medieval period. The change in theology following Henry's break with Rome entailed (as do all philosophies of revolution) a changed view of history as well. The old view of history as an artificial frame for the recurrence of divine pattern had been common to several centuries of European culture, and had been codified in interpretations of Scripture as diverse as Augustine's *City of God*, the *Meditations of the Life of Christ*, the *Biblia Pauperum*, the programme of sculpture at Chartres, and all traditions of Christian hagiography. This view saw men of every generation participating in one great *historia*—in the *speculum humanae salvationis*. In this view nothing happens for the first time. What 'happened' in the Old Testament recurs to fulfilment again in the New and again in the lives of the saints. The theme is recurrence. Christ lives and dies and is born again daily in the sacrament and in the hearts of men. There is no 'pretence' as such even in a crucifixion play, for the actor, like his audience, is participating in a divine pattern. Like Paul, Peter, or Francis, they try to come to grips in a powerful way with what it means to be 'crucified with Christ'. Nor is there false pretence in what may seem to be the extravagant common stock miracles of the typical saint's life, for while these may be as conventional and artificial as any similar device in romance, their function is not more demanding, but simply by being a *signum* of the one Christian Spirit in which all may participate, they invite that participation. This is why the medieval hagiographers saw nothing incongruous in attributing to the life of a saint who lived in the tenth century precisely the same miracles as were reported for one from the fourth century—as Reginald of Canterbury put it, 'all things are common in the communion of saints'.[6] In fact, it is better to talk about the life of the saints than the lives of the saints, according to Gregory of Tours, 'because though there may be some difference in their merits and virtues, yet the life of one body nourished them in all the world'.[7] Here is a view of history, but history *sub species*

[6] Ed. Levi R. Lind, *The Vita Sancti Malchi of Reginald of Canterbury* (Urbana, 1942), pp. 40–41.

[7] *Gregorii Eps. Turoniensis Liber Vitae Patrum* (in T. Mommsen *et al.*, *Monumenta Germaniae Historica*, Scriptores Rerum Merovingicarum, I), pp. 662–663.

æternitas—or history as poetry. It was not a view shared by English reformists of the sixteenth century.

For the late medieval dramatist, the essence of the reformists' position is their rejection of catholicity in its widest sense, in their assertion that time and space and the community of men were not, *in conspectu Dei*, continuous. To refuse the doctrine of the 'real presence' is to reject a view of history as much as a view of theology, as the awkward reconstructions of later seventeenth-century typologists make clear. By participating in its recurrent signs, the medieval dramatist celebrated the atonement, the new theologians wished to remember it.

The medieval saint's play is a kind of history play as much as a romance. Its reformist objectors saw that, and in their secularized theological perspective rejected the plays as a falsification of history. Both perspectives, medieval and reformist, now prove necessary to an appreciation of the tension between tradition and circumstance which shapes the early English saints' history plays, *St. Paul* and *Mary Magdalene*.

II

The first speech of *St. Paul* is a kind of prologue or *apologia* by the 'poeta', reminiscent of Shakespeare's choric 'Gower' in *Pericles*. After an invocation of God's blessing, the 'poeta' turns to the audience:

> Honorable frendes, besechyng yow of lycens,
> to procede owr processe, we may, vnder your correccion,
> the conuersyon of seynt paule, as the byble gyf experyens,
> whoo lyst to rede the booke · Actum Appostolorum,
> ther shall he haue the very notycyon;
> but as we can, we shall vs redres,
> Brefly with yowr fauour begynyng owr proces.
>
> (8–14)

His extra sensitivity to potential criticism, his humble leave-seeking, and careful assertion that his 'processe' truly follows the Biblical account, are peculiar, and in returning to this posture repeatedly the 'poeta' of *St. Paul* suggests that there is some circumstantial need to claim before his audience the Biblical authenticity of the play. Accompanied by some unspecified choreography (simply a 'Daunce'), he then concludes the first 'station' by appealing to the audience to check with his source, 'the holy bybull for the better spede' (159). At the outset of the second 'pagent' he again asks 'lycens' to 'redres' 'another part of the story' (164ff.) and concludes this station 'as holy scripture tellyd' (352) with a repeated submission of his play to the 'correccyon of them that letteryd be':

> How be yt vnable as I dare speke or say
> The compyler here of shuld translat veray
> so holy a story · but with fauorable correccyon
> of my fauorable masters of ther benygne supplexion
>
> (356–9)

Still, at the end of the play he finds it necessary to reassert yet again the accuracy of his translations, the proximity of his dramatic text to the historical record of the Acts, 'as the bybull sayeth' (652). Why should the author be so careful to frame his text with these protestations? The compilers of the cycle plays, for whose larger enterprise we might perhaps have expected some initial pose of this kind, did not think any apology necessary, and they took many more extreme 'liberties' with the Biblical text, if we wish to judge them by that standard, than did the dramatist of *St. Paul*. The answer presumably lies in a rising opposition by the time of these texts (1490–1530) to the open-ended exemplarist view of Biblical history that they typically contained. This criticism would come particularly from those new churchmen whose use of the Scriptures was based upon a reverence for literal historical accuracy. I doubt whether it is accidental that our only saints' plays to survive the Reformation celebrate Biblical saints.

Even before the bans, it seems that the reformists would have looked more kindly on a reasonably Biblical text like *St. Paul*, or the first part of *Mary Magdalene*, than on one which (like the second part of *Magdalene* and many other plays now lost) elaborated on the original story with spectacular miracles not found in the New Testament. Though the *St. Paul* dramatist adds a marvellously humorous debate between two turd-toting stableboys (85ff.), the spurious episode is kept short and virtually incidental to the main plot. The entrance of high priests Caypha and Anna involves the artifice of invented dialogue, but the priests were familiar figures from another portion of the Biblical text, and their role was at least consistent with the Acts story. Even the frustrated council of Belyal after Saul's conversion could be considered in the contextual spirit of the source. For the rest the author follows the Biblical text closely at all significant points, utilizing direct translation where he can. Paul's sermon on the Seven Deadly Sins, for example, is largely shaped by Scriptural paraphrase, not only of the Pauline epistles but of words of Christ from the Gospels (e.g. *Matthew* 11, 28–30):

> Lern at my-self, for I am meke in hart:
> owr lorde to hys seruantes thus he sayth:
> ffor meknes I sufferyd a spere at my hart;
> meknes all vyces annullyth and delayeth;
> rest to soulys yt shall fynd in fayth:
> *Discite a me, quia mitis sum, et corde humilis,*
> *Et invenietis requiem animabus vestris*
>
> (538–44)

The passage that follows, about fleeing sensuality and youthful lusts, comes from Paul's injunctions to Timothy (II *Timothy* 2, 3). No conventional saints' miracles are added to the Paul story, and while there is typical dramatic expansion in the speeches of Ananais, Anna, Caypha, the knights and hostelers, and typical imaginative exegesis and restructuring of the story to have Paul's conversion bewailed in Hell, all of this is self-consciously held in careful tension with an apparent need for fidelity to exact Biblical history. Presumably, a critic would find it difficult to complain of this play, 'With an O and an I, thai praysen not Seynt Poule.'

III

Mary Magdalene, on the other hand, is a Biblical saint about whom much less is given in the Scriptures, and in traditional hagiography even some of the Biblical source material for her life is conjecturally employed. The sister of Martha and Lazarus, she sits at the feet of Jesus (*Luke* 10, 38–42), is attendant upon the resurrection of her brother (*John* 11, 1–46) and anoints the feet of Jesus with costly oils and ointments, wiping them with her hair (*John* 11, 1–8). The anger of Judas at this extravagance immediately precedes his betrayal of Jesus, and since it is Magdalene to whom Christ first appears in the garden after his resurrection (*John* 20, 11–18) her role in the Gospels almost exactly outlines the chief symbolic events of his ministry, death, and resurrection. To these events she becomes a kind of representative of mankind in the story, a compelling reference for personal identification. That valuable narrative function, assisted by her own emotional character (and the general impression of her social role suggested by *John* 11, 45) probably contributed to the early attribution to her life of an incident recorded by Luke (7, 36–50). Here Jesus has been invited to dinner by a Pharisee named Simon, and while the dinner is in progress a whore of the city comes to him weeping in remorse. She washes his feet with her tears and the hair of her head, and anoints them with ointment. While this last story is clearly a separate one, coming early in Christ's ministry, its similarity to the others together with a highly dramatic potential helped it to be associated with them. As a result, Mary Magdalene became an even more attractive and enigmatic figure, in prospect a moving example of the fallen sinner, the harlot who repents in sorrow and comes to her reward. Anyone who has seen Donatello's magnificent wooden sculpture of her in the Florence Baptistry, her ragged and decaying prostitute's body rapt in an upward gaze of transcendent adoration, would expect the story to have become popular. Indeed, it was so good that the medieval hagiographers could not leave it go without a much fuller fictive supplement. This expanded to include, even in the most modest versions, her conversion of the Saracen Emir of Marseilles, a miraculous restoration of life and preservation on a desert island of the prince's wife and newborn child, numerous miracles of her ageing years in the wilderness, and up to the time of her remarkable death at Marseilles, daily ascensions into heaven assisted by ministering angels.[8] Much more than a simple saint's biography, her life acquires the stuff of legend and romance, coming to stand beside the Virgin's in terms of familiarity and popular appeal.

The first part of the saint's play follows the basic Biblical stories from which Magdalene's character is derived. But the author divides his play into two sections, giving us in the last and longer part the creative expansion of her life and miracles common to his legendary sources. The result is a play which, when both parts are taken together, is undoubtedly much more broadly representative of the saints' plays we have lost than *St. Paul*. It offers us, for one thing, that remarkably effective dramatic balance of allegorical and naturalistic technique which came to fullest flower in the saint's play, and which was theatrically realizable largely because of the old exemplarist premises

[8] A good conservative example of a legendary life is afforded by Horstmann, *Early South English Legendary*, pp. 462–80.

about truth and history, to which both the political science and the theology of Henry's new England stood resolutely opposed.

We usually think of romance and realism as natural contrasts, realism as 'a truthful depiction of nature, especially human nature', and romanticism as 'an elevation beyond the range of the familiar into aspiration'. Indeed, as C. W. Jones has shown, words like aspiration, elevation, exaltation, and edification, all used to describe the purpose of romance, are the purpose of saints' lives as well.[9] But while it would be right to see the saint's life of the legendary as thus closely related to medieval romance, the saints' plays could be much short-changed by too liberal an extension of the comparison. For, if *Mary Magdalene* is any example, the English saint's play makes superb dramatic use of its view of history, combining the conventions of romance and realism at a level of achievement not surpassed in English theatre before Shakespeare. Although his play makes much use of the allegorical and faculty psychology conventions of the morality play, with bevies of vices, virtues, devils and angels roaming about his stage, his 'real' people are more plausibly 'real' than the protagonists of his predecessors, and in sensitivity and sophistication of character revelation no medieval dramatist is closer to the psychological veri-similitude and subtlety of the best Elizabethan drama. Both 'modes' exist quite happily together.

To begin with, the author has provided a much larger and more complete social frame for the Biblical actions of Mary's life. Exploiting the tensions he knew to exist between Roman and puppet-Jewish power in the occupied Palestine of Christ's day, he builds up a drama-tically convincing foil of temporal power for what he will ultimately portray as the more powerful meekness of the Gospel. We are pre-sented with three civil authorities, each a potentate in his own right. Tyberyus Sesar's ranting claims to 'Magnifycens', chief rulership of heaven and hell, and veritable deity (4-16) stamp him as a stock-in-trade, if colourful, anti-Christ type. But he stumbles on to a richer stage characterization in his craving for fresh confidence from his courtiers:

> Lord and lad, to my law doth lowte;
> is it nat so? say yow all with on showte.
> [Here answerryt all þe pepul at ons, ȝa, my lord ȝa
>
> (43-5)

---

[9] Charles W. Jones, *Saints' Lives and Chronicles in Early England* (Ithaca, 1947), p. 52.

Like many 'imperators', in constant need of reassurance, when he finally gets enough of it for the moment his response becomes comfortably egocentric: 'Now have I told you my hart, I am well plesyd' (47).

The second *tyrannus*, Herowdes, figures in his uncontrollable temper and foul abuse a kind of barbarian egocentricity less self-conscious than Sesar's as it is less refined than Pylatt's. But, more confident than either, he needs no support beyond his own braggadocio (140–64). That marvellous paradox of the anti-intellectual who at once despises and is awed by his philosophers, he proves yet barely sensitive to their most obvious advice. After half listening to the 'phylyssoverys' prophetic answer to his rhetorical question, 'Am I nat þe grettest governower?' (165), Herowdes slumbers through their rehearsal until, at a quotation in Latin from the Vulgate (*et ambulabunt gentes in lumine, et reges / In splendore ortus tui*—175–6) he is jolted to irritable attention: 'and what seyst thow?' On hearing the rest of the prophecy he then explodes in rage, only at last to be calmed by his knights, whose welcome comfort is a denigration of the philosopher's word and a panegyric to temporal power.

Pylatt's task is to proclaim his power as judge of Jerusalem, and so he does, though with full consciousness that he is 'ondyr the emperower tiberius cesar'. Like many under the duress of middle administration, he is a prey to insecurity. Pylatt's great need is for acceptance; here, acceptance of his judgment:

> my ser-jauntes semle, quat sye ye?
> of þis rehersyd, I wyll natt spare.
> plesauntly, serrys, avnswer to me,
> for in my herte I xall haue þe lesse care
>
> (240–43)

So the Digby playwright puts before us three imperious characters, all of whom are genuinely threatening, and yet who are all in one way or another insecure. To be set with these three men is Syrus, lord of the 'castell of maudleyn', father of Mary, Martha and Lazarus. Syrus too struts with temporal splendour, and though his claim to dominion is less extravagant than Sesar's (merely Castle Magdalene, Jerusalem, Bethany and 'Berdes in my bouer'), and though his manner is more confident than Pylatt's, his dominant pose also involves an attitude towards security. Presenting us with a man worthy to be father of such notable children, even if necessarily a pagan, the Digby dramatist apparently also wants us to see him as bespeaking the impermanent virtues of temporal power. Cleverly he gives Syrus much more self-assurance than the Sesar whom he follows, but makes it a comfort built upon recognizably false foundations. Reciting his wealth, Syrus reflects on the security it gives him, naming his children as that good fortune's beneficiaries:

> I am sett in solas from al syyng sore,
> and so xall all my posteryte,
> thus for to leuen in rest and ryalte
>
> (63-5)

and further of his children,

> þey haue fulfyllyd my hart with consolacyon.
> Here is a coleccyon of cyrcumstance,
> to my cognysshon never swych a-nothyr . . .
>
> (74-6)

Here is a kind of Boethian ploy, a consolation of fortune rather than of philosophy which makes Syrus, like Sesar, think himself protected by temporal goods from a bad end. By the time old Syrus begins, Lear-like, to divide up his 'lordshep' amongst Mary, Martha and Lazarus (while 'in good mynd'), we sense how fragile is the promise of security in their father's wealth. Shortly Lazarus himself will be dead and Mary a tattered courtesan.

The Digby dramatist has added considerably to the stock characterization of villain tyrants from the medieval cycle play. In their manifestation of temporal power his characters not only form a foil for the triumph of spiritual power in Christ's resurrection and the mission of Magdalene, but also become an integral part of the framing for Mary's early role. For from a psychological point of view Mary's own greatest problem is a kind of insecurity. As her character slowly emerges in the first part of the play, the dramatist adds to our sense of his heroine's vulnerability by carefully 'framing' her position in the family. From Syrus' introduction in his opening speech, Mary is curiously placed in the middle—an unusual rhetorical arrangement—between Lazarus and Martha. Similarly, in their first speeches, a response to their father's gifts, Mary, 'ful fayr and ful of femynyte', has the middle rather than the first or final speech. Like Lazarus and unlike Martha, she appreciates in her father's gifts their power over adverse fortune and worldly labours, and welcomes her protective Castle Magdalene, a 'place of pleasans'. Her next speech on her father's death is still a 'middle' speech, and only as she realizes that she is now by her father's fortune mistress of the castle do her speeches begin to assume rhetorical and dramatic prominence (303–4). As she moves away from the protective bracketing of her siblings, however, we see that she too counts too much on the security provided by things temporal, in this case her fortune.

It is this turn of circumstance which sets the stage for the council of the traditional 'foes of man'. The Kyng of the World ('for þe whele of fortune with me hath sett his sentur'—312), the Kyng of the Flesch, and the Dylfe (on a separate 'stage and Helle ondyrneth þat stage') enter, together with their retinue of Seven Deadly Sins, a Bad Angel, and a Good Angel. World, Flesh, and the Devil, in contrast to Caesar, Herod, and Pilate, seem much more sure of themselves, and get on well together. The culmination of their dark plotting (apparently in the garden of Castle Magdalene, under the stars—313–25, 334ff.) is a decision to have Lechery tempt Mary by flattery, and in a contrivance reminiscent of the intrigues of Oberon and his fairies in *A Midsummer Night's Dream*, the Puck-like Bad Angel is stirred from his impish games to begin arousing her, apparently close by in her 'castell', yet unaware of their presence. At length Lechery and the Bad Angel gain entrance, and though there is no speaking part or direction for the Good Angel, one can only assume that he flits fretfully about in vain defensive action while the 'siege'—so reminiscent of the dramatic strategy of the *Castle of Perseverance*—is taking place. In the company of Lechery, Mary inevitably agrees to leave her castle for a tavern. There she meets the 'gallant' Curiosity. Flattery proves handy, liquor makes it quicker, and in one of the play's most sure-footed 'scenes' the gallant is soon able to dance an inebriated Mary Magdalene off stage. The Bad Angel, still the unnoticed attendant of Magdalene—Titivillus to this feminine Mankind—can now run off in glee to report his good news.

The prominent role in *Mary Magdalene* of abstract powers, vices, and good and bad angels, may seem at first glance to make it a kind of bastardized relative of the morality plays. Actually, its combination of psychological verisimilitude with these most 'unrealistic' of faculty psychology conventions is entirely appropriate to the saint's play. According to the rules of his genre, the romantic hagiographer distinguished between factual and ethical truth, 'but not in the

Baconian manner'.[10] Sesar, Herowdes, and Pylatt are different from, but no more real than, their psychogenic counterparts. The perception afforded by the council of World, Flesh and Devil, and the assault of Castle Magdalene with entrance by Bad Angel and Lechery, is as valid and important as the insights yielded up in the carefully-developed characterizations of insecurity, and they reinforce each other. The standard by which both perspectives are judged is the end in view, discovery of the surety of God's goodness, 'that unchangeable life which is not at one time foolish, another time wise, but on the contrary is wisdom itself'.[11] From his resurrection of Lazarus, the life, death and resurrection of Christ is artfully interwoven into the second half of the play and into the legendary events at Marseilles to provide the standard to which Mary will finally conform. On the level of moral virtue, the contrition for which she was usually heralded by her biographers (686ff.) is made by the Digby dramatist to transform the vices of pride, anxiety and lechery into humility, patience and charity (682ff.). As the medieval synonym has it: *miraculum = virtutes*. The wildly traumatic departure from her body of seven devils into Hell with a roll of 'thondyr' may be a spectacular feat of theatrical engineering in the allegorical style, but when the audience has recovered they see in quite another way that Mary's insecurity and anxiety have been miraculously transformed into confidence and unshakeable faith. The spiritual metamorphosis by which she becomes the unwavering saint of Marseilles and fearless hermit in the wilderness is more subtly characterized as the psychological redressment of her former personality problems:

> O þou gloryus Lord! þis rehersyd for my sped,
> sowle helth attes tyme for-to recure.
> Lord, for þat I was In whanhope, now stond I In dred,
> But þat þi gret mercy with me may endure;
> now may I trost þe techeyng of Izaye in scryptur,
> Wos report of þi nobyllnesse rennyt fer abowt.
>
> (692–8)

There is not so much a disparity of styles here as a deliberate counterpoint of generic conventions. In the range of speeches that occupies Mary from her encounter with Curiosity in the tavern to her encounter with Christ at Symond's dinner party, there is no more or

---

[10] Charles W. Jones, *op. cit.*, p. 76.
[11] St. Augustine, *On Christian Doctrine*, I, 8.

less *sublimitas* of style than in the range of speeches from Lechery in
the tavern to the final commendation of the Good Angel. The conventions involved, nevertheless, are quite opposite. While both
techniques serve the play's romantic purpose, and both are true to the
'end in view', their combination in this way amply demonstrates how
irrelevant would be a concern for literal time and place, Biblical or
otherwise.[12] As hagiographical literature, the play is a romantic
enactment of man's fall and restoration, dramatically adding an
opportunity for participation in a *signum* (the Middle English word is
usually 'tokene') of the power of God's goodness at any time to make
exemplary a human life. The presumably apocryphal miracles and
conversion of the King of Marseilles are in this context no less 'true',
theologically or dramatically, than the 'historical' events recorded in
the play. Yet as the saints were considered to be historical persons,
their plays were still a kind of history play. They were plays, however,
whose view of history—characterized by expectations of presence and
recurrence rather than change and development—seemed more
intrinsically dramatic than the modern perspective of their detractors
could afford.

IV

The proper analysis of the saint's play ought to be in performance,
of course, and while that always proves impossible to realize artificially
on paper, the directions in *St. Paul* and *Mary Magdalene* are full enough
to aid us in better appreciating the uniquely successful fusion of
techniques which is the heritage of their development. For *The Conversion of St. Paul* it may prove helpful to remember that the medieval
saint's play probably had at one time a close connection with sermon
literature. One suggestion of this comes in a thirteenth-century col-

---

[12] It was Auerbach (*Mimesis*, pp. 136–9) who demonstrated the fusion in the
twelfth-century *Jeu d'Adam* of two *styles* in the cycle drama: *sublimitas* and
humilitas. In the saints' plays, however, what actually occurs is a fusion of
genres, whose employment of style, as in *Mary Magdalene*, is much more
even. Containing virtually none of the 'grotesquery' which Auerbach feels led
to the downfall of the plays, *Mary Magdalene* suggests that the saints' plays
problem was their particular expression of the exemplarist view of history
itself. The criticisms of even Wyclifite reformists were directed not against
grotesquery (cf. passages cited), but against a lack of faithfulness to Biblical
(or ecclesiastical) history.

lection of poems and sermons, where a St. Nicholas legend, written as a verse sermon, is apparently addressed to a general audience out of doors:

> Ye ou rede ye sitten stille
> & herknet wel wid gode wille
> of godes wordes ant is werkes
> beþe þis lewede ant þis clerkes

(1-4)

Consisting of a running series of translations and paraphrases of Biblical passages directed against worldly riches, it includes in the section that refers to St. Nicholas an explicit mention of a 'pleye' which is to follow:

> yf ye wellet stille ben
> in þis pleye ye mowen isen
> þis mon hauede lond & lede . . .[13]

(39-41)

So direct a connection between the sermon and play to follow is reminiscent of certain medieval Italian manuscripts which include both sermons and plays together, suggesting that in England as in Italy the early saint's drama may have been more directly connected with preaching occasions than has been generally supposed.[14] *The Conversion of St. Paul* is little enough direct evidence to go on, but both in its arrangement by the 'poeta' and in Paul's internal sermon to the audience on the Seven Deadly Sins the play resembles the tradition of Italian saints' plays sometimes referred to under the heading 'sermo semi-drammatico'. While not reserved exclusively for saints' plays, this kind of dramatized sermon, or homiletic narrative with parts either pantomimed or supplemented with short speeches, proved entirely compatible to the genre in Italy.[15] If, as is seems likely, there was a comparable tradition of saints' plays in England, then we can probably

[13] See Carleton Brown, 'An Early Mention of a St. Nicholas Play in England', *Studies in Philology* XXVIII (1931), pp. 594-601. Most scholars have followed Brown in regarding this reference as sufficient evidence that saints' plays were an established genre here by about 1250.

[14] See Arnaldo Fortini, *La Lauda in Assisi e le origini del Teatro Italiano* (Assisi, 1863), pp. 270ff.

[15] Arnaldo Fortini, *op. cit.*, p. 279; cf. Anderson, *Imagery*, pp. 51ff.; but see my forthcoming book, *Franciscan Spirituality and the Middle English Drama*, Ch. 3.

assume *St. Paul* to be its descendant. With *Mary Magdalene* as the representative of the more elaborate and more typical large-scale saint's play, we would thus seem by good fortune to have had spared for us examples of the two most obvious styles of saint's play performance.[16]

Either play offers the modern producer an ingenious exercise in staging, although if one wished to recreate a medieval production, *St. Paul* probably offers the least difficulty. The text seems to call for three acting areas, either as three stations within an expansive playing-area (a town square in Wickham's persuasive view, overlooked by a coaching inn), or perhaps, an alternative possibility, as a mobile stage (pageant-wagon) moving from one point to another so as to gather a larger crowd en route. At the end of the first section or 'station', for example, the 'poeta', whilst a dance is taking place, addresses the audience:

> ffynally of this stacon thus we mak a conclusyon,
> besechyng thys audyens to folow and succede
> with all your delygens this generall processyon,
>
> (155-7)

where he will offer a similar choric framing speech at the outset of the second part. Moving the audience between station one and two allows for an ingenious engagement of audience participation. No sooner has the audience reached the site (near Damascus) than rapidly following their walk between the stations 'commyth saule ryding in with hys servantes' (stage-directions, 168). Here horses can be used effectively, and members of the audience join the action as fellow travellers on the road to Damascus (Plate 1). If the mechanics for the thunder and lightning which the directions require to enhance Paul's violent apparition are provided in the same way as the thunder and fireworks for the council of devils in Hell, then with horses rearing and plunging, crowd scattering and a booming voice of God from the heavens we may assume that the conversion scene could provide some marvellous spectacle.

[16] I do not mean, of course, that these were necessarily the only styles, nor that they represent the whole range of staging. Saints' plays were performed in fields (as a St. George play at Bassingbourne), on pageant-wagons (as Canterbury's 1504 Thomas à Becket), in a small park (St. Katherine at Coventry, 1490), in the round (as *St. Meriasek* in Cornwall), or even in a church (Braintree, Essex, for a play of St. Andrew in 1525).

Mary Magdalene, as the complexity of plot and length of text will suggest (2,144 lines with more than 65 parts), requires a very different type of staging. For one thing, the producer would have had to provide for scenes in palaces and castles, taverns and graveyards, hell, shipboard and the desert. Moreover, many of the changes of place are in rapid succession, which adds to the problem. The text itself is not absolutely clear about the staging, but the general picture can be constructed with reasonable accuracy. The appearance of Sesar, Herowde and Pylatt would seem to be in three scaffolds surrounding a central *platea* where most of the main action will occur. It is here, presumably, that Syrus first appears with Lazarus, Mary and Martha, and here that the resurrection of Lazarus, temptation of Magdalene and the voyages to and from Marseilles will probably have to take place. Whether as theatre in the round or according to the more usual simultaneous-mansions convention—the two are not necessarily mutually exclusive —the performance requires a large area:

> Here xal satan go hom to his stage, and mari xal
> entyr In to þe place alone, save þe bad angyl and
> al þe seuen dedly synnes xal be conveyyd in to þe
> howse of symont leprovs, þey xal be a ray-yd like
> vij dylf: þus kept closse, mari xal be in an erbyr . . .
>   (at 563)

The scaffoldings are undoubtedly the same upon which appeared 'þe Kyng of þe World, Flesch and þe Devile', adding thus to the symmetry, and if one of the scaffolds or 'stages' is destroyed when the disgruntled chief devil herds his outcast assistants into the 'howse' (741) to be set on fire, one of the others, probably the central one, might well have served as a backframe for the double-tiered action of Mary's ascensions from the wilderness (2004–39). The directions require no small technical competence:

> Here xall to angylles desend In to wyldyrnesse;
> and other to xall bryng an oble, opynly aperyng   *wafer*
> a loft In þe clowddes; þe to be-nethyn xall bryng
> mary, and she xall receyve þe bred, and þan go
> a-ȝen In to wyldyrnesse   (at 2019)

> Her xall she be halsyd with angelles   *saluted? houseled?*
> with reverent song.

Asumpta est maria in nubibus; celi gavdent,
Angeli lavdantes felium Dei; et dicit mari . . .

(at 2031)

No less demanding is the appearance and movement about the 'place'
of the ship, which, unless the outdoor stage can somehow make use
of a small pond with an island, must have been constructed, like some
Noah's arks and a host of spectacular pageant-ships from the popular
entremets and court entertainments, upon wheels or round a pageant-
wagon.[17] (This might earlier have been the third scaffold.) The ship,
sufficient for six actors, is clearly able to enter and leave the principal
playing area, e.g. 'et tunc navis venit ad circa placeam' (18379); 'Here
goth the shep owt ofe the place' (1923).

But the playwright does not depend upon extravagant machinery
alone to gain the engagement of his audience. Ranging from farcical
comedy, in an Uncle Screwtape-like dispute between the pagan priest
and his boy, to simple but emotionally powerful dialogue at Lazarus'
death and subtle verbal game in the house of Symond the Leper, the
Digby dramatist provides for a marvellous variety and orchestration
of both tone and pace. The 'Midsummer Night's Dream' sequence,
with devils and vices plotting around the unseeing Magdalene, is as
engaging a dramatic effect as its parallel, the potentially beautiful but
awesome dream-vision appearance of white-robed Magdalene and her
candle-bearing angels to the King of Marseilles, troubled, in his sleep
(1580ff.). Yet one 'dream' sequence is congested, boisterous, and comic,
the other awesome, tranquil, and mysterious.

V

The subject of the saints' plays is conversion. More obviously
evangelical than the morality or even perhaps the cycle play in this
respect, they present us with a wayward life undergoing spiritual
revolution, and then show forth the rewards and various consequences

[17] Wickham, *EES*, Vol. I, p. 223, records directions for another possible
ship, constructed for a tournament pageant in 1501; 'a goodly shippe borne
up w^t men, w^t in himself (the hero of the day) ryding in the myddes . . . and
the sides of the ship covered w^t cloth peynted after the colour or likeness of
water.'

of that revolution. Though St. Paul's conversion is a classic illustration, Mary Magdalene provides perhaps the more appealing example of a contrite and repentant sinner who, turning from her ways, is freed from evil to become a saint (Plate 2). In a marvellous evocation of her salvation's history, and in the paradoxical language of Paul and St. Augustine, she cries,

> I was drynchyn In synne deversarye
> tyll þat lord relevyd me be his domynacy-n,
> grace to me he wold never de-nye;
> thowe I were nevyr so synful, he seyd 'revertere'!
>
> (754–7)

The familiar Augustinian play on *vertere/revertere/convertere* (from the *Confessions*) is emblematic in her description of what has taken place (cf. 768–75), helping to express how from a medieval Christian perspective conversion can be a 'dramatic' event in all senses. By his paralleling of Mary's story with the action of Christ in divine redemption, and the repetition of the pattern in the story of the converted King of Marseilles and his resurrected wife and child, the playwright gives lively dramatic form to the traditional Augustinian idea of conversion as a repetition of the Incarnation in personal guise. To participate in the one transformation produces others: from prostitute to saint, or from tyrant to pilgrim, because the Word becomes flesh. The enacting itself becomes theological statement. Both Paul and Mary Magdalene symbolize the moment by putting on new costume (*St. Paul*, 502; *Mary Magdalene*, 683; cf. 1618).

The theme of the saint's play is recurrence. In *Mary Magdalene* the story of the resurrection of Lazarus is used by Christ in his speeches to signify his own death and resurrection, and the playwright then utilizes the *signum* to imply without performance the events of Calvary and the open tomb. Space is similarly symbolic. For example, we might consider the 'erbyr' in which the drunken Mary falls asleep, waiting for her lovers, only to awaken sobered with remorse and longing to seek out Jesus. From the point of view of staging, it takes little imagination to discern that the place will be the same in which Mary's fall was plotted by the council of vices, and the flowers in which the Kyng of Flesch took such delight (334–51) still available to frame the Magdalene's last attendance 'tyll som lover wol apere' (l. 570). But the 'erbyr' will also provide the garden in which Mary is first to discover the risen Christ, whom she has

> ... porposyd in eche degre
> to have hym with me werely,   *verily*
> the wyche my specyall lord hath be,
> and I his lover and cause wyll phy.   *trust*
> (1065-8)

She takes him, of course, to be a gardener. It is hard to imagine a more effective synthesis of the naturalistic and symbolic action of the play than Christ's response:

> So I am, for sothe, Mary:
> mannys hartt is my gardyn here;
> þer In I sow sedys of vertu all þe ȝere;
> þe fowle wedes and wycys, I reynd vp be þe rote. *vices*
> whan þat gardyn is watteryd with terys clere,
> than spryng vertuus, and smelle full sote   *sweet*
> (1080-85)

One love becomes another. A complex psychological realization of such parallel and recurrence is not the sort of thing to which the classical unities (or their view of history) are much assistance. There are too many occasions in the performance of a medieval play like *Mary Magdalene* or *St. Paul* where one is not, in the classical sense, wholly a 'spectator', and as theatrical folk well recognize, there is a profound connection between the stage as a proscenium-arched set-piece and the expectation of classical unities for which the medieval playwright does not provide.

The objective of the saints' plays is participation. Whether by playing out part of the dramatic action amongst the crowd, or by appealing to shared and deeply felt ideas, the achievement and the effect of such participation is bound to be psychological and emotional. *Mary Magdalene* seems likely to have generated a great deal of emotion in performance. Following the miracle of Lazarus' resurrection, a direction for general participation suggests that the play might induce a spiritual fervour now more reminiscent of the American Deep South:

Here all þe pepull, and þe Iewys, mari, and martha with one woys sey þes wordes: we be-leve in yow savyowr, Iesus, Iesus, Iesus!

(920)

Such a response, familiar in medieval Italian saints' plays, expresses the internal characterization of Biblical history as personal present to which the whole play points.

St. Bonaventure, first and most important medieval philosopher to address himself to the aesthetics of drama, wrote in his *De Reductione Artium ad Theologiam* that the illumination of the arts can be precisely that of Scripture. They both show us 'the eternal generation and Incarnation of the Word, the pattern of human life, and the union of the soul with God'. But of all the arts, he continued, 'it is dramatic art, or the art of putting on plays, which embraces every form of entertainment, whether song, music, fiction or pantomime', which best fulfils, according to Horace, the goals of art.[18] Had he been there to see, one feels sure that he would have heartily approved *The Conversion of St. Paul* and *Mary Magdalene*, and found in their orchestration of song, dance, pantomime and spectacle some justification for his most concise appreciation of their medium: *theatrica, autem, est unica.*[19]

[18] Ed. and tr. Sister Emma Therese Healy (St. Bonaventure, N.Y., 1939), p. 38.
[19] *Ibid.*, p. 40.

Note

Texts.

The texts used and referred to in this chapter are to be found in *TFT* and *MSR*; in Dodsley and Hazlitt, *OEP*, Manly, *Specimens of the Pre-Shaksperean Drama* and Adams, *CPD*; and in Eccles, *MP*. The *Shakespeare-Jahrbuch* occasionally publishes good texts of individual plays. Useful checklists of editions of Tudor plays are included in Wilson and Hunter, *ED*, Craik, *TI* and Spivack, *SAE*.

Scholarship and Criticism.

Chambers, *MS* and *ES* remain standard reference works on staging, though they have been supplemented by Wickham, *EES* and Craik, *TI*. On the staging of a fifteenth-century morality play, *The Castle of Perseverance*, Southern, *MTR* is invaluable. A. W. Reed, *Early Tudor Drama* (London, 1926) is informative on the humanists of the Thomas More circle. On staging, see also R. Southern, 'The Contribution of the Interludes to Elizabethan Staging', in *Essays on Shakespeare and Elizabethan Drama in Honor of Hardin Craig*, ed., R. Hosley (Columbia, Missouri, 1963) and essays by Hosley in *Shakespeare 400*, ed. James McManaway (New York, 1964), *A New Companion to Shakespeare Studies*, ed. K. Muir and S. Schoenbaum (Cambridge, 1971) and *Theatre Survey* XII (May 1971).

Popular and Courtly Traditions on the Early Tudor Stage

DAVID BEVINGTON

I

CAN ONE speak of 'the Tudor Interlude' as a cohesive unit, and discuss its staging as a single phenomenon? T. W. Craik has presented the most comprehensive argument to date for doing so, in his book *The Tudor Interlude* and more recently in Volume 9 of these Stratford-upon-Avon Studies.[1] Craik broadly defines the interlude to include humanist debates, farces, polemical morality plays (both Protestant and Catholic), schoolboys' Prodigal Son drama, 'regular' neo-classical comedies, and others. In spite of this heterogeneity, Craik argues, one can discern a basic similarity of performance uniting these plays. They were, he says, designed primarily for indoor performance, in the banqueting halls of the aristocracy or in similarly-appointed rooms. While conceding that travelling players also acted on trestle stages in inn-yards and in public streets, Craik maintains that the indoor hall was the essential milieu for all English secular drama down to the building of the first Elizabethan public stage in 1576. Richard Hosley offers supportive evidence when he proposes that the banqueting hall, and particularly its screen, exerted a dominant formative influence on the tiring-house façade of the Shakespearean playhouse.[2] The animal-

[1] Craik, *TI* and 'The Tudor Interlude and Later Elizabethan Drama', in *Elizabethan Theatre*, ed. John Russell Brown and Bernard Harris, Stratford-upon-Avon Studies 9 (London, 1966). Chambers, *ES*, Vol. III, pp. 1–46, similarly intermingles discussion of both popular and courtly 'interludes' in his study of staging at court; so also Southern, 'The Contribution of the Interludes to Elizabethan Staging'.

[2] Hosley, 'The Origins of the Shakespearian Playhouse' in *Shakespeare 400*. See also Hosley's admirably concise and balanced chapter on 'The Playhouses and the Stage' in *A New Companion to Shakespeare Studies*. Hosley freely concedes that inn-yards were used for dramatic performances and that booth-

baiting houses of London provided a model for the theatre building, but the actual stage was derived from the banqueting hall. Glynne Wickham similarly regards the Interlude as 'an indoor entertainment for festive, social occasions', and argues that 'the Public Theatres of the late sixteenth century drew many of their conventions from the Court and Private Theatres'.[3] Much recent criticism, then, has tended to stress the coherent nature of the interlude and the unifying function of the hall for which it was presumably designed.

This argument has considerable merit. By stressing the interconnection of the various kinds of early Tudor drama, this approach underscores the happy fact that the English ruling class never isolated itself from the kinds of drama that also appealed to popular audiences. Travelling players did unquestionably bring their plays to court and to the banqueting halls of the well-to-do. Popular and courtly drama did, moreover, share many staging conventions. From the outdoor theatres of the popular religious stage, courtly drama learned a good deal about the simultaneous use of separate acting locations. Conversely, indoor acting became common for early Tudor popular plays as it was for courtly drama. During the later Elizabethan period, in London, plays performed at the Globe or the Rose did not differ fundamentally in their staging requirements from plays performed at Blackfriars.

Was this apparent similarity the result, however, of the itinerant players' indebtedness to staging methods at court, or did the popular theatre maintain throughout the Tudor period a staging tradition peculiarly its own? I will contend that it did maintain such a tradition. A play like *Horestes* (1567) was far more likely to have developed features such as sieges and scaling operations by being staged in a London inn-yard than in a banqueting hall, though this play also had to adapt itself to performance at court. The adult actors may often have moved indoors with their popular moralities, such as *Mankind* (c. 1465-70), but when they did so on tours of rural communities they could not count on an elaborate hall-screen and gallery. We are more likely to be dealing with a booth-stage transported

stages may have been moved into banqueting halls, but argues the dominant influence of the animal-baiting house and hall-screen. (Hosley has read this essay and has offered valuable suggestions.)

3 Wickham, *EES*, Vol. I, pp. 180, 234. Cf. C. Walter Hodges, *The Globe Restored* (London, 1953) on the importance of the booth-stage.

indoors, and with plays that could be taken outdoors again as conditions permitted. In short, the tendency to visualize all Tudor secular drama as played in front of a hall-screen may give too much prominence to an essentially aristocratic environment.

The intention of this chapter is not to deny the continuity between popular and courtly traditions, as revealed in Craik's forceful presentation, but to examine the other side—the separateness of these traditions which the inclusive term 'interlude' may tend to conceal. In Tudor England, this term was applied to every kind of play imaginable, even to a Corpus Christi pageant or to a devout morality play; the word meant, simply, a stage presentation.[4] I would prefer to leave it in this entirely undifferentiated sense, and look for other ways of describing patterns of dramatic activity during the years before 1576.

The actors of Tudor plays came from various sorts of backgrounds, and earned their livelihood by various means. To be sure, adult travelling players were often liveried retainers of the aristocracy, and were expected to be in attendance on their patrons at certain periods of the year. When they travelled, they often visited other noble households. Their obligations to their noble patrons were, however, limited. They wore livery chiefly to avoid being arrested as vagabonds as they travelled the length and breadth of England. They came usually from the artisan class, like so many of their followers on the later Elizabethan public stage. Acting was their livelihood, and they had to take up a collection among the spectators or restrict access to their playing-area and charge at the gate (in inn-yards, for example) or seek payment from the Lord Mayor or nobleman in whose hall they proposed to play. Such payments were never vast, and their productions had to be both inexpensive and easy to transport. Their props, costumes, stage-structures (if any) and their very stage had to be sufficiently flexible and simple to meet all foreseeable conditions of performance. These troupes were of limited size, consisting often of four to six men and one or two boys, and so their plays had to have small casts or to provide wide opportunity for doubling.

The choristers who performed exclusively for the court or for great aristocrats, on the other hand, never travelled beyond the precincts of their own households. With many more actors at their disposal, they

4 Chambers, *MS*, Vol. II, pp. 181–4.

ordinarily had no reason to double parts or to limit the number of roles in their plays. Costumes, props and stage-structures did not need to be designed for easy removal from one location to another. Although painted scenery did not come into general use, courtly drama did innovate with permanent stage-structures. Inns-of-court productions such as *Gorboduc* (1562) could be lavish. One of the purposes of courtly entertainment, after all, was the tasteful display of wealth—what Veblen has called 'conspicuous consumption'. Most courtly drama was designed for a single impressive occasion; it was not a repertory drama having to pay for itself by repeated performances. School and university drama similarly avoided commercialism. Amateur thespians at Cambridge or Eton prepared their stages for one kind of hall and one kind of audience. They had no need to double parts.

Medieval forms of drama were still very much alive in Tudor England, and can further illuminate for us the distinction between popular drama and courtly entertainment. Popular drama often appeared under religious auspices, though seasoned with much comedy and spectacle. There were the Corpus Christi cycles of York, Wakefield, Chester, and other communities, the saints' plays such as the Cornish *Life of St. Meriasek* (1504) or the Scottish *St. Erasmus* (1518), and the ubiquitous morality plays. The popular tradition also included folk-dramas and May Day ceremonials of Robin Hood or St. George, and civic pageantry. No doubt mimes, jongleurs and animal-trainers toured the countryside. Courtly entertainment, on the other hand, specialized in the tilt or tournament, and in the fashionable 'mumming' that came to be called the 'disguising' and later the 'mask'.[5] The court must also have enjoyed a good deal of secular indoor entertainment provided by minstrels, of which the merest trace may remain in the fourteenth-century fabliau fragment called *Interludium de Clerico et Puella*.[6] The cultural gap between popular and aristocratic traditions was generally vast: Chaucer's references to the Corpus Christi cycles, for example, are uniformly sardonic, whereas in 'The Knight's Tale' he gives a vivid and sympathetic impression of the sort of chivalric panoply with which he was familiar.

Even though popular drama of the itinerant troupes often moved indoors to avoid inclement weather, it belonged originally to a tradi-

[5] Wickham, *EES*, Vol. I, pp. 13–228.
[6] For text, see Chambers, *MS*, Vol. II, pp. 324–6.

tion in which outdoor performance was common. Basically, three outdoor stages were available: the pageant-wagon, the circular arena or *platea* backed or flanked by 'mansions' or acting scaffolds, and the booth or trestle stage.[7] The pageant-wagons may have been used more often as *tableaux vivants* in a Corpus Christi procession than as stages for uncut performances of the cycles; the problems of producing a complete York cycle on moving wagons, for example, must have been virtually overwhelming. Nevertheless in some instances the wagons did apparently move from acting station to acting station along a prescribed route, displaying their 'pageants' before a succession of fixed audiences. Arena staging, as reconstructed by Richard Southern for a performance of an early morality play, *The Castle of Perseverance*, may sometimes have allowed spectators within the acting area but in that case made provision for the actors to pass across the *platea* from one scaffold to another: the usual place for spectators was on the periphery of the circular arena.[8] The acting took place in the *platea* or on the scaffolds, which were simultaneously visible throughout the drama. Heaven and Hell would thus remain as fixed locales, witnessing the spiritual struggles of the Mankind hero from birth until death and eventual salvation. *Perseverance* required five scaffolds, plus the Castle of Perseverance itself at the centre of the arena. When actors on those various scaffolds were not involved in the action, they could apparently withdraw from view behind curtains.

Besides *The Castle of Perseverance*, other late medieval or early Tudor plays were performed on arena stages: the Digby *Mary Magdalene*, for example, and the Passion sequence from the so-called N-Town ('Hegge') cycle (see Martial Rose's chapter below). It may be highly significant that the morality play began on a stage that was also used for Corpus Christi productions and saints' plays. The morality play, which was to become in the early Tudor period the staple of the travelling adult troupes, began as theatre in the round. What the adult troupes inherited, then, was an impulse towards the simultaneous presentation of panoramic spectacle, with much action taking place in the midst of the audience. The comic manipulators of

[7] Richard Hosley, 'Three Kinds of Outdoor Theatre before Shakespeare', *Theatre Survey* XII (May 1971).

[8] Southern, *MTR*.

the morality plays, later to be called 'Vices', learned their routines as devils and insolent messengers in the arena stage of *The Castle of Perseverance*. Most important, arena staging bequeathed to the Tudor popular morality a sense of cosmic presence overseeing the affairs of men, and a multiplicity of events in man's saga of soul-struggle. The Tudor popular morality had to manage somehow to compress all this cosmic multiplicity onto a simple booth-stage with a curtained back-drop for exits and entrances. Remarkably, it did so without losing the sense of panoramic vastness with which the morality had begun.

Courtly entertainment, on the other hand, preserved an atmosphere of chivalric magnificence and elegant debate. The numerous tilts and disguisings that are on record during the early Tudor period suggest by their titles that they were sumptuously fitted out in the trappings of allegorical romance: 'The Joust of the Wild Knight and the Black Lady', 1507, 'The Garden of Pleasure', 1511, 'The Castle Dangerous', 1512.[9] Mummings and masks, such as the 'Mask of Venus, Cupid, Six Damsels, and Six Old Men' (1527), involved the courtiers them-selves as masked dancers and orchestrated their appearance with music, spectacle, and a slender fictional narrative based on some mythological or pastoral commonplace. Courtly drama evolved chiefly from this sort of elegant indoor entertainment, and employed the same 'stage' used for masks—the aristocratic banqueting hall.

II

Let us now compare the staging of two early plays, one popular and one courtly: the anonymous *Mankind* and Henry Medwall's *Fulgens and Lucrece*. *Mankind* predates the Tudor era by a few years (*c.* 1465-70), but the gap in time is not serious since other popular moralities of the same genre (e.g. *Mundus et Infans* or *The Interlude of Youth*) date from the early sixteenth century. *Mankind* is a good place to start because it is so clearly designed for itinerant professional actors. They actually interrupt their performance to take up a collection among the audience, and do so just when the audience's curiosity

[9] See Harbage, *Annals*, for these and other such tilts and disguisings in the Tudor period. The dating of plays in this chapter is generally indebted to these *Annals*.

Plate 1. 'The Conversion of St. Paul', painted by Jean Fouquet (1415–81), from *The Book of Hours of Etienne Chevalier*. (*Musée Condé, Chantilly*)

Plate 2. 'Mary Magdalene and the Pot of Ointment', a fifteenth-century MS. illumination. (*Victoria and Albert Museum*)

has been whetted by the offstage shouting of the chief comic attraction, Titivillus. The spectators are urged to pay 'if ye wyll se hys abhomyn-abull presens' (465). These spectators are unquestionably rural, for the play makes quite a point of mentioning places and names that would be familiar to the audience. From the places named we gather that the play toured in Cambridgeshire and Norfolk, visiting a group of villages near Cambridge and another group near King's Lynn. We gather too from the play that its author was a local man, perhaps a Cambridge-shire clergyman teaching his predominantly rural audience the virtues of patient acceptance of their agricultural way of life. With all its emphasis on local colour, *Mankind* does not seem like a play that would also have been taken to court.

For what sort of stage was this rural play designed? Several indica-tions point to an inn, or series of inns. When the players begin their collection, they first ask money from 'the goode man of this house' (467). His title suggests that he is the innkeeper, though he may also be simply the head of some household in which the play is being per-formed. In either case, the phrase 'goode man' is hardly dignified enough to honour a noble patron or a Lord Mayor. Further hints of an inn occur when the revellers in the play call for a 'tapster', and bid the 'hostlere' lend them a football (729, 732).

If we are dealing with an inn, should we visualize the play as performed in the inn-yard or in a large public room? Some scholars have preferred the inn-yard,[10] on the assumption that the two social classes present in the audience ('ye souerens that sytt, and ye brothern that stonde ryght wppe', 29) would then occupy respectively the galleries of the inn and the inn-yard itself. The London inns of the 1560s may well have used their inn-yards in this fashion for the performance of plays, despite the fact that the galleries of inn-yards were not designed as spectators' galleries and cannot have been very convenient. The arrangement of spectators in an inn-yard would nonetheless have anticipated the later Elizabethan public theatres, with their higher-priced seating in the galleries and cheaper standing room on the ground near the stage. The arrangement also recalls that

[10] See for example Adams, *CDP*, p. 305, n. 5, and my own *From 'Mankind' to Marlowe*, p. 15—though I should now like to modify my earlier view. On this matter and several others I am indebted to T. W. Craik, who has graciously read this essay and offered helpful comment.

of *The Castle of Perseverance*, or of Corpus Christi pageants played at crowded street corners with scaffold seats for dignitaries.

Yet the allusion to sitters and standers could apply just as well to a large room, and we must allow for the real possibility that *Mankind* was taken indoors. The mention of cold weather and the need for a fire (323), the Christmas song (332–43) and the general appropriateness of the play to the pre-Lenten season all suggest performance at a time of year when indoor performance would have been desirable. The protagonist, Mankind, exits at one point to relieve himself with the apology that 'I wyll into thi yerde, souerens, and cum ageyn son' (561), perhaps implying that he and the audience are not at present in the 'yerde'. In such a case, the distinction between 'souerens that sytt' and 'brothern that stonde ryght wppe' would mean simply that the respected leaders of the community are seated while the humbler sort crowd in at the door.

This arrangement of the spectators does not differ materially from that found at court, as for example in *Fulgens and Lucrece*. Does this similarity mean, however, that the popular stage of *Mankind* must also resemble that of the court? To an extent, some resemblances are inevitable once any play is acted indoors before socially stratified audiences. Yet we cannot assume that the inns of rural England, or even the private houses of commoners, would have provided the architectural facilities to be found in a great hall. We are surely safer in assuming that the itinerant troupes simply moved their booth-stage indoors, rather than assuming that they relied on hall-screens and galleried superstructures. The actors of *Mankind* would not even have to use the door or doors of the room in which they acted; the curtain of their booth would handle all entrances, exits, and offstage conversation. We are still dealing here with a tradition derived from outdoor public performances rather than with the indoor entertainments of the ruling class.

The nature and function of this indoor booth-stage, if such it was, can only be deduced from internal evidence of the play itself. The actors need a back-stage area for their costumes and hand props. If Mercy and Titivillus double parts, as seems likely, their costume-changing could be effected behind the curtain. When the revellers repeatedly take away Mankind's long coat to shorten it according to the latest fashion, they probably take it behind the curtain and return with another coat cut to a shorter length. Titivillus removes Mankind's sack of grain and agricultural tools, hiding them behind the curtain. Other easily transportable hand-props are brought forth: Titivillus' net for making him invisible, a broken noose, fetters, a portable gallows-tree on which New Guise nearly hangs himself. In addition to simple exits and entrances, the actors must have means for offstage conversation. Titivillus' shouts can be heard before he appears. At another point, the comic tempters New Guise, Nowadays and Nought speak aloud and yet are invisible to Mercy and Mankind who are on stage. The revellers comment satirically on what Mankind is saying, whereupon Mercy warns his pupil Mankind that his spiritual enemies 'wyll be here ryght son, yf I owt departe' (257). The curtained tiring-area of a simple booth-stage would produce the simplest and most flexible means of rendering this effect. The actors do not need a door, for none is mentioned in the text.

At no point is the scene very localized, though we get the impression of a village and of fields in which Mankind attempts to sow his grain. The scene is cosmic at the same time, for Mercy represents Godhead and Mankind is a generically human delver of the soil like Adam. The stage is thus flexible in space and time, and flexible too in the ease with which it could be transported from one rural community to another or from outdoor to indoor performance.

The stage required for Henry Medwall's *Fulgens and Lucrece* (c. 1497) bears an outward resemblance to that of *Mankind*, but the effect is strikingly different. To be sure, the comic servants 'A' and 'B' joke with the humbler members of the audience and elbow their way through the crowd standing around the door. Medwall was, after all, in touch with popular forms of drama, as were the humanist writers generally: he wrote an orthodox morality play, *Nature* (c. 1490–1501), possibly for performance in the hall of his patron, Cardinal Morton. Nevertheless, his *Fulgens and Lucrece* is designed for a single impressive courtly occasion. Whether that occasion was the visit of the Flemish and Spanish ambassadors during the Christmas festivities of 1497, as argued by Boas and Reed,[11] cannot be positively determined, but the play was not intended to be taken on tour. Seemingly topical jests about 'the gyse Of Spayne' and the 'wylde Irissh Portyngales' and the comic use of Flemish dialogue (II, 380–94) point to some special celebration. Minstrels and dancers perform an elaborate mumming

[11] F. S. Boas and A. W. Reed, eds., *Fulgens & Lucres* (London, 1926), pp. xix–xx.

in the courtly style (II, 389). The spectators are guests at a patrician banquet who have already dined when the first part of the play commences (I, 9–16) and who expect to feast again between the two halves. 'A' and 'B' call a halt to the first part of their play at 'the wyll and commaundement Of the master of the fest', and promise they will play out the remnant 'At my lordis pleasure' (I, 1425–32). This is the kind of play to which the term 'interlude' is sometimes applied in the most literal sense, of providing intervals of entertainment for a banquet. (The title page calls the play a 'godely interlude'.)

Fulgens and Lucrece makes a rigorous distinction between its comic and serious scenes. The comic scenes are intended to 'make folke myrth and game'; the serious disputations on true nobility are offered so that 'gentilmen of name May be somwhat mouyd By this example' (II, 890–93). The comic servants 'A' and 'B' rub shoulders with the audience, bidding someone answer a knock at the door and then complaining when that spectator responds slowly: 'A man may rappe tyll his naylis ake' (II, 73–80). Conversely, the disputants of the main action seldom acknowledge the presence of the spectators. The comic scenes exploit the milieu of the Tudor banqueting hall; the serious action, set in ancient Rome, presents a supposedly historical narrative. In the comic sequences the hall-screen, its doors, the banqueting tables, the guests, and the fire are all an indispensable part of the dramatic illusion whereby 'A' and 'B' attempt to pass themselves off as gentlemen-spectators watching the play just like everyone else; in the serious action we witness an entirely different sort of dramatic illusion according to which the audience eavesdrops on a historically remote event. In one, the audience is anachronistically involved; in the other, the audience retreats behind a 'fourth wall' and adopts a stance of 'willing suspension of disbelief'. The brilliant interplay of the two modes of illusion exploits the banqueting hall in two ways, as a contemporary presence forming part of the dramatic scene and as a neutral playing area imagined to be ancient Rome.

The serious action of *Fulgens and Lucrece* is what especially distinguishes this play from *Mankind*. The disputation on true nobility is cast as a *débat*, in a literary tradition that is both courtly and humanist. The dramatic form comes from courtly debate—as found, for example, in John Lydgate's mummings written for Henry VI—whereas the rhetoric and intellectual argument come from an Italian humanist tract by Buonaccorso called *De Vera Nobilitate* (as translated into

English by the Earl of Worcester). The tone of the argument is courtly throughout, just as *Mankind's* is essentially popular. *Fulgens and Lucrece* depicts a serious rivalry at court between two contending forces that were very much at odds with one another in the court of Henry VII: the titled aristocracy, represented by the insolent Publius Cornelius, and the 'new men' of low-born background, represented by Gaius Flaminius. The analogy between ancient Rome and Tudor England is abundantly clear in this contest between a feudal baron and a new administrator who justifies his political prominence on the basis of deeds rather than family titles. Lucrece's preference for Gaius is not so much a romantic triumph as an endorsement of the new political order to which Medwall, and his patron Cardinal Morton, were deeply indebted. (In Medwall's source, the issue, left meekly by Lucrece to her father, is unannounced.) The argument must have been so potentially offensive to the older aristocracy, in fact, that Medwall needed to introduce the antics of 'A' and 'B' to mollify his patrician spectators. The comic servants ape the contentiousness of their masters and thereby reduce strife to laughable absurdity. They 'distance' the action by their comic indifference to the rivalry of their social superiors and by their witty observation that their patrician auditors ought to be similarly indifferent: 'Why shulde they care? I trow here is no man of the kyn or sede Of either partie, for why they were bore In the cytie of Rome' (I, 177–80). Medwall's use of comedy, then, is motivated chiefly by the need for disclaimer of his serious political intention. The play borrows techniques of popular dramaturgy, but its central action originates in a milieu of courtly entertainment and directs its themes at a courtly audience.

III

Later examples confirm our impression that courtly and popular drama retained separate identities and separate stages throughout the early Tudor era, even though the two traditions certainly influenced one another. John Heywood, for example, knew how to write plays in the popular style, as in the case of his *Four PP* (c. 1520–22). This play requires no scenery or elaborate stage-structures and could be performed anywhere, using curtains or doors for exits and entrances. Its broad fabliau humour exploits popular tastes in anti-feminism and scatology. The play could certainly have been performed at court, and is in the tradition of Chaucer's fabliaux, but does not limit itself to patrician surroundings. So too with Heywood's *The Pardoner and the Frere* and *Johan Johan*. On the other hand, Heywood's more courtly disputations in the style of Medwall's *Fulgens and Lucrece* are exclusively aristocratic in their auspices. *The Play of the Wether* (1525–33) is seemingly designed for boy actors, all ten of whom assemble at the end of the play to 'synge moste ioyfully' (1252). Similar gatherings of the entire cast are found in *Respublica*, *Disobedient Child*, *Jacob and Esau*, and other children's plays. The scene of *Wether* is a banqueting hall: Jupiter has come 'This nyght to suppe here wyth my lorde' (1027). The play requires a throne where Jupiter can hear music played to him and into which he can withdraw from view. Evidently this throne is fitted with curtains and is a substantial edifice. Although we may be tempted to suppose that it was set up against the hall-screen between the doors, where the entire effect would somewhat resemble the façade of the later Elizabethan public stage, we in fact have no idea where the throne was located.

At least one other early play at court features a similar stage-structure. *Godly Queen Hester* (1525–9) calls for a 'travers' (seemingly a curtained structure) into which King Assuerus can retire and hear music played to him without leaving the stage, like Jupiter in *Wether*. At one point, for example, 'the kynge entryth the trauers & aman goeth out' (138). Later, 'the chappell' sings a hymn while the king meditates in private (860). A 'travess', perhaps similarly constructed, was actually used by Queen Elizabeth in the royal chapel for Easter Communion in 1593.[12] Although this historical illustration is comparatively late for the period we are studying, it does point to the use of a private compartment where a royal figure could be screened off from view when not actually participating in a ceremony.

Other functional stage 'houses' or *domus* are fairly common in courtly or school plays of the early Tudor period. They give quite a different impression from the usual single curtain and open stage of the popular theatre; these structures are multiple, separate, and simultaneously visible locations such as we later find in the plays of John Lyly. *Wit and Science* (1531–47) may require a den for Tediousness (perhaps a decorated doorway) and some representation of Mount Parnassus. *The Marriage of Wit and Science* (1567–8?), a court play on the same subject, also features the 'house' of Lady Science with a functional

[12] Chambers, *ES*, Vol. III, pp. 26–7.

'gate' through which Wit and the others are invited. *Gammer Gurton's Needle* (*c.* 1552–63), a Cambridge play, seems to require two functional stage houses for Gammer Gurton and for Dame Chat, with a hole in the latter house through which Dr. Rat climbs and is beaten for his pains. *Thersites* (1537), acted perhaps at Eton or Oxford, must have a shop for Mulciber and another *domus* for Thersites' mother. *Jacob and Esau* (*c.* 1547–53), a court play, must provide a 'tent' for Isaac and historical costuming for its characters: they are 'to be consydered to be Hebrews, and so should be apparailed with attire'. *Virtuous and Godly Susanna* by Thomas Garter (1563–9) seems to have required a partition running from front to back, serving as an orchard wall, with a real door leading into the orchard where the elders spy on Susanna. All these structures tend to move away from the unlocalized stage to a historical, Biblical or mythological setting. This impulse towards the verisimilar seems to come chiefly from neo-classical example, although medieval staging, courtly and popular, also played its part.

Popular drama prior to Elizabeth's reign seldom varied in its use of the unlocalized stage. The staging requirements of *Mankind* are essentially those of *Impatient Poverty*, *Lusty Juventus*, and a host of mid-century moralities. *The Life and Repentance of Mary Magdalen* (*c.* 1550–66) refers, like *Mankind*, to the taking up of a collection—'halfpence or pence'—among popular audiences. Such plays customarily refer to their *mise en scène* as 'thys place' and to their auditors as 'my maysters' or 'the persons here present'. As the more successful troupes gravitated towards London during the early Elizabethan years, however, a desire for more ambitious staging began to reveal itself in plays like *Cambises* and *Horestes*. These plays were probably performed both in London inns and at court; did the players learn their new staging methods from courtly example? When the best of these troupes (such as Leicester's Men) built permanent theatres in 1576 and onwards, were they influenced in their conception of a theatre more by their experiences as travelling players or by their opportunities to perform in patrician banqueting halls? Perhaps we can obtain a tentative answer by comparing two plays from the 1560s, one popular and one courtly—*Horestes* (1567) and *Gorboduc* (1562).

IV

An 'Orestes' was performed at court during the Christmas revels of 1567, either by Paul's Boys or Lord Rich's Men. In the same year was

published a play by John Pickering called *A New Interlude of Vice,
Conteyninge the Historye of Horestes*. Whether this published version
represents the performance at court has been questioned, chiefly by
those who regard the extant play as too vulgar and crude for the
delectation of a courtly audience.[13] Nevertheless, the coincidence of
date and subject makes it likely that text and performance are related.
If so, the actors must have been Lord Rich's Men rather than Paul's
Boys, for the violent action and extensive doubling of roles are entirely
unsuited to juvenile players. Popular plays of this 'unsophisticated' sort
did appear at court. Moreover, *Horestes* is by no means lacking in
political advice that pertains to the crown as well as to the country at
large. It is a *mirror*-type play demonstrating the nature of tyranny and
its opposite. Clytemnestra and Egistus are usurpers and wantons, whereas young Horestes is a true prince. He must make the difficult choice
between mercy and justice in pronouncing sentence on his mother and
her lover Egistus, who are guilty of the death of Horestes' father. The
prince learns that he must be prudent, slow to act, responsive above
all to the good counsel of his advisers, and yet firm. If he proceeds in
a spirit of public correction, what might otherwise be spiteful revenge
in him will be seen as true justice. However much this lesson may
apply by extension to Queen Elizabeth's problem with Mary Queen of
Scots, who had just been forced to abdicate in 1567, the lesson is also
broadly political. *Horestes* reflects the ever-increasing fascination of
popular drama with matters of statecraft, and looks at politics from the
point of view of those who are governed.

In staging, *Horestes* is more ambitious than earlier plays of the
popular canon. The extensive stage-directions speak often of drums,
trumpets and marching armies: 'Let the drum play and enter Horestis
with his band; marche about the stage' (546); 'Let the trumpet blowe
within' (717). The main action is Horestes' siege of Mycoene, represented by a city wall and gate facing the stage. Clytemnestra speaks
from atop this façade, looking down at Horestes' army on the stage:
'Let the trumpet leaue soundyng and let Harrauld speake and Clitem-
nestra speake ouer the wal' (697). The battle is a vivid one, and
requires that Horestes and his soldiers break through the façade and
drag Clytemnestra forth: 'Let it be longe eare you can win the Citie,
and when you haue wone it, let Horestes bringe out his mother by

---

[13] See, for example, John W. Cunliffe, ed., *Early English Classical Tragedies*
(Oxford, 1912), p. lxx.

the arme' (864). Subsequently, Egistus is also defeated in battle and is hanged by Horestes' men: 'fling him off the lader . . . Take downe Egistus and bear him out' (943–70).

Although this amount of military activity is new to popular drama, we should be very hesitant to ascribe the newness of it to courtly influence. Except for *Liberality and Prodigality* (*c.* 1567–8, revised *c.* 1601), we find nothing like this city façade in Tudor court plays, and *Liberality* is a late text into which late staging methods may very well have been incorporated. We have certainly seen nothing in courtly drama of soldiers marching, alarums, excursions, sieges, drums, trumpets and the like. These staging gymnastics of *Horestes* markedly anticipate those of the later Elizabethan public stage, of 1 *Henry VI*, for example, with its scaling operations and its use of the tiring-house façade or—as John Elliott argues (see below p. 230)—of separate mansions to represent the city walls of Orleans and Rouen, or *Henry V* with its gates of Harfleur. Courtly drama, on the other hand, studiously avoids the chronicle play both before and after the date of *Horestes*.

Furthermore, we must not assume that *Horestes* was written exclusively or even primarily for the court. It is just the kind of play that must have been shown in the public inns of London—the Red Lion, the Bull, the Cross Keys—which were showing signs of rapidly increasing dramatic activity in the 1560s.[14] Here the inn-yard rather than an interior room would have been a virtual necessity, in order to accommodate larger audiences and extended playing space for assaults and scaling operations. With a booth-stage set against one wall of an inn-yard, Clytemnestra could speak from a gallery above the stage, and scaling ladders could be used to gain access to her fortress. At court, the screen itself was sometimes too ornately carved to permit much rough handling, but the evidence seems to confirm that special scenic structures were used for such set-pieces in court entertainments (see Chapter 10 below). Even though such an arrangement were used, however, the vigour of *Horestes*' assault on 'Mycoene' may suggest that an inn-yard served as the original theatrical environment.

Certainly every other staging aspect of *Horestes* is in the popular tradition. The play doubles its twenty-seven roles for six players, much as *Cambises* (*c.* 1561) doubles thirty-eight parts for six men and two boys. Because the Vice and Horestes are demanding roles and hence are doubled with as few other characters as possible, the four remaining

[14] Chambers, *ES*, Vol. II, pp. 355–8, 379–83.

actors of *Horestes* must double parts constantly. The rollicking
humour of the comic scenes involves much slapstick physical abuse:
'let the Vice thwacke them both and run out', 'give him a box on the
eare', and so on. The comic types look forward to their counterparts
in Shakespeare's later histories: they are cowardly soldiers, camp
followers, highwaymen, or rustic countrymen learning to survive in
a time of war. For such a play in the 1560s, the London inns offered
exciting new possibilities. Court performance had to be kept in mind
as well, for the occasional performance at court was a great cachet
—and windfall—for the players. Nevertheless, *Horestes* does not indicate any extensive indebtedness to the staging traditions of the boy
actors.

To see a characteristically different kind of elaboration in courtly
staging of the 1560s, let us conclude with a look at *Gorboduc* (1562).
It is, like *Horestes*, a *mirror*-type play about the dangers of inadequate
political leadership. Like *Horestes*, its advice to the throne stresses the
crucial importance of good counsel bestowed on a monarch. Its
political orientation, however, is more patrician. It demands a major
role for Parliament in naming a successor to the English throne. One
of its authors, Thomas Norton, was chairman of a Parliamentary
committee in 1565–6 urging petitions on Elizabeth in the name of
Parliamentary prerogative. The play spells out the manifest dangers of
an unsettled succession and clearly implies that the heir to the throne
must be English-born and Protestant—someone, that is, other than
Mary Queen of Scots. Many popular plays were equally fearful of
Catholicism, of course, but the point of view of *Gorboduc* remains
exclusively that of the ruling classes.

Gorboduc was designed for a single extravagant occasion. It was
part of the elaborate Christmas festivities of the Inner Temple, and
was performed on 18 January 1562 at court, in the presence of Queen
Elizabeth. Her presence was indeed crucial for a play of such pointed
advice. Once she had seen it, the play became history; the text we
have is the record of an event, not (as in the case of *Horestes*) a script
for players. The Inner Temple authors wished to impress their advice
on Queen Elizabeth as vividly as possible. They caused a 'grett skaffold'
to be erected in the Queen's hall at Westminster, and to be dismantled
the next day. *Gorboduc* was only part of that day's entertainment, for
it was followed by a 'grett maske'.[15]

[15] J. G. Nichols, ed., *The Diary of Henry Machyn* (London, 1848), p. 275.

The play itself owes something to the courtly traditions of mask and *débat*, as well as to Senecan tragedy and *A Mirror for Magistrates*. Long rhetorical speeches are antithetically balanced against one another, almost unrelieved by stage action. At the same time, the visual effect is often spectacular. The dumb-shows between the acts call for elaborate staging and expensive costuming. Before Act IV, for example, 'there came forth from vnder the stage, as though out of hell, three Furies, Alecto, Megera, and Ctesiphone, clad in black garmentes sprinkled with bloud and flames, their bodies girt with snakes, their heds spred with serpentes in stead of heare.' Evidently the 'grett skaffold' erected for the occasion was a raised stage, complete with a trapdoor, though there may also have been scaffold-seating for members of the court. The dumb-show before Act V features 'a company of hargabusiers and of armed men, all in order of battaile', who discharge their pieces and march three times about the stage to the accompaniment of drums and fifes. These dumb-shows are extravagant in their demands for large casts and for several consorts of musicians. Act I requires violins, Act II cornets, Act III flutes, Act IV hautboys, and Act V drums and flutes. For Act III a 'company of mourners' are clad all in black; for Act I 'sixe wilde men' are clad in leaves. All this is particularly expensive for a single performance. Extravagance was, after all, an essential part of the display.

Despite the opulence of its spectacle, however, *Gorboduc* is revealingly devoid of the muscular stage effects we find in *Horestes*. Although *Gorboduc* tells of political strife and ends in open rebellion, violence is banished from the stage in accord with classical precept. Marching armies are limited strictly to the dumb-shows. A *Nuntius* informs us of Fergus's campaign and his twenty thousand men. Eubulus speaks eloquently and lengthily on the evils of civil war, but we see no sieges of cities or hangings on stage. Classical decorum of this kind gained ascendancy at court; popular history plays never became fashionable there. The popular tradition was left pretty much on its own to devise the staging methods we find in *Horestes* and later in the English history plays of Shakespeare.

Note

Texts.
The editions used for this chapter are Deimling and Matthews, *CP*; Block, *LC*; England and Pollard, *TP*; Toulmin Smith, *YP*; Norris, *CC*; Craig, *CCP*; Furnivall, *DP*; and Davis, *NCP*.

Scholarship and Criticism.
Kolve, *PCC* is sound and illuminating on psychological aspects of medieval festive drama (on 'game' and 'play' elements in the cycle plays particularly). Glynne Wickham's chapter, 'Stage and Drama till 1660', in *History of Literature in the English Language*, Vol. III (ed. Christopher Ricks, London, 1971), is also interesting on the same subject.

C. L. Barber, *Shakespeare's Festive Comedy* (Princeton, 1959) and John Spiers, 'The Mystery Cycle: Some Towneley Cycle plays', *Scrutiny* XVIII (1951–2), are helpful on the festive and folk elements in English drama, as is J. L. Styan, *The Dark Comedy* (Cambridge, 1968) on an equally important but until recently little understood variant of the comic mode. The comments of all three critics have interesting implications where the medieval cycles are concerned.

V

The Comic in the Cycles

ARNOLD WILLIAMS

I

IF ALL drama must be either comedy or tragedy, it is obvious that the cycle plays must be comedy, for they cannot be tragedy. To the Middle Ages tragedy meant chiefly a story with an unhappy ending, one whose main character, as Chaucer's monk phrased it, 'is yfallen out of heigh degree / Into miserie, and endeth wrecchedly'. More sophisticated critics added that it had to concern magnates and kings and be written in high style.[1] The Scriptural drama of the cycle plays fits none of these criteria. If the cycle ended with the fall of Adam and Eve, or the punishment of the wicked in the Last Judgment, perhaps the requirement of going from joy to misery would be met. No cycle is so arranged. Those episodes which in themselves have the possibility of tragedy, the Crucifixion, for example, are followed or accompanied by other episodes which reverse the movement. The Fall is a fortunate fall, for it opens the way for the great manifestation of love in the redemption. The horrors of the Crucifixion are really prologue to the joys of the Resurrection. The condemnation of the wicked is preceded and nullified by the rewarding of the just.

This holds true for the other criteria. The history of the human race, which is the subject of the cycle plays, involves kings and magnates, but not exclusively. In fact the emphasis is rather more on the humble. The Shepherds worship the infant Jesus before the Kings. Common people like the man born blind or the woman taken in adultery play quite as large a role as those in absolute authority like Pharaoh, Caesar Augustus, the two Herods, Pilate, Annas and Caiaphas, all of whom are tyrants and villains. Some of the playwrights attempted to differentiate between high and low characters by assigning the

---

[1] Paul Strohm, 'Storie, Spelle, Geste, Romaunce, Tragedie', *Speculum* XLVI (1971), pp. 356-9.

high characters mixtures of French and English, as in the Cornish and Chester cycles, or macaronic Latin-English, as in the Towneley Pilate, or 'aureate' English, as in the two Coventry plays. The results, however, do not appeal, at least to the modern reader, as 'high style' in the sense that Shakespeare or Milton achieved it.

If, as a common medieval belief voiced by Vincent of Beauvais and Dante held,[2] the main requirement of comedy is a happy ending, the cycle plays are comedy. However, we are accustomed to expect other things of comedy. One of these is a unity, which in the ancient drama of Greece and Rome is achieved in either or both of two ways. The Old Comedy of Aristophanes is unified by the target of its satire, often a specific person or an identifiable group. *The Clouds* is aimed directly at Socrates, whom Aristophanes saw as a perverter of morals. The target of *Lysistrata* is more diffuse, the war party concretized in the chorus of old men, who continued the wasteful and hopeless war with Sparta.

In the New Comedy of Menander and his Roman followers, Terence and Plautus, plot is the unifying element, and in its basic elements the plot is almost invariable: a man, nearly always young, desires a woman and overcomes obstacles to attain her finally. The devices by which this standard plot is worked out include intrigue, mistaken identity, disguise, misunderstanding, surprise, discovery. Classical comedy also created certain stereotyped characters, for instance the braggart, the parasite, the foolish old man, the shrew.

Some of the stereotypes have parallels in the cycle plays. The soldiers sent out by Herod to massacre the infants easily fall into the mould of the 'miles gloriosus' or braggart, as do those sent by Pilate to guard the sepulchre. The discomfiture of Herod's soldiers by the women produces farce in some of the plays (see T. W. Craik's chapter below, pp. 178-81), especially in the Digby play of the *Killing of the Children*, which develops a boasting coward named Watkyn. In both York and Towneley Cain is given a comic servant, Brewbarret and Pikeharness

---

[2] 'Comedy is poetry reversing a sad beginning by a glad end'—Vincent of Beauvais quoted in C. S. Baldwin, *Medieval Rhetoric* (originally published in 1928, reprinted Gloucester, Mass., 1959), p. 176. 'Comedy begins with sundry adverse conditions but ends happily'—Dante, letter to Can Grande, in Paget Toynbee, *Epistolae* (2nd edn., Oxford, 1966), pp. 200-01. It is perhaps significant that Dante calls his great work both a comedy (*Inferno* XVI, 128) and a tragedy (*Inferno* XX, 113). We shall see a similar ambivalence in the cycle plays.

respectively. The greatest development is of the *senex*, the foolish old man. Two characters lend themselves to this role; Noah, who is five hundred years old when commanded to build the ark, and St. Joseph, who is not only the grumbling and self-pitying old man called on for tasks beyond his strength (catching doves for the presentation in the temple in the Coventry *Weavers' Pageant*, 461–520) but also convinced that he is cuckolded. In all treatments he addresses the men in the audience, warning them not to take young wives. York and Towneley are especially notable for the rapid changes in tone, as Joseph first perceives Mary's pregnancy and breaks forth into denunciation; then is enlightened by the angel in a dream, and becomes solicitous for his wife's welfare and reverently adores the infant; then begins grumbling again when he has to pack the family off to Egypt.

In other respects, the cycle plays resemble neither the Old nor the New Comedy. Since they tell the story of mankind from creation to doomsday, they cannot have unity of plot in any conventional sense. They do not have a single cast of personages for the whole of the cycle. Adam and Eve are succeeded by Cain and Abel and they by Noah and his family, and so on. It would be hard to imagine a plot structure that would accommodate all the episodes shown in even the most abbreviated cycles, such as the one at Coventry, which was limited to New Testament scenes alone. To my knowledge the only post-medieval play having a different cast for each of its episodes is Gerhard Hauptmann's *The Weavers*, which like the cycle plays is unclassifiable as comedy or tragedy.

If the cycle as a whole can be neither comedy nor tragedy, can a single episode? Generally not, because the action of the episodes is an element uncontrollable by the dramatist. The material of the cycles is history, which has often provided characters and actions to the tragic writer, seldom to the comic. When, partly in reaction to the theology of the medieval Scriptural drama and partly in deference to the new respect for the classics, sixteenth-century authors tried to write regular plays on Scriptural subjects, they chose the tragic form but had, for theological reasons, to give their plays a happy ending. The results were generally feeble, as in Beza's *Abraham Sacrifiant*. Only Milton's *Samson Agonistes* commands respect from the modern reader, and then principally as a closet drama. So far as I know no Renaissance, Reformation or Counter-Reformation playwright attempted a comic treatment of a Scriptural subject. Probably it would have appeared indecorous.

Fortunately, the authors of the cycle plays were little troubled with decorum in the restricted sense in which critical theorists use the word. That opened a channel into the comic, and the incorporation of non-Scriptural materials furnished an opportunity for a freer development that might approach formal comedy. Only one play in the entire corpus of cycle plays has something like a formal plot. This is the *Second Shepherds' Play* of the Towneley Cycle, a dramatization of the adoration of the shepherds. Scripture says nothing except that while the shepherds were watching their flocks, an angel appeared to them announcing the birth of the Messiah, they went to see the infant, and subsequently spread the news abroad. Several of the authors of the cycle plays expand the characterization of the shepherds; only the Wakefield Master (and then apparently only in his second attempt) introduces the element of plot in the episode in which the scroundrelly Mak, despite the precautions of the shepherds, succeeds in stealing one of their sheep and almost succeeds in concealing it. This is the nearest approach to a comic plot in the whole of medieval Scriptural drama. It is not, of course, the standard boy-meets-girl plot, but it does incorporate some of the standard devices: disguise (Mak trying to pass himself off as a stranger from the south, the sheep disguised as baby), mistaken identity (the sheep as a babe in the cradle), discovery (when Third Shepherd lifts the coverlet and finds a sheep) and, most important, burlesque, for the whole scene of the visit of the shepherds to Mak's cottage is a parody of the later visit to the Christ child in the stable.

One other element needs a bit of explanation. Comedy has its villains or antagonists as well as tragedy. The difference is that the comic antagonist is punished, but never mortally. Slaves are beaten, Malvolio is gulled, Harpagon becomes ridiculous, but nobody is killed, or even imprisoned. Mak suffers just this kind of punishment. Legally he could be executed for sheep-stealing—but the shepherds content themselves with tossing him in a blanket.

If the *Second Shepherds' Play* is the nearest approach to formal plotted comedy, comic elements appear elsewhere in the cycles. Some of the stereotyped characters occur—the shrew in several of the Noah plays, the foolish old man with a young wife in the characterization of

Joseph, the braggart in soldiers who guard the tomb of Jesus. In all such instances it is safer to suppose that they are independent inventions rather than imitations of the classics. Generally speaking, the comic comes in quite different forms and from quite different sources.

Comedy's requirements are more basic than agreement with the classic tradition. Comedy should be fantastic, festive, and above all funny. Comedy deals mainly with the impossible or the illogical. The sudden multiplication of Falstaff's assailants is a sample of the fantastic, as is also Socrates in his basket between heaven and earth in *The Clouds*. These can be matched by the scene in the Towneley *First Shepherds' Play* in which two shepherds almost come to blows over the pasturing of some non-existent sheep.[3]

Greek comedy takes its name from the revels accompanying the festival of Dionysius. The drama of the Middle Ages arose from the celebration of the two great Christian festivals, Easter and Christmas. Just as the festival elements are still prominent in Shakespeare's 'romantic' comedies, two of which, *A Midsummer Night's Dream* and *Twelfth Night*, are named from holidays,[4] so are they in the cycle plays, most of which were given on the feasts of Whitsuntide or Corpus Christi. They incorporate elements derived from folk festivals, which in turn contain the remnants of pagan rituals, for example the wrestling contests in the Chester Nativity and Cornish Passion plays,[5] and the meal in both the Chester *Nativity* and the Towneley *First Shepherds'*.[6]

We should probably not be too far wrong in seeing many of the great farce situations in the cycles as primarily festive high spirits. Such are the fight between Noah and his wife in the dramatizations of the deluge; the debates of the shepherds over the words of the angels'

---

[3] Cf. Lope de Rueda's amusing *Los Olivos* (included in *Medieval Interludes*), where a similar brawl erupts over an as yet non-existent achievement.

[4] Barber, *Shakespeare's Festive Comedy*, esp. pp. 3–57.

[5] Norris, *CC: Passio*, 2509. The wrestling was enacted in full view of the audience in the Piran Round revival of the Cycle, as the in-the-round staging situation would seem to demand. (See Neville Denny's discussion of multiple-action staging below, pp. 136ff.)

[6] For samples of these elements from folk festivals see Speirs, 'The Mystery Cycle: Some Towneley Cycle Plays', pp. 86–117, 246–65.

song, whether it was 'gle, glo, glas glum' or 'glorum, glarum with a glo / and much of celsis', or what not (Chester VII, 387; Ludus XVI, 85; Coventry Shearmen and Tailor's Pageant, 272–7—the incident, evidently made familiar by dramatic representations and a favourite with audiences, is depicted in the Holkham Bible Picture Book); and the knockabout business that was evidently included as an accompaniment to those great set-pieces, the Ark and Temple-building sequences.

II

The important last requirement, that comedy be funny, furnishes the opportunities, but also the problems. Philosophers and critics display a striking lack of unanimity in their definitions of what is funny, what makes us laugh or even smile. The probable source of the difficulty is that the laughable always involves some violation of the decorous, and the decorous differs widely from one society to another. Comedy is notoriously subject to the accidents of time and space. Undergraduates rarely need any convincing to accept *Oedipus the King* as tragic. It requires a great deal of labour to get them to see *The Clouds* as funny. (The best example from my own experience was seeing a Japanese kabuki tragedy, *Kanjincho*, followed by a comedy, the *Zen Substitute*. Despite my complete ignorance of the conventions of Japanese drama, even of the essential attitudes of Japanese society, *Kanjincho* produced in me, as in most of the Western audience, much the same response as *Oedipus* or *Lear*. The *Zen Substitute* elicited no response at all.)

The society of fifteenth-century England is perhaps closer to our own than is that of eighteenth-century Japan; but the question of what is comic is no less puzzling. How, for instance, are we to take the numerous situations in which an evil personage goes into a rage that seems to us comic? Herod is the stock example. After learning that the three kings have gone home another way and so evaded the trap he has set for them, the Coventry Herod breaks forth into this ridiculous speech:

> I stampe! I stare! I loke all abowtt!
> Myght I them take, I schuld them bren at a glede!   *fire*
> I rent! I rawe! and now run I wode!   *mad*

A! thatt these velen traylurs hath mard this my mode!
The schalbe hangid yf I ma cum them to!

and the stage-directions read, 'Here Erode ragis in the pagond and in the strete also' (*Shearmen and Tailors' Pageant*, 779–83). The whole corpus of English Scriptural drama must contain more than a score of such scenes, in which Cain, Pharaoh, the two Herods, Pilate, and even Satan himself go into such apparently comic rages. Were they comic to the spectators?

It is quite possible that what we see as funny was utterly serious, in fact terrifying to the audience. The nineteenth-century tear-jerker melodramas like *Thorns and Orange Blossoms* are invariably played nowadays as comedy, but we know that the audiences for whom they were written took them seriously, weeping at the heroine's tribulations and hissing the villain.

Beyond this ambiguity is still another: laughter is a possible response to something threatening. This can be the so-called nervous laughter. Under certain circumstances the downright terrifying can produce laughter. When either the supposedly terrifying is shown to be harmless (the noise is being made by the wind, not by a ghost) or when the terror is not actual but only make-believe, the recognition of that fact may produce laughter. Film-makers have capitalized on this close association of terror and laughter in horror pictures of the 'Abbott and Costello Meet Frankenstein' sort. The conditions for this comic resolution of terror are met over and over again in the cycle plays in the threatening speeches of the tyrant figures, Pharaoh, Caesar Augustus, both Herods, Pilate, the devils that burst onto the stage singly or in troops. It is hard for a sophisticated modern reader to see how the medieval actors could have played these scenes straight or the audience taken them seriously. But we cannot be sure.

Even less knowable is the attitude of the medieval audience towards two other effects that are enormously amusing to us. These are the constant anachronisms and the proneness of the style to become burlesque. Both flow from the essential purpose of the craft cycles, to reach the sensibility of the common man by representing the great events of Christian history as strictly contemporary happenings. The authors seemed to have bent every effort towards portraying the Crucifixion as an execution that might have happened in York the week before. Thus evil personages like Cain, Pharaoh, the two Herods,

Pilate, even the Jewish high priests swear by Mahound. Annas and
Caiaphas are 'bishops'. St. Joseph becomes the foolish old man wed to
a young wife—the January–May motif of folk humour—in constant
fear of being cuckolded.

It is a great temptation to the critic to explain these anachronisms
in terms of the naivety of the audience, perhaps of the playwrights also,
for instance in the numerous vows and greetings of a Christian nature
peppering the Old Testament sequences. In the Towneley *Second
Shepherds' Play*, Second Shepherd salutes First Shepherd thus:

> He saue you and me / ouerthwart and endlong   *across along*
> that hang on a tre / I say you no wrang
> Cryst saue vs.   (48–50)

The fact that Christ is not yet born is of no significance. If you want
your audience to accept the Judean shepherds who watched their
flocks near Bethlehem as exactly like the Yorkshire ones who watch
theirs near Wakefield, you cannot have them greet each other with
the historically appropriate 'sholom aleichem' or its English translation,
'peace be unto you'. The operative principle, as in costuming and
portraiture, is contemporaneity of reference. Invocations of Christ,
Our Lady, or one of the saints establish the virtue and religion of
the character, just as oaths by Mahound establish the opposite—it is
the only oath an audience will recognize as non-Christian, as heathen,
and hence as indicative of utter villainy.

But this is not the whole story. Later in the same play First Shepherd
awakes and, after another anachronistic oath partly in mangled Latin,
'Iudas carnas dominus', proceeds to describe his experiences while
sleeping:

> My foytt slepis, by ihesus / and I water fastand
> I thought that we layd us / full nere yngland.   (351–3)

This is an obvious double-take, much like the lines which Shaw gives
Britannus in *Caesar and Cleopatra*. Assuring Rufio that the enormous
lighthouse crane is operated by an old man and a boy, he admits he
does not understand its mechanics: 'They have counterweights, and
a machine with boiling water in it which I do not understand: it is
not of British design.' Shaw was pulling someone's leg, and so was
the Wakefield Master. This comic use of anachronism, though rare
in the cycle plays, surfaces often enough to warn the critic to be wary.

Its most common form is the inclusion of a local place-name in an evocative catalogue of far-away places like Syria and India. Thus Nuntius in the Towneley *Herod the Great* enumerates Herod's dominions:

> Tuskane and turky
> All Inde and Italy
> Cecyll and surry

which are sufficiently confused and anachronistic, but then he caps the list with

> ffrom Egyp to mantua vnto kemp towne.[7]
> (XVI, 42–50)

This is, of course, the work of the Wakefield Master, but the use of local place-names to draw a laugh is common in the cycles. One of the Chester shepherds has led his sheep from 'comlie conway unto clyde', and the magnates in the plays of the Cornish Cycle customarily reward their followers with gifts of local estates, as when King David bestows on his Herald 'charter rights to Carnsew and Trehembis' for organizing the work on the temple (*Origo Mundi*, 2311–12).

The total effect of such passages, whether or not intended by the author, is one of disparity, a chief producer of the comic. In fact, disparity lies at the root of all burlesque, and there is much of that in the cycle plays. We have already noted that the visit to Mak's cottage is an anticipatory parody of the visit to the manger. All the treatments of the adoration of the shepherds except that of the Hegge ('N-town') Cycle anticipate the gifts of the magi with the gifts of the shepherds— a bob of cherries, a pair of old hose, a pipe, a spoon that holds forty or a hundred peas. Authors seem to vie with one another to see who can invent the most outrageous gifts.

Nearly all the burlesque in the cycles is of the same sort, sometimes called diminishing burlesque or travesty. As against the mock heroic, represented by Pope's *Rape of the Lock*, in which trivial matter is augmented by being expressed in high style, travesty creates a disparity by expressing high matter in low style. The vehicle of the cycles is rhymed stanzaic verse, too often of the jog-trot variety parodied by

[7] Clarence Steinberg, '*Kemp Town* in the Towneley *Herod* Play', *Neuphilologische Mitteilungen* LXXI (1970), pp. 253–60, considers it likely that this was a local place-name.

Chaucer in *Sir Thopas*. Imagery, too, is often derived from everyday life, as when the Chester St. Joseph, worshipping the newborn Christ, uses the image of brewing:

> for thou art come mans blisse to brewe
> to all that thy law will shewe.   (VI, 525–6)

Even the Hegge plays, which have the least comic content of any of the cycles, occasionally show this disparity between matter and expression. Speaking to the soldiers returning from their unsuccessful watch over the tomb of the dead Christ, Pilate says more in sorrow than in anger:

> Now all ȝour wurchep is lorn
> And euery man may ȝow wel scorn
> And bidde ȝow go sytten in þe corn
> And chare a-way þe ravyn.   *scare*
> (XXXIV, 1548–51)

The image diminishes one of the great failures of all time to the dimensions of a scarecrow.

A common quality emerges from all these comic rages, anachronisms, parodies and travesties: an essential ambiguity which adds the dimension of irony characteristic of all great comedy. The ambiguity of the cycles is multiple. We cannot be sure that what we perceive as funny was so perceived in the fifteenth century. We can partly solve this puzzle by abandoning all historical perspective and agreeing that whatever we find funny is in fact funny. But even then much of the ambiguity remains. Are the comic gifts of the shepherds really comic? When we have finished laughing it may strike us that the significance goes deeper. These are poor men. They have no gold, frankincense or myrrh to give, but what they have they give joyously, even if it is only a pair of old hose. If we choose we can pursue this line of feeling into sentimentality. Or we can pursue Pilate's figure into dizzying heights of theological speculation: compared to the power of God, the uttermost efforts of evil men have only the terror of a scarecrow put in a field to frighten birds. Perhaps St. Joseph is not comparing the divine gift of salvation to a mash of malted barley; perhaps his brew is medicinal (the more likely interpretation perhaps) and Christ the healer. On the other hand 'brewe' may be of much humbler derivation, from domestic cooking, used simply to suggest 'preparation' or 'accomplishment'. Or the choice of image may merely reflect the playwright's lack of expertise; 'brewe' is the only word he can think of that rhymes with 'Ihesu', 'knewe', 'trewe', 'new' and 'shewe'.

III

We have noted that the cycle plays slightly resemble the New Comedy in the treatment of certain comic stereotypes, but differ in their lack of plot. They also resemble the Old Comedy in their satire, but differ in the lack of specificity. The cycle plays contain a good bit of topical satire, little of it directed at specific individuals. The best-known sample is the complaints of the shepherds in the Towneley *Second Shepherds' Play*. One grumbles about the gentry who oppress the peasantry by taxation and confiscation; another is bitter about women, particularly his wife; and the third vents his spleen on the weather. This rather broad spectrum of targets is thoroughly representative of the satire of the cycles.

In the Towneley *Judgment* the devil Titivillus, created by the same hand as the shepherds, recites a long and miscellaneous roll of sinners: false swearers, extortioners, simonists, women who wear horned headdresses (XXX, 206–385—see, too, *Imagery*, pl. 3b). Cheats and corrupters are a common target. The Chester *Harrowing of Hell* contains a confession of a 'tavernere, a gentill gossippe and a tapster', who adulterated the beer, watered the wine, and gave short measure (XVII, 261–308).[8] Perhaps the most pointed of such satires is the character Den (probably 'dean') in the Hegge *Trial of Joseph and Mary*. The episode opens with a monologue in which he warns all evil-doers. Two 'detractors' have reported Mary to the 'bishop' Abijachar for adultery. Den is sent to summon them. Like Chaucer's Summoner he uses his office for extortion:

> But ʒit sum mede and ʒe me take
> I wyl withdrawe my gret rough toth
> gold or sylvyr I wol not forsake.

and the author is then careful to universalize the characterization: 'evyn as all sumnorys doth' (XIV, prologue by Den and 113–36).

The root cause of the satire in the cycles is the point of view. This

---

[8] This piece, not found in all manuscripts, looks as though it originally belonged to the Judgment play.

is particularly apparent in the treatment of kings and ecclesiastical dignitaries. With the exception of the Three Kings, who are after all away from home and without authority, all kings and 'bishops' are villains. Somewhere in every cycle we have a situation in which some humble person has to confront established authority, and always he hates or fears it, often with good reason. In the common York and Towneley *Doctors*, when Joseph and Mary discover Jesus in the temple teaching the doctors of the law, Joseph hesitates to enter. 'With men of myght can I not mell,' he says, 'they are so gay in furry fyne.' And Mary has to lead the way and reprove the young Jesus (York XX, 229–32; Towneley XVIII, 217–20).

Perhaps Joseph's reluctance is more awe than fear, but in the healing of the man born blind, Chester definitely makes fear the motivation. The parents of Chelidonius, as the blind man is called, find themselves summoned to testify before the Pharisees. In fact, they are in a crossfire, for the two Pharisees disagree among themselves about the validity of the miracle, and both are anxious to convict Jesus of fraud or blasphemy. The mother says bitterly, 'a vengeaunce on them . . . / the neuer did poore man good.' The father, however, points out that they must go, 'or ells they would without delay / cursse us and take our good' (XIII, 162–9).

A similar theme, but with a different emphasis, appears in the N-town (Hegge) dramatization of the woman taken in adultery (Play XXIV). Again the attempt of the Pharisees to score a point against Jesus furnishes the motivation, but the Pharisees appear not only vindictive but also cowardly. The play opens with Jesus preaching repentance and forgiveness of sins. Accusator suddenly appears to tell the Pharisees that he knows where they can catch a pair of adulterers, which one of the Pharisees sees as an opportunity for tripping up Jesus. The three break in on the sinners. The young man flees, dressed in a doublet with the points untied and carrying his breeches in his hand, as the very explicit directions tell us. When the three try to stop him, he pulls a knife and threatens that if anyone tries to stop him, 'I xal þis daggare put in his crop'. The reaction of one of the Pharisees reminds us of Dogberry's instructions to the watch: 'With such a shrew wyll I not melle.' The poor woman is, of course, left to bear the entire burden of guilt. When the Pharisees call on Jesus for judgment he underlines their cowardice by writing their sins in the earth, whereupon they sneak off.

The exploitation of this worm's-eye view of established authority produces as its ultimate extension something like the 'dark comedy' or 'sick humour' of contemporary literature.[9] This tragic-comic mood breaks through when the Towneley Cain, the smoke from his rejected sacrifice still blinding him, invites his virtuous brother 'com kys the dwill right in the ars', a prelude to murder, and then, when God summons him, blasphemously calls God 'that hob-ouer-the-wall' (II, 287-97). The attitude is even more evident in the responses of the soldiers Herod sends out to kill the Innocents. In one cycle they enjoy the task, in another they feel it beneath them to kill babies and fight women, in still another they fear that Herod's actions will precipitate a revolt, which of course they will have to suppress. It seems likely that the attack of the women was sometimes played for laughs, and one play, the Digby *Killing of the Children*, creates a comic braggart-coward Watkin, who fears the mothers.

This sort of grim humour reaches its apogee in the Passion sequences, particularly in the York and Towneley cycles. The behaviour of the soldiers detailed to nail Christ on the cross might have been written as an illustration of Bergson's theory that comedy results when human beings act as though they were mechanical automatons.[10] To the York Soldiers the Crucifixion is simply a job. As good craftsmen they would like to do it well, but everything goes wrong. The hole into which they should drive the nail for the feet is bored in the wrong place—'it failis a foote and more'—so that they have to pull on the body with ropes to stretch it into a fit. The hole in the ground into which the cross must slot has been dug too wide, and they have to drive in wedges to keep the cross from wobbling (XXXV, 107-248). The Towneley Torturers are a little less professional, and a little more personal. They take the old motif of Jesus the Jouster, familiar to us from *Piers Plowman* (B, XVIII, 10-28) and up-end it. As Jesus is a king he must joust in a tournament. They have just the horse for him, the cross, and he will not fall off. They would be 'full lothe on any wyse that ye fell downe', and so on and on, squeezing every drop of oafish raillery from the occasion (XXIII, esp. 89-118).

The triumph of dark comedy is the Towneley *Talents*. Much about

[9] See Styan, *The Dark Comedy*, for a thorough analysis of this phenomenon. Most of what follows is theoretically based on Styan's discussion.

[10] *Laughter*, tr. Cloudesley Brereton and Fred Rothwell (New York, 1937), esp. pp. 86-8.

this play is puzzling. It duplicates material already presented in the preceding play. It seems to have been borrowed from some area further to the south than Wakefield.[11] The title 'Processus Talentorum' is manifestly a scribal error; it should be *talorum*, 'bones', for it deals with the dicing for the clothes of the crucified Christ. This Scriptural incident (*Matthew* 27, 35) is briefly treated in all the cycles, but only Towneley devotes a whole play to it.

Positioned between the Crucifixion and the Harrowing of Hell, the *Talents* also falls between comedy and tragedy. It begins with the usual boasting and threatening speech by Pilate. Then the three Torturers enter one after the other, each in a hurry. They have brought with them Jesus's clothes, which each is anxious to possess, or at least get a fair share of. The question is how to keep Pilate from taking all for himself. Pilate is somewhat grumpy on being awakened. The Torturers are right in fearing that Pilate will want everything for himself. When they grumble, Pilate suggests dividing up the garments. They cannot find a seam on which to divide the gown and Pilate will not have the garment cut up. Finally, Third Torturer remembers he has three dice, and all agree that high throw will win all. Pilate is, of course, first and when two of the Torturers fail to beat his thirteen, it looks as if he will get the clothes after all. However, Third Torturer throws fifteen, which ought to win. But Pilate is determined to have the clothes and suggests, as only one in absolute authority can 'suggest', that the winner give them to him as a favour. Reluctantly Third Torturer gives up the garments—after all Pilate is his commanding general. The play closes with the three Torturers moralizing, somewhat in the vein of Chaucer's Pardoner, on the evils of gambling.[12]

On the more serious level, the play is an apt summation of the forces of greed and selfishness that have killed Christ. This is their highest moment, for the next play begins the ascent into light and love with the Harrowing of Hell, to be followed by the triumph of truth in the Resurrection, after which even Pilate and the high priests have to admit that their 'law is lorn'. It is a remarkable achievement that Pilate in

---

[11] Martin Stevens, 'The Composition of the Towneley *Talents* Play: A Linguistic Examination', *Journal of English and Germanic Philology* LVIII (1959), pp. 423–33.

[12] The robe is magic, and hence of immense value. In the Cornish *Death of Pilate* sequence it preserves Pilate from the punishment he deserves as long as he wears it.

his moment of triumph is not heroic evil but meanness, a Roman procurator who cheats a common soldier out of his winnings in a game of chance. The subtlety of this play has escaped many critics. For instance, anyone who finds the moralizations of the Torturers naive is reading his own naivety into the play. What has actually happened is that the modulation from the tragic mood of the Crucifixion to the comic one of the Resurrection has resulted in a thorough mixture of the two kinds, grim humour, jesting seriousness.

Though the cycle plays because of their very nature never achieved formal comedy, the comic still bulks large in their total effect. With a few exceptions—the Mak episode of the Towneley *Second Shepherds' Play* is the most notable—the comic is always intrinsic to the dramatic structure of the piece. We find no examples of the sort of thing represented by the episode of the quack-doctor in the Croxton *Play of the Sacrament* (525–652), an episode not at all necessarily connected with the purpose of the piece, but apparently written only to provide an opportunity for a pair of comics. In the cycle plays the comic always flows directly from the method of the cycles, which is the attempt to make Scriptural story human and contemporary. We see everything through the eyes of the common citizen, and the disparity between that point of view and the one we are accustomed to in 'religious' literature produces a comic irony that is never absent for long in any of the cycles. It is probably this effect more than any other that has produced the great popularity of the cycles in their modern revivals. In fact, they are entirely consonant with the modern temper in their frequent transition to dark comedy. Certainly the constant undertone of comic irony preserves them from the sanctimoniousness which mars most post-medieval dramatic treatments of Scriptural themes.

Note

Texts.

Quotations used in this chapter are from my own forthcoming *The Cornish Cycle*. The original Cornish text (with minor imperfections) is available, together with a fairly useful line-for-line translation, in Norris, *CC*, and in *The Ordinalia* (unpublished), ed. and tr. R. Morton Nance and A. S. D. Smith (Nance Bequest, Royal Institution of Cornwall, Truro). Markham Harris has recently produced a prose translation, *The Cornish Ordinalia*.

Scholarship and Criticism.

F. E. Halliday, *The Legend of the Rood* (London, 1955) offers some speculations on Cornish staging, as does Richard Southern, in passing, in *MTR*. D. C. Fowler (*Medieval Studies* 23 (1961), pp. 91–125) has ventured the only serious calculation of the Cornish Cycle's dating.

Among much interesting material contained in the Nance Bequest are five unpublished lectures delivered by Henry Jenner at the University of Exeter, four in 1928 and one in 1932, on the subject of Cornish drama and its sources.

Abbreviations.

SD—stage-direction (occurring immediately after the line-number cited)
PP I—Passion Play I (Hegge)
PP II—Passion Play II (Hegge)

VI

Arena Staging and Dramatic Quality in the Cornish Passion Play

NEVILLE DENNY

I

THE PASSION plays of medieval Europe represent an astonishing artistic achievement, expressions of the popular imagination as ardent and pure as those that produced the Gothic cathedrals. The best of them belong on merit in any supranational 'classical' dramatic repertoire: even among the best the Cornish Passion Play stands apart, a work of remarkable dramatic power and authority.[1] In fact I know of no other medieval dramatic work to set above it for sustained dramatic power, theatrical virtuosity, pebbly simplicity of vernacular verse dialogue, symmetry of form. Other works may challenge it under one or other of these heads—*Ludus Danielis* for formal beauty, the Wakefield Master sections of the Towneley Plays for poetic artistry, certain Italian and Spanish entertainments for bravura spectacle—but none can approach the Cornish Passion for impressiveness of achievement in all these sectors simultaneously. Even in today's terms the work rivets attention and engages the full imaginative participation of the most diverse of audiences.

Its achievement is primitivist rather than sophisticated or self-consciously artistic. Certainly the play is reminiscent of all the best work of this kind, bold, direct, artless. One of the first things to strike one about it is its limpid simplicity and sincerity, its 'reverence' (in D. H. Lawrence's sense as well as any pious one), an attitude growing out of a profound respect for and attempt to do proper justice to

[1] It survives as part of the fifteenth-century Cornish Cycle—Day Two (*Passio Domini*) plus Resurrection sequences of Day Three (*Resurrexione Domini*). Versification, local references and overall unity of structure all seem to point to its independent existence, to prior composition, almost certainly on French models, cyclic shape coming about later as a result of the success of the English cycles.

the truth and reality of the subject-matter, a determination one senses everywhere faithfully to represent 'historic' events, however hallowed or important to the human race, taking place in a real and familiar universe (recognizable human types and situations, in a recognizable social environment)—to represent 'history', in other words, rather than myth or fancy, in properly responsible terms, without any of the stridency or inflated heroics or exotic fairy-tale effects one might be forgiven for having expected.

Mary Magdalene Now this box of special ointment,
              Worth much in gold it is so rare,
              I here take up and break in two,
                  And pour the oil on head, and feet.

Simon the Leper If he were a proper prophet
              Surely he would know the woman
              Is a common trollop, and would
                  Not allow her to anoint him!

Jesus   O Simon, listen carefully
              To what I have to say to you.

Simon   Speak your full mind, gentle master,
                  And I will hark attentively.

Jesus   Once upon a time, it doesn't
              Matter where, there were three men,
              Two debtors and one creditor.
                  The one man owed the creditor
              Five hundred marks in all, while the
              Second owed him merely fifty.
              Both debts the first man cancelled though,
                  Since neither had the wherewithal
              To pay him back. Tell me this, then,
              Briefly—which of the two had cause
                  To love this man the more?

Simon   Oh, I can answer that at once—
              He who is forgiven most will
                  Love the most, any time!

Jesus   A very wise deduction! . . .

Judas   Was it really necessary
              To waste the precious ointment, though?

> We might well have sold it
> For full three hundred marks or more,
> And distributed the proceeds
> Among the county's poor!

Jesus   Oh do not harbour any grudge
               Against her who has anointed
               Me . . .   (485–540)

I am not here talking about diction or the quality of the verse (in the
original Cornish language, of course—one can do no more than hint
at its quality in translation),[2] though this obviously plays an important part in the securing of such an overall effect. Rather, it is the total
dramatic experience I am referring to, appealing simultaneously to a
range of the senses. It is the *play* to which we are attending (rather than
the lines alone) that addresses us in this way. What emerges in consequence is a kind of granular dramatic reportage, documentary narrative as it were, immediately and powerfully arresting, operating on
its own empirical terms and standing or falling by those terms (even
when supernatural elements—angels, devils—fall within its compass).
The point is an important one. The affinities of this drama are with
popular art and ordinary experience, not with sophisticated courtly
art and ritual on the one hand, or abstract didactic art and ecclesiastical
ritual on the other; with carols, wall-painting and stained glass, roof-
boss and alabaster carving and the feeling inherent in these activities,
rather than with systematized theology or extravagant romance. In
feeling and tone—in overall character and 'style'—we are much closer
to the Limbourgs, Fouquet, and the various miniaturist Masters than

---

[2] The translation used in this chapter was prepared expressly for production
purposes and not with the ends of textual scholarship in mind. (None of the
other versions is easily speakable by actors, nor even easily readable, Norris and
Nance-Smith because of their cumbrous line-by-line mode of attack, Harris
because of its pronounced American rhythm and idiom.) The aim was the
highest degree of accuracy commensurate with idiomatic liveliness (the rhythms
and idiom of ordinary speech) and a verse-form (a variant of the *rime coué*
quite widely used in the English cycles) as close to the original as could be
found in contemporary English practice. Fidelity to the general drift of any
speech or passage, and to the tone and spirit of the original, was felt to be of
more importance, for these purposes, than literal, word-for-word accuracy.
The line-numbering is that of the original MS, accessible in Norris, *CC*.

anything else, to the tradition that was to go on to produce the miracle of Flemish art—intensely felt, meticulously observed.

> *Pilate* So now, Lord Caiaphas, Annas,
>   Doctors—you have brought the fellow
>   Back again to Pilate,
>   Alleging that he alienates
>   Your people from the God of Heaven.
>   Well, by Lucifer, when
>   I examined him I found no
>   Fault in him, and now neither does
>   His puissant majesty
>   King Herod! It seems to me it
>   Would be better to release the
>   Man at once, without
>   Further argument, if he just
>   Undertakes to keep the peace and
>   Stop promoting discord! ...
>   Open up your prison, Jailor,
>   And entertain this Jesus for
>   A spell while we debate
>   The matter. Bring in a wench for
>   Him. Make him at home ...   (1850–76)

What one senses here are much deeper impulses at work than intellectual didactic ones, or even idly romantic ones, impulses within the folk itself and ultimately responsible, whoever the actual playwrights were, for this quality of response—direct, innocent, absolutely honest—in the presentation of events of such momentous and living importance.

However that may be, this quality of treatment, this attitude to subject-matter and childlike openness before it, make for drama of extraordinarily effective modulation and strength, totally disarming in its candour and transparency. One can see this quality everywhere at work—in the diction, in portraiture, in motivation, in the sketching of a social context. Together they add up to a primitivist realism of unusually compelling dramatic power, very close to *actualité* film and television techniques in some of its effects (it is intriguing how often film and television are called to mind in the attempt to understand how this drama operates). One can see it in the important opening scene where the tone for the whole work is so surely established. It is there in the dramatically tense and skilfully modulated confrontations between the captive Jesus and the Judean authorities; in the

Plate 3. De Witt's drawing of the Swan Playhouse, c. 1596. (*University Library, Utrecht*)

Plate 4. Fouquet's miniature of the Martyrdom of St. Apollonia, from the *Book of Hours of Etienne Chevalier*. Based upon a contemporary in-the-round saints' play production that seems to be very close in detail and in character to Cornish in-the-round staging practice. (*Musée Condé, Chantilly*)

deftly handled Trial scene that these confrontations lead up to; in the deeply moving Deposition and Burial; in the Resurrection; in the risen Christ's bitter-sweet meetings with Mary and with Mary Magdalen. It is there, later in the cycle, in the confident structuring of the Incredulity and, superlatively, in the poetry of the concluding Ascension.

These are all scenes of exceptional dramatic potential in their own right, of course, ably presented in a variety of dramatic versions, just as the qualities I have been discussing—the primitivist realism, the ardency and reverence, the honesty—feature so prominently in other contemporary artistic treatments of them as well. The difference lies in the nature of the presentation. Far more crucially than with most dramatic works, the Cornish *Passio* owes its distinctive character and authority to the theatrical 'environment' for which it was designed, and it is only in relation to this that one can talk intelligibly about the dramatic and theatrical qualities that the work possesses (the literary and poetic qualities, insofar as it is ever useful to separate them from the theatrical in a dramatic work, can be of interest only to a handful of celticists and Cornish language experts because of the extinct linguistic medium—Middle Cornish—in which it was composed). The theatrical matrix in Cornwall was an open-air amphitheatrical one in which a form of native European staging reached a pitch of maturity from any consolidation and evolutionary development of which it was deflected only by the mesmerizing false promises of the Renaissance. This was the fluid, immensely versatile form of 'open', so-called 'simultaneous mansions' staging in which a handful of *domus* or 'mansions' (seats, tents, booths, emblematic scenic units) embraced or fronted a *platea* or acting-area from which the spectators were roped off or kept back by marshals, the mansions representing localities of whatever 'distance' from each other in the context of the play (e.g. Rome and Jerusalem in the Death of Pilate play in the Cornish *Resurrexio*), but conferring on the (neighbouring or entire) *platea* the temporary locational status (Italy, Palestine) of whatever mansion is the principle focus of the action at that moment.

The stroke of genius on the part of the Cornish play-makers (a development that was duplicated in the East Midlands and may well have been much more widely prevalent in Southern England—even dominantly so—than we appreciate) was to stretch the arc of mansions right round to form a circle, using for the purpose what seem to have

E

been traditional places of assembly and recreation, the ubiquitous *plan-an-gwarry* or 'playing-place', earthwork amphitheatres improvised from prehistoric fortifications and early cattle enclosures (of which Piran Round near Perranporth is a miraculously surviving example). They simply sited the *domus* equidistantly round the embankment and disposed the audience between them, on tiered rows of seating capable of accommodating two or three thousand spectators. The circular grass plain contained within it became the stage or acting-area, the *platea* or 'place'.[3]

II

Not the least valuable feature of the Cornish Cycle MS is the inclusion in it of plans that seem to depict the staging layout for each of the three days of cyclic presentation. These show the disposition of eight stations round the circumference of the *plan-an-gwarry*, all but one of them almost certainly on the top of the embankment. What form these stations took is not very important. Originally they are likely to have been simple stools or thrones or benches ('*sedes*'), as they were in the older form of church-nave presentation from which the tradition ultimately derives; but an early development would have been the improvising of some form of shrouding feature that freed the occupant from needless presence for the full duration of the performance. By the early fifteenth century they may have become tents (as they had in various parts of Europe), though the strong winds in most parts of western Cornwall at any time of the year would seem to militate against this. More likely they had become little huts, roofed and curtained timber structures, like rudimentary bus-shelters, of a kind one can see depicted in a contemporary miniature by Fouquet representing a dramatic performance of the Martyrdom of St. Apollonia (see Plate 4).

[3] 'Guirremears (i.e. *gwary myrs*—miracle plays) . . . were used at the great conventions of the people, at which they had famous interludes celebrated with great preparations, and not without shews of devotion in them, solemnized in open and spacious downs of great capacity, encompassed about with earthen banks, and in some part stone work of largeness to contain thousands, the shapes of which remain in many places at this day . . .' (John Scawen, mid-seventeenth century, quoted in *The Parochial History of Cornwall*, ed. Davies Gilbert (London, 1838, 4 vols.), Vol. IV, pp. 204-5.)

Very little else in the way of scenic embellishment was required. Only three scenic features are demanded by the Passion play, a Mount or Mounts (emblematic almost certainly, probably reinforced structures that could double as pedestals for trees and posts and crucifixes); the Temple of Jerusalem (probably also emblematic and miniaturized but not to the extent that seems to have been customary for the period, because of the eclipsing scale of a typical *plan-an-gwarry*); and a Sepulchre (which might conceivably have been accommodated under Heaven in much the same way as a Prison was probably accommodated under the Torturers' scaffold, but which could also have utilized the same structure—or elements of it—that served for the Temple). Two or three other *loca* (odd rooms or houses, an Inn, the Atrium, a Smithy) could be suggested easily enough by the context plus a few props, no special scenic unit being necessary (though again, part of the Temple unit could be so utilized—as it was for instance in the Trial scene in the Hegge plays—or indeed any of the peripheral scaffolds not at the moment in use, though this I think was unlikely).

It is by no means clear where these different *loca* would be situated in the arena. The analogy of *The Castle of Perseverance* might seem to suggest that the central scenic unit of any play or sequence of plays should be situated in the middle of the *platea*. Problems arise, however, some of them relating to sight-lines, if the structures are of any size (as the sheer scale of a *plan-an-gwarry* would seem to demand). More important would be the lurching, fits-and-starts rhythm that would be compelled by periodic interruption of the flow of the action for dismantling and removal of every unit, in the very centre of the arena, every time a new unit was called for by the narrative.

Analysis of the play's structure seems rather to recommend, if not to dictate, a staging pattern based on a three-point ground-plan as offering the most promising and least unwieldy means of production. These pivotal points—areas anything between four and twelve yards in diameter at the imaginary corners of an equilateral triangle occupying the centre of the *platea* (ABC in fig. 3)—could be used alternately, indeed in any order, as principle foci of action. Both the few scenic units required and the principal dramatic localities could usefully be located in these areas, and the position always so manipulated as to leave one focal point free, for scene-shifting etc., while the audience's attention is concentrated on another, leaving the powerful—indeed the dominant—stage-position of in-the-round theatre, the centre,

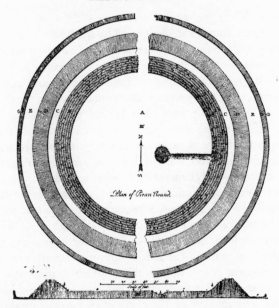

Fig. 1. William Borlase's plan of Piran Round (from the *Natural History of Cornwall*, reproduced by courtesy of the University Library, Cambridge).

always free for its proper exploitation in the overall *mise-en-scène*. (The staging principle works very effectively in practice.)[4]

4 This is not of course the only way in which the *plan-an-gwarry* stage could have been used for a production of the Cornish Passion, and neither is this discussion of the play's theatrical viability critically predicated on it. It remains conceivable that the centre, or even position A, was used for the principal scenic units, despite the disadvantages noted. Alternatively a two-point or even a four-point system could have been used instead. The other, more impressionistically defined, *loca* would still need to have been sited around the *platea*, though, however haphazardly. The same would be true, in a more limited sense, for yet another way in which the *plan-an-gwarry* could have been used, where the Temple, and no doubt the Sepulchre too, were somehow incorporated into the Heaven structure, the adjacent bits of embankment serving for the various Mounts (including Calvary) called for by the action. The corollary to this, though, would have been to convert an in-the-round staging situation into a crypto-Elizabethan one, approaching the Lincoln ('Hegge') and Valenciennes modes—a development that I believe only began to take place at a much later date. On balance, I think some variation of the staging principle here conjectured would have been the more likely.

To set the scene: a *plan-an-gwarry* audience come to see the Passion play would enter an earthwork amphitheatre some 100 feet in diameter comprising a circular flat grass *platea* or 'place' surrounded by an embankment ten to twelve feet high, terraced into seven or eight rows of seating. Set up on this embankment in the eastern quadrant would be Heaven, a grand and commanding presence, as splendid and radiant as the dawn, the dominating visual element in the entire theatrical environment. Opposed to this as a visual and thematic (even psychological) element would be '*Infernum*'—at ground level almost certainly—an enormous monster's head, 'hell-mouth', the Leviathan of *Isaiah* 27, 1: a lividly painted, nightmare creation of fanged and gaping jaws, glaring eyes and smoking nostrils, possibly set into a breach in the embankment opposite the one containing the gate the audience would enter by.[5] Both *loca* would constitute important points of entrance to and exit from the arena, the only one for angels and devils respectively, though both places play an important part in the Harrowing of Hell, when the just and blessed from the old Mosaic dispensation are delivered by Christ from Hell's bondage into the new,

[5] The eight stations or mansions for the *Passio Domini* in the MS plan are labelled as follows (reading from twelve o'clock, the two breaches in the round occurring at three and nine o'clock respectively): Heaven; Centurion; Caiaphas; Annas; Herod; Pilate; Doctors; Torturers. The principle of distribution clearly relates to the dramatic (and perhaps social) importance of the personages involved in the action. For this reason I am inclined to question the complete accuracy of the MS stage-plans for Day Two in respect of the Centurion (a character who makes the briefest of appearances in the concluding two minutes of the Crucifixion), an allocation that effectively removes station 2 (S2) in any functional sense from the action. One must also doubt the attribution of S7 to the Doctors. Station 7 is attributed to Hell (*Infernum*) on Days One and Three, a sizeable and expensively prepared structure, of course, and (one would have thought) fixed and permanent for the six days and two run-throughs of the Cycle that seem to have constituted the customary practice. (The St. Ives Borough Accounts for 1575, for instance, record receipts for performances of 'the playe' over six apparently consecutive days.) Satan and his cohorts make an important contribution to the action in Day Two, more-over, and have an even greater part to play in the Harrowing sequence. Hence the *loca* would seem to be as indispensable on Day Two (as in any independent Passion play) as it is on the other days of the Cycle. It is true the Doctors may have been accommodated in some *domus* atop *Infernum*, but if so, who occupied the structure on the other two days? My own solution would be to assign station 2 to the Doctors (or preferably, S2 to Caiaphas and S3 to the Doctors, which would make for some interesting patterns of movement across the *platea* in the course of the play), retaining S7 for Hell-mouth. (see Fig. 3.)

and led across the arena and up into Heaven by angels to the accompaniment of celestial song. The other points of entry for the actors would be the gate itself and the six remaining *domus* on the six-foot-wide embankment top, access to them being from the rear, up the outer slope of the earthwork. Round the rim of the embankment the little booths would be closed and silent as the audience took their places on the terraces below and between them. In the *platea* itself the Temple would be standing (perhaps at C), an emblematic structure, in no way a realistic imitation, perhaps even a miniature some six or seven feet high, but more likely to be two or three times that size. In another quarter of the arena, possibly at A (in some close or symbolic proximity to Heaven, in other words), a Mount or system of Mounts, again emblematic and miniaturized, would be situated. For the rest, apart from decorative flags and banners and of course the speckled colour and movement of the audience itself, the theatre would be quite bare.[6]

The signal for the commencement of the play would be the closing of the entrance-gates and the sudden opening of Heaven's curtains to reveal God seated in splendour and majesty on His throne, costumed like some ecclesiastical potentate and flanked by two archangels. One imagines the theatre bowl stilling to a hush and almost simultaneously the gates being flung wide again for Jesus to enter, a charismatic, traditionally presented figure, instantly recognizable, in the midst of his twelve disciples. 'Disciples,' he says, moving into the *platea*, secur-

[6] See Figs. 2 and 4. The MS stage-plan, augmented by stage-directions and internal evidence in the text, together with what we know about the configuration of the Cornish *plan-an-gwarry* from surviving examples (Piran Round in particular) and from antiquarian sources (and of its use in medieval play-production from such writers as Richard Carew and John Scawen), provide most of the evidence we need to reconstruct the theatrical context. The *St. Apollonia* miniature provides useful supporting evidence, and so too does a second, very important medieval stage-plan included in the *Castle of Perseverance* MS and reproduced on the cover of this volume. (On the interpretation of this stage-plan, and on the subject of medieval in-the-round staging generally, see Richard Southern's pioneering study *Medieval Theatre in the Round*.) William Borlase, the eighteenth-century antiquarian, attests to the rows of terraced seating in Piran Round and the round at St. Just-in-Penwith (*Natural History of Cornwall*, Oxford, 1758)—see Fig. 1. The existence of these in Piran Round is confirmed by Professor Charles Thomas's recent excavations. Piran Round was prepared along these lines for the revival of the Cornish Cycle in 1969.

ing the attention of any who may not yet be aware the play has
started,

> . . . this is my message—
> Pray together, unitedly,
> That God Almighty who's on high
> Will send his grace to you, so that
>   At last you may be saved;
> That with all his shining angels
> Radiantly in heaven your souls
> Shall dwell for evermore at peace,
>   In joy that knows no end . . .   (1–9)

And the play is launched, immediately compelling in its directness and
human relevance, with Jesus, in this prelude to the Temptation,
teaching his disciples (and by extension ourselves, the theatre audience)
like some wandering friar or holy man, giving a telling new pertinence
and urgency to the familiar utterances.

Like the other scenes earlier enumerated—Interrogations, Trial,
Deposition and Burial, Resurrection, Incredulity, Ascension—able
treatments of this scene can be found in many Passion plays from all
over Europe. Skilful exploitation of the *plan-an-gwarry* resources by
the Cornish play-makers (given the superlative sight-lines and acous-
tics they start off with) might enhance the dramatic quality here and
there, as for instance by imaginative use of space and numbers, and in
this Temptation scene by the simultaneous presence in the arena of
the three main *loca* or pivotal points of the action, 'wilderness' (with
its 'stones', say at B), Temple (at C) and 'mountain' (at A), with the
consequent fluent transition of sequences that this makes possible.
Essentially, however, it is a scene, like the others referred to, that
lends itself to rewarding presentation in any theatrical environment,
that could indeed be realized on any fixed stage, medieval or post-
Renaissance. What sets the Cornish play emphatically apart is the
astonishing use that can be made, and brilliantly is made by the playwright, of certain other resources made possible by the Cornish
theatrical situation. I have in mind particularly two remarkable characteristics of the region's Biblical drama: first, a unique mode of
theatrical 'cutting' from scene to scene or place to place within the
platea delayed, as an evolutionary development, from the demise of
Cornish theatre until the advent of film in our own times; and second,
an equally unprecedented and as yet unparalleled style of 'panoramic'

or 'multiple-action' staging which finds its nearest echo in the twen-
tieth-century three-ring circus (though never with any verbal conflict), or—much more crudely and ineptly (largely because of depth-of-
field focusing considerations)—in wide-screen, 'epic' film techniques.

A hint of the dramatic possibilities of both modes is contained in the
opening scene already referred to, in our consciousness throughout of
the benign, loving and controlling presence of God and his archangels
overseeing all from the Heaven mansion, and also of the equally telling
presence, louring and malevolent, of Hell (the twin poles of man's
moral universe, between which flawed, pathetic humankind must
quite literally act out its divine comedy). There is also the striking
business, antedating Macbeth's haunted banquet by two hundred years,
of Jesus's first Temptation—by a Satan visible only to himself—within
the framework of a seminar with his disciples quite undisturbed by
the exchanges:

Jesus	Penance too is needful, if the
	Malevolence of Hell's to fail—
	As I well know from hungry days
	Spent praying in the wilderness.
Satan (aside)	Spent hungry days? If he craves food
	We'll know for sure he can't be God,
	Beyond a single doubt!
	I'll tempt him to eat. Hopefully
	I'll get him to commit the sin
	Of brutish gluttony!
	If notwithstanding all my power
	We fail, and can't enmesh him in
	Sin's tangling net, why then
	He is the man who Man redeems,
	But for whose work and holy teaching
	All mankind should perish.
(to Jesus)	I charge you if you are indeed
	The Son of God on high, command
	These stones to turn to bread!
(aside)	And on the instant I shall know
	The nature and the magnitude
	Of all his charm and power!
Jesus	Man shall not live by bread alone,
	Nor should desire so to live,

But rather in the saving words
  The Trinity has uttered.
By this figure, my disciples,
You should understand this bread's the
Word of God, which alone sustains
  The man who will accept it.

John　　　　O dear and beloved Master,
Just as you have taught us, so do
We believe, that the word of God
  Will feed and satisfy our souls . . .　　　(43–76)

The full orchestral development of both modes must wait for the
succeeding Palm Sunday episode, however; for the Maundy Thursday–
Last Supper sequences; for certain sections of the Interrogation
scenes; supremely, for the Crucifixion itself.

III

An amazing number of things begin to happen simultaneously as the
Palm Sunday Entry approaches, in ways we had to wait for the advent
of cinema to see duplicated. In one quarter of the *platea* (possibly at A)
Jesus rejoins his disciples after his descent from the 'mountain' where
Satan's third, make-or-break Temptation was made and where God's
archangels had come down to bless and hearten him. John and Peter
go at Jesus's direction to fetch the ass (almost certainly at the gate).
A crowd filters in and begins to line a sinuous route (say from A to B
via Hp-M-3p) as the ass is led back to the little knot round Jesus (and
for a crowd to look anything like a crowd in such a vast arena at
least fifty 'extras' would be required over and above the named and
appropriately present characters). A bazaar is simultaneously being set
up in the Temple (at C), complete with produce, pottery, ale-jars,
bolts of cloth, baskets of pigeons and (one imagines, in this region)
sheep. Representatives of the nobility emerge from the dignitaries'
mansions, wives and womenfolk, children and retainers to descend
and join the crowd, while their menfolk—like the Torturers and the
Doctors—position themselves on their scaffolds surveying the bustling
scene below. Jesus mounts the donkey and the ambiguously rapturous
'royal entry' of this King, this man of sorrows, begins, amid cheers
and hosannas and frond-waving and triumphal song that must fill the

bowl like coronation acclamation. Further, as the procession nears its end some of the crowd (the mansion women notably) will have to drift over to the market in the Temple while the rest must surely be sat down apart (at B perhaps), possibly to be taught or ministered to by the disciples, so as to leave the Temple area clear for the dramatically important Cleansing that is about to ensue.

At this juncture then, at the climax to the joyful Entry, an unusual

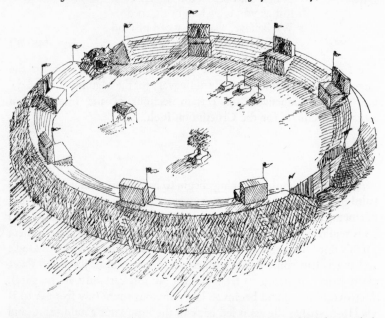

Fig. 2. Reconstruction of a Cornish *plan-an-gwarry* as prepared for the concluding sequences of the Cornish Passion play, based on MS stage-plan, Fouquet's miniature, and the configuration of Piran Round (as filled out by Borlase's survey).

and extremely subtle theatrical situation has been set up by the playwright, 'epic' in a second, Brechtian sense (since the entire audience knows the story in advance, and the significant part that will be played in the action by each of the groups and individuals taking up positions in the arena around them). Occupants of all the scaffolds are outside their mansions (Devils, Torturers, God and his archangels, Caiaphas and attendants, Doctors, Annas and attendants, Herod and his court, Pilate and his officials) looking down into the extraordinary scene unfolding in the world or cockpit of the play. In the *platea* the animated crowd is perhaps resolving itself into two vaguely contrasted groups, one contributing to a surge of bustle in the Temple bazaar, the other simmering down to an attentive audience, a sort of early catechetical class, apart. This is the time, the links and flexing tensions between all these elements in the overall theatrical situation having been so adroitly established, when Jesus cracks a whip that must echo like a pistol-shot round the amphitheatre and strides over to break up the 'fair'.

> Out, money-grubbers! Out!
> You make a mockery of God
>   And of our holy church!
> Turning this place of sanctuary,
> A house of prayer, into a loud
>   Bazaar, a den of thieves! (331–6)

Goods and produce go sprawling, bolts of cloth unroll, ale-jars spill and shatter, sheep scatter, pigeons explode upwards from overturned baskets, merchants are tumbled helter-skelter out of the way, yelling in protest but scattering as the whip cracks anew, flying in all directions from the cyclonic rage within the Temple.

The point of interest is the number of things happening simultaneously over such a wide area: sheep, pigeons, fleeing chapmen, screaming women; the commanding, wrathful figure of Jesus; the startled catechumens at B; the equally startled ring of observers up on the embankment top. The audience's eyes must be darting everywhere, like spectators' at an ice-hockey match. In theatrical terms, the effect is electric and quite unique.

This effect is clarified and sharpened over the next few minutes. Jesus returns to the catechetical group while Pilate descends from his scaffold to saunter over to the Temple to inspect the damage. The outraged Merchants are simultaneously bustling across to make their arm-waving complaints to Caiaphas. He too descends and Pilate, ladies, merchants and prelates meet apart (probably at A), so that a bi-polar staging situation begins to resolve itself out of the confusion of the previous scene, with the audience's attention swivelling now between Jesus and his followers in one quarter (the sick being ministered to) and the worried dignitaries in another, the upheaval in the Temple providing a subordinate focus of interest at C. A subtly changing sequence of theatrical patterns of a kaleidoscopic or radar-screen nature has been effected, beginning with an initial, classically simple focus in the messianic group around Jesus, two little stars of brightness burning on the edges where Heaven and Hell bracket the action. This crisp pattern then blurs, loses form, assumes a much larger, looser shape as the numbers in the arena are augmented, while the flowers of light on the periphery suddenly multiply and go sparkling right round the circle. The sprawling S-shape within the coronet of stars then itself dissolves, resolves itself into two cloudy areas of focus, the one—at the Temple—scarcely having time to acquire any definition before it fragments and scatters outwards at the Cleansing. Finally the whole pattern blurs again and crystallizes for a third time into two vividly clear foci of attention, the positive and negative poles within this world as Heaven and Hell are outside it, with a third, less sharply defined, to one side where the false god Mammon lies rudely overthrown. Light is poised against darkness, love against self-love, good against evil. And the ultimate challenge, the unequivocal and irrevocable act towards which all history has been gathering, is thrown down in that havoc in the Temple.

The theatrical patterns break up yet again shortly after this, when the dignitaries return to their mansions and the crowd is conducted from the arena by seven of the disciples, leaving Jesus and the remaining disciples to accompany Simon the Leper to 'Bethany' for wine and hospitality (possibly at Tp, the temporary *loca* simply being suggested by stools and table; alternatively at C, the Temple having been converted into an open-sided 'house' or 'room', perhaps with the removal of the upper storeys). Here the moving Maundy Thursday scenes are enacted, the Magdalene washing and anointing the feet of the Master and Judas objecting to the 'waste' (*'skullye'*—'waste', 'spill', 'splash about'). But while the scene unfolds itself another action is building up at Caiphas's scaffold, where the Archbishop is dispatching his Boy or Crozier-bearer to summon Annas for discussions about the threat they feel Jesus has come to represent.

(*And then he shall go to Prince Annas, and the Crozier-bearer speaks:*)

Acolyte   Most illustrious of princes,
             Lord Caiaphas says joy to you,
                 Desiring you to come
             To him, to favour him with best
             Advice on what to do about
                 The agitator Jesus.

Annas   I shall be glad to join his grace,
                     To search out means with him to trap
                     This fellow and dispose of him
                        If he has preached seditiously.

(He descends, and then he shall go to the Bishop)

                     Hail, lord, most potent archbishop!
                     Oh joy to you a thousand times!

Caiaphas   Welcome, by Mohammed's blood!
                       Come up, Annas, and sit by me.

(Annas goes up to him)

                     What are we to do? This upstart
                     Turns the whole county from Allah,
                     I swear it by my mitre, and
                        Undermines all our sacred laws!

Annas   Send trusty men to spy him out.
                     If they find him in some cottage
                     Let them pounce on him and tie him
                        Up, then bring him here to us . . .

                                         (563–84)

Sophisticated 'cutting', in other words, switches our attention from the feet-washing scene to Caiaphas's mansion, to Annas's mansion, to Caiaphas's mansion again, and back again to Bethany—in time for us to observe Judas slinking away on a roundabout course to Caiaphas's palace where the first sordid moves of the Conspiracy are to be enacted.

Judas   What will you give me, reverend sir,
                     If I help you to capture Christ,
                        And that without delay?

Caiaphas   Whatever price you name, my child!
                     You shall have it, every penny,
                        I swear by Magog's bones!

Judas   Thirty pieces of silver is
                     What I ask for this. I will not
                        Take a penny less.

[*Caiaphas*]   Done!

Iudas   Detail some men to help me then
            And we shall seize him covertly
               And bring him in tonight . . .

[*Annas*]   By Allah, Judas, you have proved
            Yourself a champion tonight! . . .

                                              (586–611)

At this very moment, and present in our single field of view, Jesus
is breaking bread and offering thanks in Simon the Leper's 'house',
blessing his hosts, leading the household in prayer.

                        IV

Even as the bargain is being struck (at S3), and while Christ is
simultaneously being entertained at Bethany (at Tp or at C), the Last
Supper 'room' is being set up somewhere across the *platea* from both
places (probably at B), a table and stools or benches again being all
that is required to suggest the new *loca*. And the dazzling 'cutting'
continues, with all the polish and assurance of an avant-garde television
film. The action cuts from Caiaphas's palace to Simon the Leper's
where Jesus is directing John and Peter to seek out a room for their
Passover supper. It cuts to the 'room' or 'inn' itself; to Peter and John
en route into Jerusalem; to the inn-yard or common well where the
Servant is drawing water; to the disciples' arrival at the inn and hiring
of the room and their commencement with the supper preparations;
back to Jesus taking his leave; to the confluence of the two groups of
disciples, one from Bethany, one having come in at the gate where
earlier they had exited; finally settling for a while on the serene beauty
and calm of the Last Supper itself, though the implacable hostility of
the established order (as represented by the personages on Caiaphas's
scaffold) and the snorting, almost casual brutality of the 'world', ourselves (as represented by the uncouth bully-boys on the Torturers'
scaffold) are a significant presence in the arena, as palpable as Heaven
and Hell themselves. Indeed Judas is soon slinking away again, on
another circuitous path to Caiaphas's palace, to set the betrayal in train.

Judas   Hail, my lord archbishop, seated
               There in cope and mitre!
            Hail, most venerable Annas!
               To both of you, much joy!

Caiaphas   Ah, master Judas. Joy to *you*!
By the creed of holy Mahound
  Welcome to my palace!
Welcome a thousand times! Is it
Time yet for the ambush party
  To apprehend the traitor?

Judas   Your grace, it is . . .

(931–41)

And for the next few minutes two extraordinary scenes are again simultaneously enacted in opposing corners of the *platea*—Christ washing the disciples' feet in the 'upper room', the sacrament of the Mass having just been instituted, in a symbolic rite of love and service ('*yn creys me re ysethas avel seruont ow seruye*'—'I have taken my place among you as a servant serving . . .'), while in the palace courtyard the ambush party makes its grisly preparations, arming itself, sharpening weapons, lighting cressets and lanterns, bolstering its courage with ale. Again the juxtaposition is a calculated one, delicately contrived despite its being facilitated by this staging situation, presenting the timeless opposition between Christ's love and gentleness and the malice of the world in one superbly controlled image, of which so many luminously abound in this play.

The effect is modulated and intensified as the Last Supper draws to its close and Jesus takes his departure, with three of his disciples, to go to Olivet (probably at A, utilizing the same Mounts that had served for the earlier Temptation scene), the remaining disciples leaving the arena again. While Jesus is at prayer and in his agony, the disciples nodding on their watch; while God sends down his archangel to comfort him, the Judas posse leaves the archbishop's mansion and begins to steal round the arena for the ambush, producing yet another remarkable example of the panoramic staging made possible by the Cornish theatre, focusing our attention in shuttlecock fashion on the anguish and human frailty on Olivet and the brute animosity remorselessly approaching. It may have become a familiar enough convention in our own times, in film and television, even a hoary and melodramatic one (hero—or more often than not heroine—oblivious of the monster/murderer/Indians closing in; cut to villain/s; cut to hero; etc. etc., while the more youthful spectators scream 'Look out!' 'Behind you!' 'Run!'). The difference here is in the *simultaneous* presence in one field of vision of both elements of the dramatic equation, and of course in the moral qualities both have been so powerfully invested with: the holy figure bent in prayer, and the agents of a value system and a power structure inimical to everything a Jesus stands for and incapable of accommodating it. Love, again, at the centre; power and ready vindictiveness—Them and Us—closing in, entered into ugly alliance to destroy it. The actual Betrayal, in all its archetypal ugliness,

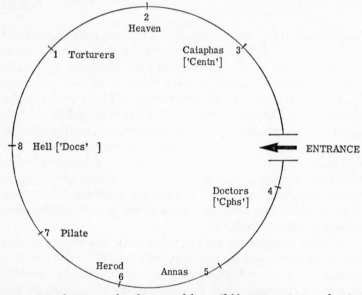

Fig. 3. Cornish Passion play: lay-out of the scaffolds. MS ascription of stations 3, 4 and 8 is indicated in square brackets (see footnote 5).

comes, at the climax of all this beautifully engineered staging, with the violence of two opposing electrical charges meeting in a vacuum:

Judas   Joy to you everywhere, O Lord!

   (*And he kisses Jesus*)

Jesus   Good friend, why do you kiss me now?
                 For surely, Judas, you have come
                 To sell me to my enemies!

   (*Here Jesus says to Prince Annas and the rest of the Jews:*)

                 Tell me, whom do ye seek, O Jews?

Annas   Jesus of Nazareth, *par dieu*—
                 The abominable Christian!

Jesus   Look this way then, for I am he,
                 Jesus himself, from Nazareth. . . .

3 Torturer   Jump on him, mates, and hold him fast!

(*And then they shall seize him*)

[*4 Torturer*]   Come! Get ropes around the bugger
                 Fast, but only hurry!

[*1 Torturer*]   Truss him up just like a chicken!

[*2 Torturer*]   Then run him off to Caiaphas
                 Without a pause for breath!

Peter   Tell me quickly, Master, if it's
                 Not sound judgment and your Father's
                     Will to swing my sword
                 Among these blackguards ruthlessly!

(*Here Peter cuts off the ear of Malchus*)

4 Torturer   Ow, my ear! Oh, comrades, help me!
                 My ear has been cut off!

Jesus   Enough, you idiots, enough!
                 Poor man, peace . . .

                                                  (1103–50)

The curtains of Heaven probably close at this moment, allowing the full enormity of the historic moment to strike home, to remain closed, as God's signs and symbols in the churches themselves are shrouded, on Good Friday, not to be uncovered until the glorious accomplishment of God's purposes at the Easter Day Resurrection.

Perhaps the most dramatic use of all is made of these staging possibilities in the painful Interrogation scenes that follow. It is a striking fact that Jesus's active or vocal part in the Passion plays is terminated very early. For most of the play he is the unresisting target of the world's insensate fury, the still centre round which all its unleashed and uncomprehended passions boil and seethe. Saying next to nothing, doing nothing, he nonetheless grows by virtue of that very immobility and calm at the heart of all this turbulence to overshadow and dominate the action like a colossus. Again, this is a quality shared by most of the medieval Passion plays, particularly those in which a single actor plays the role of Christ. In the Cornish Interrogations—as in the Entry, the Trial and Crucifixion, of course—an enormous difference is once more made by the staging situation, particularly and most obviously in the use that can be made of crowd participation. But 'cutting', 'panoramic staging' and 'wide-screen' effects of a more precise and studied kind continue to be employed, in two scenes most conspicuously, Peter's Denial and the Dream of Pilate's Wife (though the Death of Judas is another, as varied in theatrical interest, in its own way, as any of those already referred to).

The first of these is a justly famous example. The wonderfully controlled cutting between Caiaphas's palace (Jesus bound and silent in the arena before and below him) and the little crowd huddled round the brazier in the 'atrio' (SD 1218) drinking ale, is impressive enough, but the simple, in theatrical terms nonetheless still very advanced, bi-polar character of the early interrogation scenes, with our attention being shuttled between the doomed and vulnerable figure at Caiaphas's feet and the defiant Peter hotly denying his master by the courtyard fire, elaborates swiftly into a tri-polar one for the Buffeting, enacted apart (say at Tp or Hp). Our attention is swung here between the brutal beating, the raucous plebeian group—and Peter—at the brazier, and the leisured detachment of the play's aristocratic world on Caiaphas's scaffold, the complex orchestration reaching a pitch of dramatic intensity as the episode accelerates to its climax and the semi-conscious Jesus slumps to the ground, the cock crows, and Peter's cry of horror rings round the arena and he stumbles away from the gaping huddle at the fire:

> Do not forsake me now! Forgive
> My dreadful sin and treachery!
>   Fear and madness over-
> Came me. Lord! I throw myself at
> The feet of your mercy, torn and
>   Broken with remorse!

(1435-40)

Not even cinema, even in its 'epic', wide-screen form, has been able to match, never mind excel, the dramatic possibilities, the intensities of contrast and irony and emphasis, made possible by such simultaneity of action—largely because the camera would have to move so far back (to get everything it wanted in the same sharpness of focus) that everything would be swamped in a plethora of detail. The Cornish play-makers were spared this complication. Neither were they crippled, as again the film-makers are, by unwieldy conventions of realistic presentation. Even the wide-screen cannot contain both the courtyard and the council chamber in its single view—architectural features get in the way that the Cornishmen could totally ignore.

The same considerations are true of Pilate's Wife's Dream. A similarly effective staging pattern, again only possible in the Cornish theatrical context, is employed when Jesus is packed off into gaol for a spell. Pilate and the Jewish elders go into gesticulating (mimed) conference (at B perhaps, or 3p), Lady Pilate dozes on a couch in Pilate's scaffold (S7), and in, or upon, or just outside Hell-mouth Satan and the devils seethe and gibber in agitated conclave. They dispatch a representative to warn Lady Pilate 'in a dream' of the consequences to her husband and family if Pilate goes ahead and allows the (for them) catastrophic execution to take place. Our attention, once more, is effortlessly swung between these corporate components of the total theatrical scene, to produce yet another effect unique in theatrical experience, analogous only to the modes in which poetry operates. Here every salient feature of the moral equation is being presented to the mind and senses *simultaneously*—the gentle revolutionary chained up with criminals; a determined, no-nonsense 'Establishment'; Pilate impersonal and unassailable within his office; the active agents of evil, of chaos, playing on a pliant mind (the sleeping Julia Procula) in order to neutralize the threat that love and gentleness represent; even a handful of citizens—*our* representatives—being manipulated by the powers-that-be.[7]

[7] The nearest approach to the Cornish staging modes that I know of occurs, significantly enough, in the Hegge Plays, where a staging situation seems to have obtained that was very close in character to the Cornish one (i.e. a system of 'simultaneous mansions' fronting or partially embracing—even perhaps completely embracing—an expansive 'place' or acting-area. Curiously, the full dramatic potential of the theatrical environment seems not to have been discerned or exploited by the Lincolnshire play-makers. In the Conspiracy, for example, when Judas steals away to sell his services to the ecclesiastical Establishment, the Last Supper is not permitted to continue concurrently but has a curtain drawn on it, which is opened again once the contract has been concluded ('þan xal þe place þer cryst is in xal sodeynly vn-close...'—*PPI, SD* 669). A similar shutting off of one otherwise simultaneous scene from another also occurs in the Simon the Leper sequence, where the Bethany 'house' and the

The effect is echoed, though subtly different in quality, in the
dark scenes that follow, when Jesus is abused and scourged and mocked
by loutish and uncouth tormentors before a gaping, enthusiastic pro-
letarian audience (the same people who had welcomed him so
wildly such a short time before), while the patricians once more
nibble titbits afar off, chat and laugh easily, lick their fingers, sip wine
—all of this punctuated by cheers, blows, lashes, grunts, curses, cries,
cocktail-party noises. It makes yet again for an extraordinarily unset-
tling balance and contrast of impressions, a stretching and bending of
the mind, a *controlled* complexity of response, in which perceptions of
basic human realities (man's inhumanity to man, the quarantined re-
moteness of Them, suggestible and malleable Us) are presented side-
by-side with moral implications of a cosmic order: the accomplishment
of God's purposes *by means of* the very nest-feathering and pragmatism
('It's better that one man should die, I do assure you, than that all the
faithful should be lost'—446-8) of rulers and officialdom, and the
malice and casual brutality of an easily-led and entertained populace.

V

An extraordinary scene ensues as the court or 'bar' is being set up
('*ordneugh bar the ysethe*'—2225), the 'Tribunal' or Judgment-seat
either in the *platea* itself, say at B, or utilizing part of the Temple
structure (as was done at Lincoln), or perhaps in Pilate's mansion, the
'Justice' flanked for the occasion by Caiaphas and Annas, with the
prisoners, guards, lawyers, crowd arranged in the arena before them.
While the court is being prepared Pilate calls for the prisoners to be
brought out. But the Jailor and his Apprentice are involved in a

---

Jews' 'council-house' seem to be alternately shrouded whenever the focus of
the action shifts ('þe cownsel hous befornseyd xal sodeynly onclose schewyng
þe buschopys prestys and jewgys syttyng in here Astat ...' *PPI, SD* 397). But
in Pilate's Wife's Dream something very close to the Cornish patterns is
allowed to take place. Here Satan enters the 'place' ('in þe most orryble wyse')
while Jesus is being marched back in fool's outlandish garb from Herod's
mansion to Pilate's (i.e. circuitously round the 'place'). During the course of
this march ('þei xal . . . ledyn hym A-bowth þe place and þan to pylat be
þe tyme þat hese wyf hath pleyd'—*PPII, SD* 465) the devils' exchange takes
place (at Hell-mouth) that issues in the visit to the sleeping Julia Procula. The
'dream' is merely mimed here, Satan having no lines to address to her (he
has apprised us in advance of the import of the 'dream') as Beelzebub has in
the Cornish Passion, but the two scenes do take place concurrently. (See,
though, Paula Neuss's remarks on this scene, p. 58 above.)

private squabble, over wages and working conditions, the Apprentice having chosen this awkward moment to go on strike, or to work to rule, sending his master apoplectic with rage at his lack of consideration compounded by his ribald insolence:

Jailor   By Allah's tail, he's foaming at
          The mouth already! For Satan's
              Sake, give over now and
          Get the buggers out!

Boy   You owe me
          Too much back pay, mate, and that's the
              Honest truth—I strike!

Jailor   You're under indentures, little
          Runt! And you'll do your job whether
              You feel like it or not!

Boy   I've never had no wages! I've
          Not had a halfpenny from you yet!

[Pilate] Jailor! Will you hurry!

Jailor   By God, I'm warning you, I'll have
          You whipped along at the cart's tail,
              And then thrown into gaol!

Boy   Just try! A fart for your threats and
          Contracts. They don't bother me at
              All, awake or sleeping!

Jailor   Oh, what a big fellow he is!
          Full of big brave words—and swagger—
              All to try his betters!

Boy   I couldn't find a worse master
          Between here and Tregear!

[Pilate]   Jailor!

                                    (2252–75)

Pilate and the dignitaries are growing very annoyed at this delay, the commons no doubt enjoying every hilarious minute of it, though (nimble menial outfencing lumbering authority—Private Jenkins and Captain Trevelyan of a later age—according to an age-old, ever-popular routine). For us in the audience another clever pingpong situation has been engineered, our attention being batted back and forth this time between the slapstick clowning outside the gaol (Tp—

the prisoners themselves, including Jesus, cooped up behind them like
beasts in a cage), the exasperated dignitaries and the delighted crowd.
At a more serious level, the unbearable culmination of events the
action is rushing towards, and its cosmic significance, are here being
counterpointed—and framed—by the mundane and the farcical; things

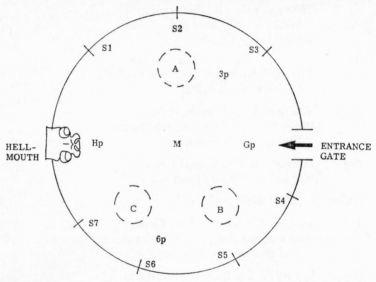

Fig. 4. Cornish Passion play: staging plan. S—scaffold; p—position in the
platea, in relation to some adjacent feature (e.g. Gp = in the vicinity of, in
front of, the Gate); M—middle; ABC—focal points of the action where
principal locations or scenic units are sited.

celestial and august by things vulgar and scatological. The framework
for God's murder, in other words, is being presented as the topsy-
turvy and untidy goings-on of daily life: while we bicker, jape and go
on strike, Christ is being prepared for sacrifice.

In exasperation Pilate finally sends soldiers to crack the jailors' heads
together and they abandon their brawling and get the prisoners out.

> Dismas, Jesmas, come out! And you
> Too, Jesus and Barabbas. You're
>   To be tried and sentenced,
> My fine gallows-birds! Come, Pilate's
> On the judgment-seat already,
>   And waits impatiently!   (2337–42)

And the Trial gets under way. For the first time in the entire play, it is interesting to note, the amphitheatre becomes the focus of a single action. All the mansions round the circumference, including Heaven and Infernum, are blankly closed and silent, while in the *platea* itself only one locality is represented and rivets all attention, the atrium where the Trial is taking place. In simple technical terms, the unusualness of this structuring is enough to invest the scene with immense dramatic urgency. Only twice more is this to happen: at the Crucifixion itself and at the concluding Ascension.

VI

The unique staging dynamic of the Cornish Passion reaches its perfection, some may feel, in the painful Calvary scenes to which everything has been leading. As the intensely dramatic Trial breaks up (Barabbas scooping up ale and girls rejoicing) the holiday crowd swarms eagerly over the arena to line a Dolorosa route which becomes the immediate, mocking echo of that other holiday route, at the play's gay beginning, when this same crowd—our representatives, in medieval times indistinguishable from ourselves in speech or dress—waved palms and sang hosannas at another procession containing Jesus as its chief element. A medieval audience, moreover, like any Catholic one today, would be equally keenly aware of the pitiful Stations of the Cross about to be enacted before their eyes, which eyes would dart round the *platea* ahead of the stumbling figure to identify here a Blessed Virgin, there a Simon of Cyrene, here a St. Veronica with her vernicle, there a huddle of weeping Women of Jerusalem—at the termination of the processional route the dreadful hill itself. The point I am making is that, however ably the scene (like many others) may happen to be treated elsewhere, in the open expanse of a Cornish *plan-an-gwarry*, as treated by the distinctive Cornish staging conventions, the immensely moving Via Dolorosa episode takes on a scope and texture that are quite unique.

The point is reinforced by the ensuing scene, the introit to the appalling execution itself, where the Torturers discover that they have no nails and dispatch one of their number to the Smithy's (set up with the aid of a bellows and anvil—at C? at 6p?—moments before) to get some. A remarkable scene ensues, our attention and the quality of our response once more being skilfully controlled by the dramatist.

At 'Calvary' the preparations for the execution proceed with loud and grisly zestfulness, with Jesus and the felons being lashed to their crosses and the crowd jostling for favourable vantage points. Apart (in one of the palaces) the dignitaries relax in sociable comfort, drinking wine, exchanging pleasantries, waiting for the gala to begin. And at the Smithy's the First Torturer and the Smith's Wife forge the spikes, syncopating clangs on the anvil with lewd flirtation and love-play that stop the breath with their daring, in this context:

1 Torturer	I'll pump for you like a yeoman,
	Lass! I tell you no lie there's not
	A smith in all wide Cornwall what
	Works his bellows better!
Smith's Wife	You pump like a baboon! Gently
	Now, goddam it! Or not a spark
	Stays in the forge. Enough!
	Oaf! Now beat the iron with me
	Stroke for stroke—I'll kill you if you
	Let it go cold on me!
1 Torturer	God catch my soul I'll beat so slow
	And gentle we'll draw it out for
	You real lovely. There! Ah,
	There's not a bully-boy in all
	The duchy can match me at it—
	As everybody knows!
Smith's Wife	Well, do it in the right place, then,
	You silly twit! If your aim's wrong
	And meanwhile it cools off,
	It'll go all limp and bent! Watch
	The beat, you bloody ox![8] *Stroke* it!
	One, two. One, two. So! So!
1 Torturer	There's nothing wrong with *my* beat, sweet
	Heart!
Smith's Wife	No? Look, it's all drooped and goose-
	Pimpled! Oh, well, so much the worse
	For the gallows-bird, who'll get them
	Roughly through his hands! . . .

(2709–36)

[8] The last four lines of the passage (Smith's wife's speech) occur at this point in the MS, erroneously, it seems to me.

Compared to what we ordinarily understand by the term, this is dramatic irony concentrated or intensified to an extraordinary degree. But more than irony or ironic contrast, however bitter, is involved here. Life goes on, the scene seems to say at one level, fertility and death, sin and sanctity, appetite and sacrifice, grossness and trans-cendency—a bleak philosophical observation. But the very ordinari-ness of the scene, a man and a woman in flirtatious byplay (you could find its counterpart, as brazen or more muted, in pubs all over the country at any time these past six hundred years or more), in every respect our mirror-images—speaking our language, wearing our clothes, enjoying a few moments' harmless diversion—underlines the quotidian nature of the episode's context. Christ's sacrifice is a timeless one; in doctrinal terms it is taking place now; beyond the tavern walls where customer and barmaid dally, limbs are being stretched on the crucifix, nails are being got ready, that momentous sacrifice is about to take place yet again. In one quarter of the arena one kind of life-promoting ritual is being enacted, crudely and debasedly; in another a purer kind, the ultimate kind, is being enacted too, where life for all of us is being underwritten. Two kinds of 'love' are being contrasted, two kinds of 'bride'-hood. The scene works with amazing, and deeply disturbing, boldness and authority, and lends an extra dimension, an intenser, more sharply etched perspective, to the Crucifixion itself.

Many factors, then, can be seen working in association with the playwright's initial ardency of impulse and coherency of vision to produce the distinctive texturing of the finished play as it unfolded in a medieval *plan-an-gwarry*. Capitalizing on the initial story, in other words, presented with such immediacy and 'reverence', the drama was incalculably enhanced by its unusual unity of impact (one Jesus, one cast, one ambiance of action), its crisp symmetry of form, the supple continuity forced upon it by the amphitheatrical, 'simultaneous mansions' staging situation. (This continuity and flow from scene to scene is equally long before its time, resembling the cinematic 'fade' more than anything else, and contributes extensively to the dramatic stature the play enjoys.) But more important than all these factors, the play's remarkable techniques of scene-cutting and panoramic presen-tation admit of a range of theatrical possibilities unrivalled by any other dramatic form up to and including the scope made possible by the technology of our own day.

Note

Texts.
The texts referred to in this chapter are included in Young, *DMC*; Deimling and Matthews, *CP*; Block, *LC*; England and Pollard, *TP*; Toulmin Smith, *YP*; and Furnivall, *DP*.

Non-dramatic texts used are the *Gospel of Nicodemus*, ed. William Henry Hulme (EETS, Oxford, 1907), and *Heliand*, ed. and tr. Marianna Scott (Section XLVII, *University of North Carolina Studies in the Germanic Languages and Literatures*, No. 52, 1966).

Scholarship and Criticism.
Chambers, *MS* remains the standard, most basic work of reference for any student of the drama of the Middle Ages. On the epic genre, E. M. W. Tillyard, *The English Epic and its Background* (Oxford, 1954), is as important; and Auerbach, *Mimesis*, is indispensable to any inquirer into the nature of dramatic experience.

The epic quality of medieval cyclic drama has not been much examined. The place of the hero in the cycle plays, and the status of the cycles as history, have been glanced at *inter alia*, by Wickham, *Shakespeare's Dramatic Heritage* (London, 1969), *passim*, and Denny, introduction to his forthcoming *The Cornish Cycle*.

Abbreviations.
PG—*Patrologia Graeca*
PL—*Patrologia Latina*

VII

Epic Qualities in the Cycle Plays

K. P. RODDY

I

THE ENGLISH cycle drama's dependence on the Bible as a source is usually acknowledged, but the relationship remains undetermined because instances of modifying a specific Biblical text have not been fully documented. Scholars have only recently investigated the range and degree of the expansion, omission or displacement of the Biblical narrative. The complicated problem demands studies of selected plays which demonstrate the effect that a single aspect of medieval culture may have had upon their construction. Liturgy, folk themes and literary realism have all been examined as dominating influences upon certain plays. Erwin Wolff has discovered one of the more important determinants, namely the contributions of the early Biblical epic to the York plays.[1] Classifying certain extra-Biblical elements in the cycles as epic in nature is a promising approach; but a broad, descriptive application of epic characteristics is needed.

The epic genre is correctly associated with the noblest and largest of activities: the migration of nations, the fate of kings, the conduct of gods, the heroic struggle between good and evil. An epic subject is determined not by battle or courage alone but by the momentous impact of the action upon men's lives. Such considerations led J. Dover Wilson to term Shakespeare's history plays epic; in his view *Henry V* in particular cannot be fully appreciated unless its epic conventions are understood. For many scholars the moral and social dimensions of *Beowulf* distinguish it as an epic; raising it above works merely heroic such as the *Battle of Maldon*. The utilization of this elusive criterion of grandeur facilitates the task at hand, that of identifying epic features in the mystery cycles. E. M. W. Tillyard, in *The English Epic and Its*

---

[1] 'Proculas Traum: Der Yorker Misterienzyklus und die epische Tradition', in *Chaucer und seine Zeit*, ed. Arno Esch (Tübingen, 1968), pp. 419–50.

Background, provides the necessary framework by establishing four epic characteristics: high seriousness, amplitude and breadth, a sense of controlling will, and a representation of the feelings of the people. Although not constituting a definition, these requirements by their presence in a work indicate that the subject-matter has been infused with the high significance proper to epics.

The four epic characteristics are exceptionally useful in criticism because they are pervasive and can be observed at any point throughout a work. Thus if the requirements are relevant to the appreciation of cycle drama, they can be recognized in any individual play chosen at random. There are several advantages in using the raising of Lazarus episode for this study, though it has been arbitrarily selected: the Lazarus miracle exists in all four extant Corpus Christi cycles and in the Digby *Mary Magdalene*, yielding sufficient material for comparison; the plays have seemed to be simple dramatizations of the Gospel text (*John* 11, 1–45), so there has been a virtual absence of scholarly commentary. Actually the modifications which occur are as varied as any in the cycles. The case for an epic aspect in the cycles can be proven: the modifications in this relatively minor play, if shown to conform to epic characteristics, will demonstrate an epic function for the cycles.

The most important of Tillyard's four requirements is the postulation in the work of a great will governing the action. The epic presumes as ascendant power which assures eventual order and degree. The presence of this quality in the Scriptural plays seems quite obviously derived from the Bible itself. The Bible's authority is based both on its claim to have recorded the will of God as manifest in history and on its promise that God's purpose will conclude time in harmonic resolution. The extraordinary power of the Bible to impose an intelligible pattern upon the course of history has been one of its most compelling attributes. As Erich Auerbach wrote, 'Far from seeking, like Homer, merely to make us forget our own reality for a few hours, [the Bible] seeks to overcome our reality; we are to fit our own life into its world, feel ourselves to be elements in its structure of universal history.'[2] An essential dramatic change which the cycles effected was that of presenting the promise of ultimate resolution as a reality. The existence of the Last Judgment play in the cycles is an outstanding example of such a change, but it is by no means the only one. The God of the Bible is eternal, and any manifestation of Him in time implicitly

[2] *Mimesis*, p. 15.

contains all other manifestations. Medieval cycle drama adopts this outlook: time can be condensed and the Scriptural past made to demonstrate future perfection in an explicit and emphatic way. The phenomenon of eschatological anticipation occurs most frequently in the plays which comprise the life of Christ. Because Christ's divinity had been emphasized in medieval popular theology, His will was represented as consciously directing the action towards its conclusion. Christ is depicted throughout the New Testament plays as entirely dedicated to the pattern which He Himself has ordained.

The Johannine account of the Lazarus miracle may suggest a sense of Christ's controlling will, but the cycle play ascribes greater powers and clearer purpose to that will than could possibly be justified by the Scriptural narrative. For example, when Christ in the Gospel is told of Lazarus's sickness He says, 'This sicknesse is not to death' (verse 4). Yet while Christ speaks Lazarus is dying or has died, and Christ as portrayed in the Middle Ages would have been absolutely cognizant of this. The words must therefore have had some meaning which coincided with Christ's divine intent. Cyril of Alexandria explained that Christ was not considering intermediate events in this verse, but finalities: Christ foresees the miracle He will accomplish and thus indicates that Lazarus's death at this point is not permanent.[3] Cyril's gloss may have been the basis for the expansion of the verse in the Digby play, but the playwright broadened the scope of reference considerably. The Digby Christ asserts an overriding will which has eternally provided for heavenly life and thus abolished death:

> of all In-firmyte, þer is non to deth,
> for of all peynnes þat is Inpossyble.
> To vndyr-stond be reson, to know þe werke,
> the Ioye þat is in Ierusallem heuenly,
> Can never be compylyd be covnnyng of clerke,
> to se þe Ioyys of þe fathyr In glory
> the Ioyys of þe sonne whych owth to be magnyfyed,
> And of þe therd person, þe holy gost truly,
> & alle iij but on In heuen gloryfyed.   (802–10)

The theme of indescribable happiness in heaven has little bearing on the Lazarus play and can be explained only in terms of a sacred pronouncement directed to all Christians. Christ reminds the audience to

---

[3] *Commentarium in Joannem*, in PG 74, col. 40.

contemplate the perfection of heaven and to value it over the con-
tinuation of physical life. There is the epic sense that God's will and
power concern more than the life of one man.

II

Through such assertions, the audience affirms its collective belief
in the ineffability of God and thereby accomplishes a communion
with the divine will. As Northrop Frye has suggested, 'The scriptural
plays . . . present to the audience a myth already familiar to and
significant for that audience, and they are designed to remind the
audience of their communal possession of that myth.'[4] This characteristic of 'spiritual and corporeal communion' lends quite naturally to
a second requirement for an epic, the 'choric' response, the impression
that 'public feelings have been expressed'. The values which permeate
an epic poem are the remarkably uniform and deep-seated asseverations
of popular culture; as C. M. Bowra indicated,

> The gatherings which listen to heroic poetry have something like
> a common consciousness, not merely in the sense that they all enjoy
> the same performance together, but in the sense that they all feel
> much the same about it because their own lives conform to custom-
> ary rules of which they are largely unconscious and therefore
> uncritical.

The epic poet, according to Bowra, 'is really the voice of the people
whom he addresses and whose feelings and thoughts are his own'.[5] The
playwrights of the cycles similarly complemented and fostered this
'common consciousness' by adding details which are purely within
the cultural idiom. A bond of identity between play and life, character and audience, spectator and spectator is thus assured. Placed
throughout the cycles are secondary incidents whose primary function
is to articulate basic attitudes. Such incidents may proceed independently of the action, and in this respect are similar to examples of the
characteristic of controlling will. However, the focus of culturally-
determined material is much more narrow—even domestic—and the
purpose is representational.

An episode has been inserted in the Hegge ('N-town'—probably

---

[4] *Anatomy of Criticism* (Princeton, New Jersey, 1957), p. 282.
[5] *Heroic Poetry* (London, 1952), p. 476.

Lincoln) Lazarus play which can only be explained as the compact embodiment of culturally-approved behaviour, almost in contradiction to the central movement of the drama. In the Johannine narrative the fundamental concern is the raising of a man dead for four days, so one might naturally expect the incidents in a dramatization of that narrative to flow towards the miracle itself. But at Lincoln the action is frozen in order to express cultural values. Lazarus dies on stage, and the two sisters begin an elaborate and lengthy lament; remarkably, this lament is answered by an equally elaborate solace offered in turn by three characters, who are called in the script simply *consolator i, ii,* and *iii.* Although John only briefly suggests such comfort (verse 19), the solace in the Lincoln play masterfully counteracts and relieves the sisters' intensive mourning.

The conventions of dramatic consistency prescribe that the sympathy offered to the sisters must be unsatisfying and ineffectual; otherwise, the climax is robbed of its necessity and importance. Like the consolation in the Book of Job, the consolation in the Lazarus play must seem a pitiful attempt to comprehend what can be resolved by God's will alone. Moreover, according to the *Legenda Aurea* and the York *Breviary*, Magdalen's grief is an essential, almost causal, element in the miracle.[6] And in most commentaries on John, Christ's own tears (verse 33) are noted and commended. But contrary to the rules of thematic treatment and in opposition to the vindication of grief, the consolation from the three comforters is straightforward, not ironic. It is actually a sane and thoroughly Christian effort to curb excessive lamentation:

> Arys for shame ʒe do not ryght
> streyth from þis grave ʒe xul go hens
> þus for to grugge ageyns godys myght
> Aʒens hyʒ god ʒe do offens.   (25. 173–6)

> hom to ʒour place we xal ʒow wysse   *direct*
> Ffor goddys loue be of good chere
> In dede ʒe do ryght sore amys
> so sore to wepe as ʒe do here.   (181–4)

These are the expressions of general popular feeling, of an authentic

---

[6] In the Th. Graesse 3rd edition (1890; Ösnabrück, 1965), p. 409. *Breviarum ad insignis ecclesie Eboracensis*, Surtees Society Vol. 75 (1882), col. 402, 'In Festo S. Marie Magdalene'.

cultural stance. The contention can be proved by examining other medieval descriptions and representations of the Lazarus miracle. For example, Thomas Aquinas repeats verse 19 in his lectures on John and approves of the comfort which the Jews came to Bethany to offer, 'because it was indeed a pious thing'. To support his opinion, he quotes *Romans* 12, 15 and *Ecclesiasticus* 7, 38.[7] Still stronger parallels are found in imaginative literature, since it is a better index of cultural pre-occupations than exegetical commentary.

In medieval drama itself, analogues to the Hegge consolation can be identified that exhibit a similar disregard for consistency. Two Latin plays survive on the subject of Lazarus's resuscitation, one by the twelfth-century wandering scholar-poet Hilarius. In his play the consoling Jews answer the sisters verse for verse, singing at one point:

> Cease tears, we beg you,
> we can advance nothing indeed
> through tears:
> persisting in tears would be sensible
> if one with so many of them
> could revivify.[8]

It might be supposed that Hilarius means such comfort to be taken ironically: Lazarus actually is revivified through tears. This supposition is inaccurate, for the consolation offered is in direct response to these lines of pathological lamentation which Martha has sung:

> I do not refuse to die
> For a dead brother,
> Neither do I fear death. . . .
> Following the death of a brother
> I refuse to live.
> Alas! Have mercy on me. . . .[9]

In the other Latin play, found in the Fleury manuscript and dated about a hundred years later, the Jews propose these sentiments:

> It is enough, you know, that it pleases God,
> that He wished the death of your brother;

---

[7] *Super Evangelium S. Joannis lectura*, Caput XI, lectio iv, ii, ed. P. Cai (Turin, 1952), p. 281.

[8] Young, *DMC*, Vol. II, p. 214, ll. 89–94.

[9] *Ibid.*, ll. 77–9, 83–5.

> for things willed by His power
> our sorrow is forbidden
> at the risk of his anger.[10]

This comfort is obviously a capsulization of the basic Christian disposition towards death. Obviously, too, the function is publicly to affirm central truths about death that the audience holds in common.

It is improbable that Hilarius's *Lazarus* or the Fleury play were sources for the Lincoln consolation. Rather, all three playwrights shared homogeneous values which limited grief through definite patterns of comfort. The three parallel consolations probably developed independently, each reflecting culture in the Middle Ages. Medieval literature contains other examples which also amplify the Jews' condolence, but one more will suffice to show the diffusion and antiquity of the tradition. The ninth-century Old Saxon epic *Heliand* extends Scripture in its version of the Lazarus miracle, which suggests the same mirroring purpose as that of the Lincoln consolation. *Heliand* represents Caedmon's formula for translating Biblical material into available cultural forms; it is thus helpful in comprehending the epic nature of the cycles, as Wolff cogently argued. The passage which mentions the consolation is a paraphrase of verses 18 and 19 of *John*:

> Here was gathered together
> Much folk of the Jews from Jerusalem,
> Who wanted to comfort the women with words,
> So that they would lament less the death of Lazarus,
> The loss of the child-young man.[11]

Though only a clause, the rationale for offering comfort, 'so that they would lament less', has the flavour of a cultural maxim. It has been maintained here that one of the primary functions of an epic is to articulate cultural wisdom both in aphorism and in episodic action.

III

Beyond the cultural aspect there is an intellectual dimension to the epic which necessitates a third epic requirement, that of amplitude and breadth. The epic must incorporate a magnitude that is held in balance

[10] *Ibid.*, pp. 204–5, ll. 172–7.
[11] Section XLVII, *University of North Carolina Studies in the Germanic, Languages and Literatures*, No. 52, p. 137.

F

by the fundamental sanity of the epic poet. In the cycles, the sanity springs from a conviction that, since the divine pattern is known, undifferentiated matters in Scripture can be made to correlate with the entire Christian system. Amplification yields material which is quite similar to culturally-based episodes like the Lincoln consolation, but the function of the latter is to mirror and of the former to enlighten, to illuminate Scripture and clarify its implications. When an interpretation of an ambiguous Biblical passage had been legitimatized by common acceptance and hallowed by tradition, it became inseparable from the text it was meant to augment. The Reformation's reaction against the practice of aggregation was unfortunate in its zeal, 'for,' to quote Joseph Campbell, 'the function of such myth-building is to interpret the sense, not to chronicle the facts, of a life, and to offer the art work of the legend, then, as an activating symbol for the inspiration and shaping of lives, and even civilizations, to come'.[12] (See too, David Jeffrey's chapter above, pp. 72–3.) The epic amplitude which is the result of myth-building is rooted in a serious, not gratuitous, attempt to complete the workings of divine will.

Epic amplitude as it appears in the cycles was most often derived from patristic commentary or apocryphal legends. The Church Fathers themselves were guided in their Biblical criticism by the attitude of the New Testament towards the Old: the ancient mysterious covenants of God in the past were to be interpreted as foreshadowing Christ, who would be the sign of God's new presence. The obscurities in the New Testament could therefore also be explained in the light of Christ's unequivocal teaching and His continual presence in the Church. A few ambiguities exist in the Johannine Lazarus account; in one, Christ announces His decision to return to Judea and is opposed by His Disciples, who fear He will be killed. Christ answers that the day has but twelve hours and one must travel while there is sun (verses 9 and 10). Augustine understood this saying allegorically to refer to the relation between Christ and the Twelve Apostles (and therefore all bishops), who were subordinate to Christ as the hours are to the sun.[13] The Chester playwright includes this interpretation in his play, expanding it to involve a more general moralization:

> To the day my self may likned be,
> and to the twelue howers all ye,

[12] *The Masks of God: Occidental Mythology* (New York, 1964), p. 347.
[13] *In Joannis Evangelium*, Tractatus XLIX, Caput XI, in *PL* 35, vols. 1749–51.

that lightned bene through following me,
that am most lyking light.
ffor world[e]s light I am veray,
and who so followeth me, sooth to say,
he may goe no chester way,
for light in him is dight.   (13, 353–60)

The reference has been extended to apply to all Christians. In this way
the Chester playwright was entirely within the patristic tradition of
reinterpretative amplification according to contemporary conditions.
But the direct use of the Fathers was only an element in the epic amplification of the Scriptural story in the cycles; apocryphal matter had
contributed much more.

Like the Church Fathers, the creators of legends about the characters
and events in the New Testament sought to clarify the sense of Scripture according to contemporary faith. The difference seems to be that
the legends were more consciously literary than intellectual in their
approach to Scriptural history. The term 'New Testament apocrypha'
conjures associations of secret heretical sects and Church condemna-
tions, but just as often apocrypha should convey the innocuous literary
paraphrasing of the Bible. The apocryphal Apostolic Acts, for example, are most certainly indicative of the taste for Greek romance
literature among Hellenistic Christians.[14] The question of historical
verisimilitude was simply not as important as was the gratifying
embroidery of some significant concept in Christianity. The apocryphal
work most important to the cycles, the *Gospel of Nicodemus*, was also
inspired by a literary genre, in this case the Eastern myth-epics describing titanic battles in the underworld. In the *Gospel*, Christ's victory
is portrayed physically with powerful clarity, and the unmistakably
heroic stance remained the object of imitation for thirteen hundred
years. The amplified warrior ideal depicted in the *Gospel of Nicodemus*
was essential in extending a sense of dedicated struggle and conquest to
the entire Christian movement.

The presence of an heroic ideal in Christianity is frequently explained
as an early medieval concession to the Germanic preference for the
poetry of warfare; but the designation of the Christian as warrior
antedates the conversion of the North by several hundred years. The
description appears in Scripture, in explanations of Scripture, and also

[14] R. L. P. Milburn, *Early Christian Interpretations of History* (London, 1952),
p. 128.

in the Latin Christian epics of the late Classical period some time
before serious missionary activity began. The passage in *Heliand* which
amplifies verse 16 of John's account of Lazarus has often been considered a textbook example of the change in Christianity during the
Dark Ages. In the Gospel, after Christ's twelve-hour speech, Thomas
says, 'Let us also go, to die with him.' *Heliand* expands the ambiguous
statement to show Thomas's courage and loyalty:

> Then one of the twelve,
> Thomas, did speak— he was truly an excellent man,
> A loyal thane of his Lord.   'Let us never reproach His deeds,'
> Quoth he, 'nor reproach His will.   But rather we should remain
> with Him,
> Should suffer with our Lord.   For that is the choice of the thane:
> That he standeth steadfast   with his Liege together,
> Doth die with Him at his doom.   Let us all do so therefore:
> Let us follow his path,   nor let our lives
> Be worth aught against His,   unless we may die
> In this host with our Lord.   So honour will live after us,
> A good word before the kinships of men.'

This seems a fairly straightforward example of the transformation of
Scripture to meet the specific and ephemeral needs of conversion. But
the interpretation of verse 16 as an example of Thomas's heroic dedi-
cation can be found in the works of Augustine, Cyril of Alexandria,
Fulgentius, Bede, as well as Juvencus, the epic poet.[15] Naturally the
social organization of thanes and the idealization of honour were
peculiar to Germanic culture, but the heroic tradition was solidly
Western and outlived the age of conversion; thus Thomas's courage
became the usual explanation for the verse.

This specific discussion of the patristic and apocryphal attempt to
clarify and explain the Bible through controlled amplification prepared the reader for an appreciation of Thomas's remark as it appears
in the Towneley Lazarus play:

> Sir, What so euer ye bid vs do
> We assent vs well ther to:
> I hope to god ye shall not fynde

[15] Augustine and Bede are quoted in Aquinas, *Catena Aurea*, Caput XI, 3,
ed. A. Guarienti (Turin, 1953), Vol. II, p. 484; Cyril, *Commentarium in Joannem*,
cols. 44–5; Fulgentius, *Sermo XXII, De Lazaro suscitato*, in *PL* 65, col. 889;
Juvencus, *Evangelicae Historiae*, Liber IV, ll. 330–32, in *PL* 19, cols. 307–8.

None of vs shall lefe behynde;	*stay*
ffor any parell that may befall	*peril*
Weynde we With oure master all.	*go*

(31, 33–8)

A long tradition of exegesis has transformed Scriptural ambiguity into a precise and significant lucidity. The chosen emphasis is entirely consistent with the literary heroic ideal which will permeate the climactic Harrowing of Hell. It is important to note, at the same time, that Scriptural passages in which the meaning is clear (verses 21–5, for example) are translated directly and accurately. The function of commentary and legendary amplification is usually to supplement, not replace, the scriptural narrative.

IV

The conjunction of the three epic requirements of controlling will, communion, amplitude would not constitute an epic were it not for the fourth criterion which unifies and elevates them. This requirement, 'high seriousness', is an attitude that indicates matters of the most grave and solemn consequence. Passages infused with high seriousness are those that concentrate the other epic attributes simultaneously in a forceful culmination of action. At these points the epic speaks directly of those concerns that are most essential and most immediate to the audience. The Scriptural account of the raising of Lazarus supplies an opportunity for such an address in the instantaneous appearance of the dead man upon Christ's powerful command, 'Lazarus, come forth.' Lazarus, as the spectacular focal point of attention, is in an ideal position to bear witness to God's rule with high seriousness, to remind the audience of the significant spiritual and physical realities that the Christian must acknowledge.

It should not be surprising, then, that Lazarus is given speech in all five versions of the play, and that what is said has been determined by the traditional interpretations which define the deepest significance of the miracle. John recounts the raising of Lazarus to further God's glory. According to one modern commentary, 'glory' means the inevitable union of Christ with the Father through the Crucifixion. Therefore the miraculous act signifies more than the Father's approval of Christ and the life available to those who follow Jesus; the raising of Lazarus is to be the first event in what becomes an urgent sweep towards the passion. When the news of the miracle reaches the chief priests, the council immediately decides that Christ should be put to death.[16] In the cycles, however, none of John's preoccupations figures in any dominant way: Christ's union with the Father is assumed, not anticipated, and the Pharisees need no specific occasion in order to awaken their hatred and jealousy. While the York, Chester and Lincoln Lazarus plays end with Christ's declared intention to go to Jerusalem (and, in Lincoln, to death), the episode seems almost entirely separate from the Passion sequence that follows; its justification must be sought internally, especially at that moment when Lazarus speaks.

In the five Lazarus discourses taken together, three important themes emerge: first, Christ deserves thanks and praise for his mercy; second, flesh is ephemeral and death a terrifying actuality; and third, Satan awaits men, but even he is subject to Christ's power. Lazarus's personal experience of death, Hell, and Christ's redemptory might has endowed him with sacred knowledge; he is obliged to impart these crucial and serious matters at the first opportunity. In modern performance the appearance of Lazarus has been unanticipatedly and movingly effective: this effect was probably even greater on an audience awed by spectacle. Lazarus suddenly stands forth, wrapped in his winding sheet, white and moving stiffly. As he steps from his grave, he intones the most solemn intelligence man can impart; at that moment, Lazarus has an authority second only to God's.

Of the five versions, the Lazarus declamation in the York cycle has the purest expression of simple awe and gratitude. Lazarus addresses Christ, then the other characters, then the audience itself in a classic progression which gradually transcends the circumstances of the play to touch on the most serious issues in human life. There is, moreover, an almost classical incorporation of all the epic requirements isolated by Tillyard:

> A! pereles prince, full of pitee!
> Worshipped be þou in worlde alway,
> That þus hast schewed þi myght in me,
> Both dede and doluen, þis is þe fourþe day.   *dug in*
> By certayne singnes here may men see
> How þat þou art goddis sone verray.
> All þo þat trulye trastis in þe   *trusts*

[16] W. H. Cadman, 'The Raising of Lazarus', in *Studia Evangelica*, ed. K. Aland *et al.* (Berlin, 1959), pp. 423–34.

Schall neuere dye, þis dare I saye.
Therfore ʒe folke in fere,   *all together*
Menske hym with mayne and myght,   *Honour*
His lawes luke þat ʒe lere,
Þan will he lede ʒou to his light.   (24. 186–97)

The first quatrain honours Christ's power as prince, as supreme will: the 'glory' which is demonstrated in John's narrative has become 'myght', strength to overcome even death. The next two lines refer to 'men', ostensibly the sceptics and unbelievers among the Jewish bystanders, but Lazarus has already begun to refer to the present, the theatrical spectators. The progression is completed in the next two lines, which affirm to the audience in all seriousness Christ's promise in verse 26 of *John*. Finally, Lazarus concludes with a positive statement of the significance of the miracle: those who live justly, according to Christ's rule, will, like Lazarus, be saved from permanent death. These twelve lines of praise are so consistent with the play that source discussion seems unnecessary. Interestingly, Hilarius also stresses praise and thanksgiving, instructing Lazarus to begin the *Te Deum* or the *Magnificat*.

V

Other themes also attest to the epic quality with which the story is invested. Themes of the fleshly decay of Lazarus's body, for instance, occur in the Digby and Towneley plays. Although Scripture does not specifically describe the state of Lazarus's corpse before the miracle, Martha assumes that it must have begun to decompose ('Lord, by this time he stinketh: for he hath been dead four days'—verse 39.) Her words were accepted as a statement of fact, and the subject became a popular one for exegesis and in medieval art. For a graphic example, some Russian icons portray a bystander covering his nose as Lazarus steps forth.[17] The *Gospel of Nicodemus* refers to Lazarus as 'four days stinking and corrupt' when returned to life.[18] Potamius, a fourth-century bishop of Lisbon, possibly had the *Nicodemus* testimony in mind when he depicted the dissolution of Lazarus's flesh in clinical and

[17] See Konrad Onasch, *Icons*, tr. Marianne von Herzfeld (London, 1963), plates 40 and 45, descriptions pp. 364 and 366.

[18] Caput III, 3. Latin ed. C. Tischendorf, *Evangelia Apocrypha* (Leipzig, 1876), p. 424.

even grotesque detail.[19] Fulgentius similarly reminds his listeners of the extensive putrescence and vermin which appeared after four days. In the Chester play Mary, on hearing that Christ is coming, anticipates Martha's comment that the corpse now smells and Lazarus is beyond help. The Towneley playwright upholds tradition when his Lazarus thanks Christ and then addresses the audience with the words:

> your dede is Wormes coke,   *cook*
> youre myrroure here ye loke,
> And let me be youre boke,
>   youre sampill take by me;   *example*
> ffro ded you cleke in cloke,   *'clutch', wrap*
> sich shall ye all be.
>
> (119–24)

This passage may be explained as another inconsequential manifestation of the *memento mori* theme in Middle English literature, but the prevalence and vigour of the tradition makes it likely that a more integral application of controlled amplitude is involved.

The theme of Lazarus's visit to Hell, which figures in the Towneley, Chester and Hegge plays, is apparently dependent on a passage in the *Gospel of Nicodemus*. The pre-Anselmian theory of salvation is the theological basis for both the *Gospel* and the cycles. According to this theory, Satan had won the power to kill men and seize their souls, which souls became capable of enlargement only when the Devil exceeded his power by attempting to capture God Himself, in the person of Christ. Lazarus, dying before the Redemption, must therefore have descended to Hell; one thing that will urgently excite the newly-risen Lazarus, therefore, is the actuality of Hell and its torments. Again Potamius's 'Grandi fratres' emerges as a possible influence, with detailed descriptions of punishments meted out to damned sinners. An apocryphal book of Lazarus which represented his experiences in Hell is mentioned in the thirteenth century.[20] There are at least two fourteenth-century Latin accounts of the torments in Hell that he wit-

---

[19] Tractatus I, *De Lazaro*, known as 'Grandi fratres', in *PL* 8, cols. 1412–1413.

[20] Mentioned in William Smith, *A Dictionary of Christian Biography* (London, 1877–87), Vol. III, p. 635.

nessed.[21] With no exaggeration, then, does the Wakefield Lazarus inform his listeners:

> And if I myght with you dwell
> To tell you all my tyme,
> ffull mekill cowth I tell   *much could*
> That I haue harde and sene,
> Of many a great meruell
> sich as ye wolde not wene,   *believe*
> In the paynes of hell
> There as I haue bene.   (198–205)

But Lazarus has another role which is even more important than that of witness to the suffering in Hell: he is absolute proof of the power Christ holds over death and over Satan himself. Though the confrontation and victory will actually culminate in and be accomplished at the Harrowing, Christ has the power to free Lazarus's soul from hell-prison even before there is a formal conquest. In the *Gospel of Nicodemus* the raising of Lazarus is belatedly recalled by the Prince of Hell as an unmistakable sign of Christ's godhead and Satan's error in having Him killed. The Prince reminds Satan of Christ's role in Lazarus's escape as the Devil gleefully awaits his new prize:

> Perchance it is he which by the word of his command did restore to life Lazarus which was four days dead and stank and was corrupt, whom I held here dead. . . . For at that time I, when I heard the command of his word, did quake and was overwhelmed with fear, and all my ministries with me were troubled. Neither could we keep Lazarus, but he like an eagle shaking himself leaped forth with all agility and swiftness, and departed from us, and the earth also which held the dead body of Lazarus straightway gave him up alive. Wherefore now I know that that man which was able to do these things is a God strong in command and mighty in manhood, and that he is the saviour of mankind.[22]

It was apparent to Peter of Ravenna and Vincent of Beauvais that the raising of Lazarus foreshadowed the Harrowing. In their version

---

[21] MS F. IV, 94, fol. 56ᵛ–59ᵛ, Bibl. Chisiana (Rome), printed in U. Chevalier, *Gallia Christiana Novissima* (Valence, 1899), Vol. II, pp. 2–4; MS 7503–18, fol. 129ᵛ–31, Bibl. Reg. Bruxell., printed in *Analecta Bollandiana* 6 (1887), pp. 88–9.

[22] *The Apocryphal New Testament*, ed. and tr. M. R. James (2nd edn., Oxford, 1953), pp. 131–2.

Christ pounds at the gates of Hell, demanding the soul of Lazarus. When Hell asks Christ's identity, angels respond with the psalm traditionally connected with the Harrowing: 'He is the King of glory, strong in battle' (xxiv. 8).[23] The Chester playwright was aware of these associations, and he concentrated them in the thanksgiving which Lazarus offers to Christ:

> A! lord, blessed most thou be!
> from death to lyfe hast raysed me
> through thy mickle might.
> Lord, when I hard the voyce of thee,
> all Hell fayled of ther posty,   *power*
> so fast from them my soule can flee,
> all Devills were a frayd.   (455–69)

The Lazarus play is essentially an epic re-establishment of victory. It is a cultural celebration, an affirmation of the superiority of God's will, a clarification of God's work before an audience of believers. Christ is presented as a champion who protects and justifies Christianity. The struggle and victory are thereby of the highest seriousness.

The presence of Tillyard's epic characteristics in medieval cycle drama demonstrates an earnestness and continuity which have not been fully appreciated. The cycles have often been considered either as Church propaganda or as barely-disguised paganism; an exploration of the epic aspect of the cycles may correct these tendencies. An appreciation of the Lazarus play, at any rate, would be difficult without such an approach; what can be demonstrated in this play should certainly apply to the cycles as a whole. Detailed studies of sources and analogues for each of the plays are needed to aid further and deeper investigation of epic qualities in the cycles. The pre-Anselmian theory of salvation had ceased to dominate theological studies some three hundred years before it was embodied in the cycles; the survival might be traced in sermons and poetry, linking the cycles more with literary traditions and less with contemporary theology.

What also would be of service is some sense of the tastes of both the clerical playwrights and their lay audiences. The epic approach to Scriptural history that seems to arise in the cycle play must have responded to a definite literary preference among the people. Scholar-

---

[23] *Speculum Historiale*, Liber Septimus, Caput XXVIII, *De Lazari suscitatione* (Douai, Baltazaris Belleri, 1624), p. 230.

ship might establish the degree to which epic treatment reflects medieval Christianity and the degree to which it represents the mentality of the burghers of York, Chester, Lincoln, Norwich. For the present at least, the classification of certain extra-Biblical elements in the cycles as epic in character promotes an understanding of the cycles as they are. If other plays—the Doctors, John the Baptist— are found to evince a similar detailed articulation and justification in epic fashion of the audience's religious and cultural values, the cycles may regain their stature as monuments of medieval thought.

Note

Texts.

All the miracle cycles and individual plays mentioned in this essay, with the exception of the York cycle (Toulmin Smith, *YP*) and the Cornish cycle (Norris, *CC*), are published by the EETS as follows: Deimling and Matthews, *CP*; Furnivall, *DP*; Block, *LC*; England and Pollard, *TP*; Craig, *CCP*.

The contemporary non-dramatic works mentioned are also published by the EETS: *The Northern Passion*, ed. Frances A. Foster (1913, 1916) and supplement, ed. Wilhelm Heuser and Frances A. Foster (1930); *The Southern Passion*, ed. Beatrice Daw Brown (1927); *A Stanzaic Life of Christ*, ed. Frances A. Foster (1926); John Mirk, *Festial: A Collection of Homilies*, ed. Theodor Erbe (1905).

Scholarship and Criticism.

Chambers, *MS* is the most comprehensive account. Craig, *ERD* is a survey of the scholarly work on the plays as well as a critical study. Young, *DMC* examines liturgical drama and provides texts of the Latin plays.

Of the critical books, the following discuss some of the aspects included in this essay: Owst, *L–P* (see Chapter 8, 'Sermon and Drama'); Rossiter, *EDET* (see Chapter 4, 'Gothic Drama'); E. M. Salter, *Medieval Drama in Chester* (Toronto, 1955; see Lecture 4, 'A Great Reckoning', for an appreciation of the *Innocents* and *Passion*); Williams, *DME*; Prosser, *DR* (includes a chapter on the Cain plays); Anderson, *Imagery*; Kolve, *PCC*; and Murray Roston, *Biblical Drama in England from the Middle Ages to the Present Day* (London, 1968; see Chapter 1, 'The Medieval Stage'). The editorial matter in the editions cited should also be consulted, together with that in A. C. Cawley, *The Wakefield Pageants in the Townley Cycle* and R. G. Thomas, *Ten Miracle Plays*.

Abbreviation.
SP—Studies in Philology

VIII

Violence in the English Miracle Plays

T. W. CRAIK

I

ONE OF the most striking features of English medieval drama is its inclusiveness. Not only are many stories included in the miracle cycles with their vast scope from Creation to Doomsday, but also no incident is excluded from any story on the grounds that it is too theatrically difficult or aesthetically indecorous to be presented. It does not, of course, follow from this statement that the cycles are unselective in construction and crude in treatment. Their construction, it is generally agreed, is deliberate: subjects are not chosen casually, nor even for their dramatic capabilities, but because they combine into a celebration of the Redemption: 'For as in Adam all die, even so in Christ shall all be made alive' (II *Corinthians* 15, 20). There is less agreement upon their merit.

No discussion of the way the miracle plays treat their material can neglect the material itself and its origins. The plays depend heavily on their sources: this, at least, is a matter of fact. They are essentially dramatizations of parts of the Bible, augmented at times with detail that had accumulated round it during the Middle Ages. To read through a complete cycle is to recognize that the playwrights are fundamentally translators or transposers, turning narrative into drama. It is easy to lose sight of this fact when recollecting certain remarkable plays, such as the Towneley *Second Shepherds' Play* or the Hegge *Woman taken in Adultery*, plays in which the dramatist has either added quite new material or greatly amplified the material he inherited. The Chester *Creation* is more typical: in God's address to the Serpent, the only departures from the Biblical original are caused by the pressure of rhyme:

> Upon thy breast thou shalt goe,
> And eate the earth, to and froe.

This speech was too well known and too well authorized to be alterable, as Milton also was to find:

> Upon thy belly grovelling thou shalt go,
> And dust shalt eat all the days of thy life.

In that second line he writes (in a different sense from Blake's) in fetters, though his verse reasserted itself in 'Her seed shall bruise thy head, thou bruise his heel'. The Chester playwright, working in his simpler medium, seems to feel no fetters and, here at least, performs versification rather than composes poetry.

If the Bible had been as specific at every point as it is here (*Genesis* 3), the playwrights, one might think, need never have felt the necessity of dramatic creation. It might be argued that dramatic creation was thrust upon them by the need to fill out their sometimes scanty material: hence Noah's Wife and the Shepherds. Yet this explanation alone will not do, for there is no lack of material in *Genesis* 6–9 for a play about the Flood (as can be seen from the Hegge version, in which Noah's Wife is no less serious than her husband). Evidently the comic rebelliousness of Noah's Wife clamoured to get in, from popular tradition, just as the pathos of Isaac, implicit in the story of Abraham's sacrifice (*Genesis* 22), invited development.

The difference between plays on the same subject from various cycles (as in the case of the Hegge *Noah* just mentioned) shows that the medieval playwright was not the slave of his material: 'His basic story was dictated but he was clearly free to modify, rearrange, omit, and add'; he 'could, if he chose, change details and even modify major traditions'.[1] Nevertheless, it is far more characteristic of him to follow some tradition than to deviate from tradition altogether.

The tradition he followed need not, as has been said, be authorized by Scripture: the church services (the liturgy), apocryphal additions to the New Testament, Biblical commentaries and expositions, sermons, collections of religious stories such as the *Golden Legend*, vernacular verse narratives like the *Northern Passion*, all originated or transmitted material for his use, so that it is important to remember that he is not necessarily, nor even probably, inventing when he goes beyond the Biblical account which is his starting-point.

---

[1] Prosser, *DT*, pp. 16, 185.

And when the pit was made wele depe,
Ilkone toke till other kepe,
And up thai lifted the cros all
And sethin fast thai lete it fall
Into the pit to eke his paynes,
That sunder rafe both sins and vaynes;
And thai schogged it till and fra
On all manere to wirk him wa;
When it was sett so doune at anes,
Thai pinned it fast with mekill stanes.

These lines from the *Northern Passion* (p. 193) narrate an incident that was later dramatized in the Cornish, York and Towneley Crucifixion plays. In the Yorkshire plays Christ then speaks from the cross, requiring the passers-by to witness how he suffers for the sin of mankind: this appeal derives from a liturgical dialogue between Christ and Man, *O vos omnes qui transitis*, and is also to be found in the *Northern Passion* (p. 204).

The subject of violence in the miracle plays is therefore bound up with these considerations of tradition, selection, originality, and the development of pathos and of comedy; and it must also be considered in relation to medieval stage practice, which entailed the representation in action of everything that could possibly be so represented. It is because of its general bearing on medieval drama and on the medieval mind (in so far as either of these can be considered as a distinct thing) that this violence calls for discussion, even though there is relatively little of it in any single miracle cycle. The plays presenting the murder of Abel, the massacre of the Innocents, and the sufferings and death of Christ are the only ones which consistently introduce it as an indispensable element in the story. Into most of the stories it could not be introduced, nor is the attempt made to include it in any treatment of the Last Judgment, where the damned are sent to Hell but are not shown suffering its torments. Apart from the incidents mentioned, and (when they are included) Judas's suicide and Cain's accidental death at the hand of the blind archer Lamech, the violence is comic violence: the quarrel in Hell between Lucifer and the other fallen angels, who finally chase him out (York I); the conflict between Noah and his Wife (Chester III, York IX, Towneley III); Cain's cuffing his servant (Towneley II) or an angel (York VII); the wrestling of the Shepherds (Chester VII, where their servant-boy throws each of them in turn), or their tossing of Mak in a blanket (Towneley XIII). Such comic violence will not be discussed here, excepting Cain's, which is a curious element in a play in which he also murders his brother.

I propose, however, to postpone discussion of the murder of Abel (even though it comes earlier in the cycles) till after I have considered the Massacre of the Innocents and the Passion. I shall deal with these three dramatic subjects, noticing their treatment in the various cycles, rather than discussing violence at (say) Chester or York, for the obvious reason that the cycles are of composite authorship and indeed show revision within individual plays at times, a point which will have some effect on their interpretation.

II

Although the composition of the cycles in their present condition occupied a lengthy period in the fourteenth and fifteenth centuries, this period can allowably be regarded as one single age, the late medieval. Its drama has been called Gothic Drama by the late A. P. Rossiter, and he and many others have drawn attention to the resemblances between this drama and the pictorial art of the time. In both is an 'unflinching realism', a stress on the physical suffering of those who endure martyrdom and the brutality of those who inflict it. This development has often been connected with the preaching tradition of the late Middle Ages, which called men to a love of Christ and repentance of their sins by pointing out the sufferings he endured for their redemption. It is a view which is inherently probable, and should be kept in mind, though we ought not to neglect another probability, namely that in portraying realistic violence and brutal character the dramatic and pictorial artists were eagerly practising their art and exulting in their skill. In the case of the miracle plays, performed as a public festival before a lay audience, we may also try to guess, from the texts before us, what sort of drama was appropriate to that occasion and that audience.

How extreme might be the difference between a miracle play, performed under these conditions, and a Latin liturgical play on the same subject, performed in church by clerics and choristers, can be seen by comparing their treatments of the Massacre of the Innocents. The Biblical source is *Matthew* 2: the story does not appear in the other Gospels.

Four liturgical plays on this subject survive, from Laon, Limoges, Fleury and Freising. Their texts are given in full, and their content summarized, in Karl Young's *Drama of the Medieval Church*, Vol. II, Chap. 20. The following points are notable.

The Innocents are not babes in arms (of 'two years old and under', *Matthew* 2, 16), but are impersonated by boy choristers. This enables them, during their massacre, to complain to God (at Laon and Fleury), '*Quare non defendis sanguinem nostrum?*' To which an Angel responds, '*Adhuc sustinete modicum tempus, donec impleatur numerus fratrum vestrorum.*' Both these speeches come from the liturgy of matins of Innocents' Day.

They are slain in a stylized manner. This is apparent from their exchange with the Angel, and also from the fact that, in the Freising version, the one Armiger who kills all of them says (evidently to each in turn), '*Disce mori, puer.*'

The role of their mothers is undeveloped during the massacre. In only one of the plays (Fleury) do they intercede for their children, and then only with a single line: '*Oremus, tenere natorum parcite vite.*' Afterwards, however, there is in all versions a lyrical dialogue of some length between Rachel (a representative mother) and her comforters ('Rachel weeping for her children, and would not be comforted, because they are not', *Matthew* 2, 18).

The violence of Herod's character, though already present in the Fleury play, is not yet extreme: on hearing of the Three Kings' departure he wrathfully attempts suicide with a sword, but is prevented and calmed by his attendants. This is in dumb-show. In the only play where he dies (also Fleury), he does so unsensationally and again without dialogue: his body is then removed, and his son silently enthroned in his place, while an Angel addresses the dead Innocents and raises them up to partake of eternal life.

In English medieval drama the Massacre of the Innocents exists in a particularly large number of versions, for besides being included in all four cycles it figures also in one of the two Coventry plays and one of the four Digby plays. I wish to concentrate here upon the Chester version before comparing some of its elements with those in the other versions, partly because in its extant form it gives the fullest account of the story, and partly because this form in which it has come down to us raises an interesting question about its composition.

The Chester *Slaying of the Innocents* is a play of 496 lines, a medium

length for this cycle. Herod determines to make sure of killing the
newborn King of the Jews by destroying all the male infants in Bethlehem. Through a messenger he summons his two knights and gives
them their charge. They despise their task but undertake it, boast of
their valour, and depart. An angel appears to Joseph, warns him to flee
with Mary and the child, and leads them into Egypt (where, in silence,
an image falls, representing the overthrow of the pagan gods by
Christ's coming). Herod's two knights encounter two women and in
spite of their resistance kill their babies. The second woman then
reveals that her child was Herod's own son whom she was nursing.
She immediately complains to Herod, who is furious at the knights'
mistake and upbraids her for not preventing the child's death, which
he recognizes as a divine vengeance upon him. Herod is now himself
surprised by death: his legs and his arms rot, he foresees his damnation,
and he dies. A devil enters, addresses the audience, and takes him to Hell.
The angel tells Joseph that his enemy is now dead, bids him return
with his wife and the child to Judaea, and accompanies their departure
by singing '*Ex Egipto vocavi filium meum, ut salvum faciet populum
meum*'.

The falling of the pagan idols, the punishment of Herod in the
death of his child, and the nature of his own last illness, are all traditional and not invented by the playwright. They are narrated in the
fourteenth-century *Stanzaic Life of Christ*, a work compiled at Chester,
probably by a monk of St. Werburgh's Abbey, and known to have
influenced the cycle.

The playwright's energies have gone into treatment, not into plot.
He particularly dwells upon the two Knights, to whom he gives
resounding names, Sir Waradrake and Sir Grimball Launcher-deep.
There is, incidentally, some confusion about their names, for the
messenger has summoned them as 'Sir Grimbalde and Sir Launcher
depe'. Presumably the later combination of these two names into one,
and the invention of the other name, occurred during composition or
revision. They brag to the spectators as well as to the king, under-
lining their boastfulness by insisting that they never boast; and though
Herod gravely agrees, without visible ironic intent, that Samson
would be no match for them, they are obviously being prepared for
inglorious action. Encountering the two women, they are met with
contemptuous abuse such as 'rotten hunter' (rat-catcher) and 'tode',
and are threatened with blows.

> This distaff and thy head shall meete,
> Or we hethen gone!

exclaims one woman, and she exhorts her companion:

> Their basenetis be big and broad;
> Beates on now! Letis se!

The thwack of distaff upon helmeted head belongs to farce: it points
forward towards Udall's *Roister Doister*. All this is in the first part of the
encounter. It seems to me, indeed, that this first part was originally
the whole encounter. Its concluding lines run as follows:

Secundus Miles	Dame, thy sonne, in good fay,
	He must of me learne a play:
	He must hop, or I goe away,
	Upon my speare ende.
Prima Mulier	Out! Out! and well away!
	That ever I abode this day!
	One stroke yet I will assay
	To geve, or that I wende.
Secunda Mulier	Out! Out! on thee, theefe!
	My love, my lord, my lief, my leefe!
	Did never man nor woman greefe,
	To suffer such torment!
	But yet wroken I wil be: *avenged*
	Have here one, two, and three,
	Beare the king this from me,
	And that I it hym sende!

$$(X, 321-36)$$

As I read these lines, their sense is that the babies are promptly killed
and their mothers depart, leaving the Knights to go and report to
Herod. But there now follow another 56 lines leading into the Second
Woman's complaint to Herod, and in this passage (besides stage-
directions instructing the Knights to kill the first and second boys)
there is more lamentation, more anger venting itself in blows, a
repetition of the 'hop-upon-my-spear' jest, and a lively denial from
one woman that her baby is a boy:

> He hath II holes under the tayle;
> Kyss and thou may assay!

It is difficult to decide what total effect, if any, the writer or writers of this protracted scene of the killing intended it to create. There is certainly more excitement than pathos, and the excitement is heavily coloured with grotesque humour: this would be true even if the second part were not included.

In making the incident a scene of physical conflict the Chester version resembles most of the others. Only the Hegge version limits its two women to lamentation and omits all dialogue between them and the soldiers. At York, the First Soldier apprehensively cries

> As armes! For nowe is nede;   i.e. 'Aux armes'
> But yf we do yone dede,
> Ther quenys will quelle us here.

and the First Woman says that she would be unwilling to let them go 'harmeles', evidently attacking them, since the First Soldier expresses dismay:

> The devell myght spede you bothe,
> False wicchis, are ye woode?[2]   mad

The Coventry version begins with tenderness and pathos: the three mothers sing the famous 'Coventry carol', and one of them rocks her child in her arms to keep it from crying (and betraying its presence?), while another has the moving prayer

> Thatt babe thatt ys borne in Bedlem, so meke,
> He save my chyld and me from velany!

(This is the only version in which the women are aware of Herod's order before the soldiers come.) When the soldiers announce their intent, each woman speaks a stanza: the first appeals to their pity and chivalry; the second threatens them, and deals 'a stroke' to a 'fawls losyngere' ('deceiver'); the third says,

> Sytt he neyver soo hy in saddull,
> But I schall make his braynis addull,
> And here with my pott-ladull
>   With hym woll I fyght.

[2] A few further notes may be added. 'Ye slee my semely sone' (195) is premature, in view of 204-6, so 'ye slee' presumably means 'you are going to slay'. 222-5 seems wrongly distributed: I would give 222-4 to a Woman, leaving 225 for the Soldier. The soldiers leave the women at 225; what follows is the women's afterword; then, at 233, the soldiers are on their way to Herod.

> I schall ley on hym, as thogh I wode were,
> With thys same womanly geyre;
> There schall noo man steyre,
> Wheddur thatt he be kyng or knyght.

These three stanzas form a sequence, with a final deliberate descent into the grotesque ('thys same womanly geyre' drawing attention to the incongruity of the weapon). The author, though we may question his judgment, obviously knew what he was about. So did the author of the Digby play, the principal dramatic interest of which comes from the un-Biblical character Watkyn. Watkyn, Herod's messenger (thus is he worked into the traditional structure of the piece) has asked the king for a knighthood and has been sent on the Knights' mission to prove his valour. He says he will be happy to kill children but is afraid of the mothers and their distaffs; when the encounter takes place, one woman threatens to dub him knight with her distaff. '*Hic occident pueros*', the women lament and wish Herod a shameful death, Watkyn calls them traitors, and finally the long-awaited distaffs come into play:

> *1 Mulier* What, thu Javell, canst not have do?
> Thu and thi cumpany shall not depart
> Tyll of our distavys ye have take part:
> Therfor ley on gossippes with a mery hart,
> And lett them not from us goo.

'Ley on gossippes with a mery hart'! It might be Noah's Wife speaking. This play develops the semi-comic conflict between the braggart soldier and the warlike woman, which we have found at Chester, and exploits it heartily: 'Here thei shall bete Watkyn, and the knyghtes shall come to rescue hym.' One can imagine the stage action.

These plays (all but Hegge) show an uneasy mixture of pathos and farce in their treatment of their violent subject: the pathos, implicit in the story, is usually sketched in and left to look after itself (here Coventry, where the pathos is anticipatory, is the exception), while the farce is somewhat worked up. Naturally, the central action is not at all farcical but horrifying: the babies are stabbed with 'knyffe' (York), decapitated with 'swappynge swerde' (Hegge), impaled upon spears (Chester, Hegge). This brings us back to stage action.

The babies were, of course, dummies, swaddled bundles, stage properties. It is unfortunate that we have no information, other than what we can guess from the text, about their composition and how they were used. Miss M. D. Anderson, who gives instances of the incident in glass and wall-painting, comments on the Chester dialogue, 'By shaking a spitted dummy its death agonies could have been suggested with some verisimilitude, even if the producer stopped short of the disgusting realism of a sixteenth-century pageant about St. Thomas' martyrdom, given at Canterbury, when a leather bag full of blood was used.'[3] One hopes, indeed, that he did stop short of this, and we may support our hope by reflecting that the Chester play was intended for multiple repetition in the course of the day. Surely the performers would want to restrict the messiness? (Decapitation, which perhaps does call for messiness, is found only in the Hegge cycle, which is believed not to have repeated its plays in the manner of processional cycles.) The alternative to realism is stylization, and to this (even in the Hegge version) I rather incline. It would accord with the whole treatment of the massacre in the version I have not yet mentioned, Towneley.

In the Towneley version Herod's three knights arrive at Bethlehem. The first accosts a woman who enters with her child in her arms, laconically excusing himself for killing the baby; she resists and strikes him, but he kills the child; then she laments and calls for vengeance. This pattern is then repeated by the second and third knights and two other women. Finally it is the knights who drive out the women, not, as in most other versions, the other way round.

The Towneley play is the work of the Wakefield Master, and his distinctive stanza is well fitted both to the give-and-take of conflict and the rhetoric of lamentation:

> *3 Miles*　This is well-wroght gere that ever may be.
> Comys hederward here! Ye nede not to fle.

> *3 Mulier*　Wyll ye do any dere to my chyld and me?　　　　*harm*

> *3 Miles*　He shall dy, I the swere; his hart-blood shall thou se.

> *3 Mulier*　God forbede!
> Thefe, thou shedys my chyldys blood!
> Out, I cry! I go nere wood!
> Alas, my hart is all on flood,
> 　To se my chyld thus blede.

> By God, thou shall aby this dede that thou has done.
> 　　　　　　　　　　　　　　　　　　　　　　　*pay for*

---

[3] *Imagery*, p. 136, referring to Chambers, *MS*, Vol. II, p. 345.

3 Miles   I red the not, stry, by son and by moyn.   *hag*

3 Mulier Have at the, say I! Take the ther a foyn!   *thrust*

Out on the, I cry! Have at thi groyn
   An othere!
This kepe I in store.

3 Miles   Peasse now, no more!

3 Mulier I cry and I rore,
   Out on the, mans mordere!

Alas, my bab, myn Innocent, my fleshly get (for sorow!)
That God me derly sent! (Of bales who may me borow?)
                                misfortunes
Thy body is all to-rent! I cry, both even and morow,
Veniance for thi blod thus spent! 'Out!' I cry, and 'horow!'

1 Miles   Go lightly!   *quickly*
Gett out of thise wonys,   *place*
Ye trattys, all at onys,
Or by Cokys dere bonys
I make you go wyghtly!   *forcibly*
                               (XVI, 370–96)

This version seems to me the best treatment of the massacre. Its formal design controls the violence that the language insists upon (again I think there is no need to take the references to blood as a literal reflection of the stage action). The mothers' natural instinct to defend and revenge their children is dramatized, but without descending too steeply into a farce that is destructive of pathos. The Knights are not turned into grotesque comic braggarts, again to the destruction of the theme's seriousness. It is, I suppose, possible that the farcical elements, in the plays where they occur, spring not only from simple delight in farce but also from embarrassment over the dummy babies: at least, if the audience laughed, it would be at the Knights, not at the play. However, I doubt whether the authors can be credited with that kind of artistic self-consciousness. More likely, if we need any ulterior motive, the farce may be a crude form of comic relief, a safety-valve for high emotional excitement.

It goes without saying that audiences would pity the mothers and children. John Mirk's *Festial*, an early fifteenth-century book of sermons fitted to the use of parish priests on holy days, uses the

Innocents as an example of loving one's enemies: 'For thay dydden lagh on hom that slowen hem, and playde wyth hor hondes when thay seen hor bryght swerdes schyne' (p. 29). The poignancy of this picture was, by reason of the limitations of stage performance, inaccessible to the authors of the plays.

III

The Passion sequence occupies a number of plays, and possesses a focal interest, in all the cycles. I cannot, in the space at my disposal, discuss these plays in detail, but it may be that a broad discussion will not only be clearer but also more appropriate than a detailed one, since, though distinctions can be made between one cycle and another, and between one dramatist and another, these are relatively fine distinctions when we consider the massive resemblances. The copiousness of the source-material (Biblical and non-Biblical), and the reverence demanded in portraying the character of Christ, established a manner of treatment from which the dramatists would have found it difficult to depart even if they had wished to do so.

The liturgical Passion plays employed the dialogue of the New Testament augmented with *planctus* (lyrical laments) expressing the emotions of Christ and the Virgin Mary. Texts and descriptions of two such plays from Benediktbeuern are given in Young's *Drama of the Medieval Church*, Vol. I, Chap. 16. The first, which is short, dramatizes Christ's capture and his crucifixion, but not the mocking and scourging. The second, which is long, gives the whole sequence. No dialogue accompanies the ill-treatment of Christ other than the Biblically-authorized '*Ave, rex Judeorum*' and '*Prophetiza, quis est, qui te percussit?*; the scourging ('*Tunc ducitur Jhesus ad flagellandum*') and the nailing to the cross ('*Tunc Jesus suspendatur in cruce*') are indicated by stage-directions which are simply transferred from the Biblical narrative and do not concern themselves with stage technique.

By contrast, the miracle plays are much concerned with the mechanics of torture and execution. The dropping of the cross into its mortice to jar Christ's hanging body has already been noticed in connection with its earlier mention in the *Northern Passion*. The same work's account of the nailing to the cross is full of similar non-Biblical detail, as a summary will show. Christ (we are told) was stripped and laid upon the cross, which was on the ground. His hands came a foot short of the holes the executioners had made for the nails. They were unwilling to bore fresh holes, so they fastened a rope to each of his hands, so tightly that the blood burst out, and pulled them to the holes, so that his sinews burst asunder. After nailing his hands, they tied another rope to his feet, and another to his breast (or, according to one manuscript, sat on his breast), and drew down his feet a span long, over the hole, so that his legs were broken. The blood ran from his body and, according to one manuscript, from his mouth (pp. 186–92).

The account is adopted, in less or more detail, by all four English cycles and the Cornish Cycle. It would be doubly recommended, firstly as being the accepted account (the earlier *Southern Passion*, c. 1275–85, in which the cross is already standing when Christ is nailed to it, is exceptional), and, secondly, as offering opportunities for action and dialogue. The ropes also may have assisted with the practical difficulties in staging the Crucifixion, so that the soldiers could 'tie Jesus firmly to the Cross and then pretend to drive home the nails': this is suggested by Miss Anderson (*Imagery*, pp. 147–8), who gives instances of church art showing the nail driven between Christ's fingers, beside his wrist, or in such a position that he grasps it within his hand. These representations, as she says, may reflect contemporary stage practice. The crown of thorns, she likewise notes, is thrust on to Christ's head 'with forkys' in the Hegge cycle, as is also shown in church sculpture (p. 215): this detail is found also in one of the manuscripts of the *Northern Passion*:

> With staves of rede thai set it doun,
> And clapped it fast untill his crowne,
> So that the thornes went in than
> Till thai perced the hern pan.[4]

The image in this last line, traceable to the meditations of St. Bernard of Clairvaux, arrested the attention of the playwrights (York XXXIII, 400–02; Towneley XXII, 233–4; Cornish *Passio*, 2118–20). Put in the mouths of Christ's tormentors, it expressed their cruelty as well as his suffering.

Their cruelty, a necessary element in the story, is dramatized with

[4] EETS edn., p. 125. The similar passage in the *Stanzaic Life*, which contains the reference to St. Bernard and a quotation from him, is at 5977–88 (EETS edn., pp. 202–3). G. R. Owst quotes a contemporary sermon with the same detail (*L–P*, p. 508).

vigour, and some would say with an unhealthy relish. At York
(XXXIII) they scourge Christ to the accompaniment of brutal alli-
teration:

   1 Miles Rehete hym I rede you with rowtes and rappes!   *revive*

   2 Miles For all oure noy, this nygard he nappes.   *annoying*

   3 Miles We sall wakken hym with wynde of oure whippes.

   4 Miles Nowe flynge to this flaterer with flappes.

The buffeting is a scornful game. In Hegge's version, making use of
what looks like a children's rhyme, one Jew cries,

> A and now wole I a newe game begynne,
> þat we mon pley at, all þat arn here-inne.
> Whele and pylle, whele and pylle,
> Comyth to hall ho so wylle.
> Ho was þat?

> (XXIX, 168–72)

In Towneley XXI, correspondingly, we have 'We shall teche hym, I
wote, a new play of Yoyll' ('Yule'—344). This cruel playfulness is
also alluded to in medieval sermons; and ill-treatment is often called
a 'game', in medieval literature, as a form of sarcastic humour.[5] Many
examples could be produced from the cycles of this use of 'play' and
its synonyms: the Chester knight's 'he must of me learne a play' will be
recalled. In the Towneley Crucifixion, the Torturers develop an
elaborate jocular conceit whereby Christ is to joust in a tournament and
the cross is to be his steed. It has been noted by Arnold Williams[6]
that this metaphor was used seriously in contemporary religious
allegory, in *Piers Plowman*, for example. The dramatist, one supposes,
was aware of this, and the correspondence was not simple coincidence.
Whether, therefore, he intended the Torturers (by dramatic irony) to
glorify Christ by an unconscious allusion to his victory over death
and Hell, or was merely adapting an allegorical commonplace to an
irreligious joke, is open to discussion. Even if the latter is the case, it

[5] See T. McAlindon, 'Comedy and Terror in Middle English Literature:
the Diabolical Game', *MLR* 60 (1965), pp. 323–32. For medieval sermons, see
Owst, *L–P*, p. 510.
[6] Williams, *DME*, p. 129.

may be further debated whether he was dramatizing irreverence or being irreverent himself.

IV

Leaving aside that discussion for the present, together with the function and actual dramatic effect of these violent scenes in the Passion plays, we may turn next to the plays on the murder of Abel (*Genesis* 4). Cain's act of violence, by contrast with the deliberate protracted brutality of the Passion, is impulsive and momentary, a single blow with (according to the medieval English tradition) a jaw-bone. It is the accompanying elements, in some of the Cain and Abel plays, of comedy and irreverence which make them relevant to the comedy and irreverence we have found in some of the Innocents' and Passion plays.

In the Chester cycle, the story concludes the second play, *The Creation*. In marked contrast to this cycle's *Innocents*, this play is all of a piece and a work of undoubted seriousness: only Cain's departing curse to the audience hints at the author's knowledge of more boisterous treatments, if any such existed in his time.[7] God's intervention, coming straight after Cain's defiant exclamation that not God himself could defend Abel (which immediately precedes the fatal blow), is a dramatic stroke. The Hegge version is also sober and serious; but it is dramatically inferior to the Chester play, in spite of a few verbal felicities, one of which is Cain's epigrammatic argument of the uselessness of sacrificing his best corn to God:

> He wyll neyther ete nor drynke
> Ffor he doth neyther swete ne swynke.

Cain's irreverence is developed into a principal theme in the York and especially the Towneley versions. Thus Towneley:

Abell Came, of God me thynke thou has no drede.

[7] See the last three lines of the York version (as well as the end of its interpolation, quoted on p. 190), and Towneley's 443-8 (from Cain's boy) and 468-70 (from Cain himself):

> Ever ill myght hym befall
> That theder me commend,
> This tyde,

which, I take it, refers not to God but to any member of the audience who shouts 'good riddance'.

Came Now and he get more, the dwill me spede!—
 As mych as oone reepe—   *shea,*
 For that cam hym full light chepe;
 Not as mekill, grete ne small,
 As he myght wipe his ars withall.

           (II, 233–8)

This Cain goes on to deride God when the latter makes a first
appearance to reprove him for quarrelling with his brother and offering inadequate sacrifice:

  Whi, who is that hob-over-the-wall?
  We! who was that that piped so small?
  Com, go we hens, for perels all;
   God is out of hys wit!

           (297–300)

Soon after this he tells Abel that he will pay him out for pleasing God
with his sacrifice:

  With cheke-bon, or that I blyn,   *cease*
  Shal I the and thy life twyn;   *part*
  So, lig down ther and take thi rest;
  Thus shall shrewes be chastysed best.

Abell Veniance, veniance, Lord, I cry!
 For I am slayn, and not gilty.

Caym Yei, ly ther, old shrew! ly ther, ly!
 And if any of you thynk I did amys
 I shal it amend wars then it is,
  That all men may it se:
 Well wars then it is,
  Right so shall it be.
 Bot now, syn he is broght on slepe,
 Into som hole fayn wold I crepe.
 For ferd I qwake, and can no rede;   *afraid*
 For be I taken, I be bot dede.
 Here will I lig thise fourty dayes,
 And I shrew hym that me fyrst rayse.

Deus Caym, Caym!

Caym Who is that that callis me?
 I am yonder, may thou not se?

Deus Caym, where is thi brother Abell?

Caym What askys thou me? I trow at hell:
    At hell I trow he be—
    Whoso were ther then myght he se—
    Or somwher fallen on slepyng;
    When was he in my kepyng?

Deus Caym, Caym, thou was wode.
    The voyce of thi brotherys blode
    That thou has slayn on fals wise,
    From erth to heven venyance cryse.
    And, for thou has broght thi brother downe,
    Here I gif the my malison.   *malediction*

Caym Yei, dele aboute the, for I will none,
    Or take it the when I am gone.

                                  (324–57)

The murder is set in a spirited and utterly indecorous context. Cain's only fear, in spite of his perfunctory later allusions to his damnation, is of human vengeance. He treats God's momentous and traditional question with impatience (Can't God see where he is? Doesn't God know the answer?) and contempt (like Hamlet's 'seek him in the other place yourself'), and he declines the curse, saying that he will leave it behind him for God to collect again. Add to this irreverence his cool euphemisms that Abel is now resting or put to sleep and the comic-sinister indirectness of his threat to the audience; take into account the jaunty tail-rhyme movement of 'At hell I trow he be', and it is clear that the incident is neither serious nor serio-comic, but is written for laughs the whole time. Cain's habitual obscenities addressed to Abel, and the fisticuffs which he exchanges with his irrepressible boy-servant both before and after the murder, reinforce this impression.

The York version is incomplete and has moreover undergone revision. It begins seriously enough, with an Angel relating to Cain and Abel the creation, the fall of the bad angels, and the making of mankind in their place, in gratitude for which mankind should sacrifice to God. Abel gives a meek assent, Cain an aggressive refusal. Here the manuscript breaks off, to resume with Cain's comic servant Brewbarret bringing sheaves, and Cain threatening him for his slowness.[8] I

8   Come up, syr, for by my thryst   [*for* thryft],
          Ye shall drynke or ye goo.

'Drynke' is a contraction of the colloquial phrase 'drink on the whip': see agree with those who place this episode after the murder. Perhaps the sheaves were to hide the body, for Cain conceals it 'with this gresse' in the Hegge version, and in the Towneley play calls his boy to help bury it. At this point the Angel enters and asks where Abel is:

Ang.   Thowe cursyd Came, where is Abell?
Where hais thowe done thy broder dere?

Cayme What askes thowe me that taill to tell?
For yit his keper was I never.

Ang.   God hais sent the his curse downe,
Fro hevyn to hell, *maldictio dei.*

Cayme Take that thy self, evyn on thy crowne,
Quia non sum custos fratris mei,
To tyne.

Ang.   God hais sent the his malyson,
And inwardly I geve the myne.

Cayme The same curse light on thy crowne,
And right so myght it worth and be.
For he that sent that gretyng downe,
The devyll myght speyd both hym and the.
Fowl myght thowe fall!
Here is a cankerd company,
Therefore Goddes curse light on you all.   (VII, 82–98)

Here the interpolation ends, a botched stanza follows, and three more stanzas closely paraphrasing *Genesis* 4, 11–15, with Cain's valedictory curse to the audience, conclude the play. Cain's interlocutor in this last exchange is still given as the Angel, but from the nature of the botching (see ll. 103–5, 107) it is virtually certain that these speeches of his originally belonged to God, as they do in *Genesis* and in all the other cycles' treatment of the incident. Miss Prosser's reason for the substitution of the Angel for God is convincing: the playwright 'wants Cain to strike back physically at the curse-giver' and 'he certainly could not strike God'.[9]

From her survey of the Cain and Abel plays Miss Prosser concludes

---

T. W. Craik in *Notes and Queries*, July 1953, p. 279, and compare 'Ye shal lik on the whyp' in Towneley's *Noah*, 378. Cain is not offering him a drink; the error 'thryst (thirst)' springs from this misapprehension.

[9] Prosser, *DR*, p. 75.

that the Chester play is not only the most completely adapted to its religious purpose but also the best drama, while 'the late comic revisions in the York and Towneley cycles are bad drama because they are chaotic in intent and effect'.[10] In the same chapter of her book she extends her view to the violent scenes of the Passion plays, in the York and Towneley versions of which, she says, 'the torture scenes are so expanded that the entire Passion sequence appears to be thrown out of focus' and there is a danger that the audience may concentrate on the sensational actions and on the grotesque humour of the torturers rather than on the central sufferer himself.[11]

Miss Prosser's argument, which she presents with conviction and skill, demands serious consideration, and is a good starting-point to the discussion of the plays under review. Disproportion, unrestraint, and a damagingly unconventional treatment of Cain's relationship with God, are surely undeniable characteristics of the Towneley *Murder of Abel*.[12] Cain is, of course, duly condemned to exile at the end, and propriety is satisfied: but it can hardly be doubted that the playwright wanted to amuse the spectators, not to edify them. His use of colloquialism and local allusion shows that he knew his audience. The miracle play being, one supposes, his only available dramatic vehicle, he used it for his own purposes. I do not think these purposes were blasphemous, even though blasphemy is employed to raise a laugh, and though the laugh is at God's expense (as, in the York play, it is at the Angel's). Could the play have been presented, and presumably enjoyed, if all parties had not felt the irresponsible treatment of God to be quite innocent? Children, after all, have been known to mock their fathers without hating them, and there is something childish (not necessarily in a derogatory sense) in both the obscenity and the blasphemy. It is a strand in medieval humour, this humanizing ('God lukit and saw hir lattin in [the ale-loving Kynd Kittok into heaven] and lewch his hert sair'), and even ridiculing, of God the Father. '1591. April 19th. Andrew Brunner, a citizen and glass worker of Ayldorff, during a great storm when it was thundering loudly, blasphemed and railed against the Almighty, called him an old Rascal, said that the old Fool had gambled away his money and lost it at cards,

[10] *Ibid.*, p. 88.   [11] *Ibid.*, p. 85.
[12] I am confirmed in this opinion by John Gardner's unsuccessful attempt to prove the contrary ('Theme and Irony in the Wakefield *Mactacio Abel*', *PMLA* 80 (1965), pp. 515–21.

and now wished to win it back by playing at bowls.' For this flight of fancy, I am sorry to say, Brunner was severely punished by the Nuremberg authorities.[13]

V

All this may appear a digression from my main subject, violence, but it is not, for the treatment of God the Father in the Towneley *Murder of Abel* bears upon the treatment of God the Son in the Passion sequence of this and the other cycles. In Pilate's judgment-hall and at Calvary, Christ is mocked by his tormentors:

> 4 *Judeus* On lofte, sere hoberd, now ye be sett,   *clown*
> We wyll no lenger with you lett;
> We grete you wel on the newe gett,   *fashion*
> And make on you a mowe.   *grimace*
>
> 1 *Judeus* We grete you wel with a scorn,
> And pray you bothe evyn and morn,
> Take good eyd to oure corn,   *heed*
> And chare awey the crowe.   *drive*
>
> (Hegge *Crucifixion: PP* II, 883–90)

In his well-known discussion of 'ambivalence' in medieval drama, A. P. Rossiter compared the York and Towneley Passion plays with Bosch's paintings of Christ mocked, and noted the juxtaposition of pathos and cruel humour; in this juxtaposition he detected 'the presence of two rituals at once, of which the one is the negation of the faith to which the piece is ostensibly devoted. The very values of martyrdom—of *any* suffering as significant—are implicitly denied by thus making game of it.' He proceeded to define his view more clearly: 'the ambivalence reaches out towards a searching irony'; grotesque comic relief 'derives from that opposite and antithetic world of the diabolical, in which the shadows of primitive paganism survived'; there is 'a positive zest-for-unholiness', 'a ritual of defamation'.[14]

There is no sign, in any part of any cycle, of hostility towards Christianity: as V. A. Kolve convincingly shows,[15] Rossiter misinter-

[13] *A Hangman's Diary: being the Journal of Master Franz Schmidt, Public Executioner of Nuremberg, 1573–1617*, ed. A. Keller (London, 1928), p. 226.

[14] Rossiter, *EDET*, pp. 69–74.

[15] Kolve, *PCC*, pp. 134–9.

preted his historical evidence from the Feast of Fools and the Feast of the Boy Bishop, and took inadequate account of the actual dramatic effect of the Passion scenes, in which the spectators are far from responding approvingly to the Tormentors' self-applauding jokes. Rossiter also adduced, besides the Passion plays, the Towneley *Murder of Abel*: but surely we must distinguish sharply between Cain's mockery of God and the Jews' mockery of Christ. In the Towneley *Murder of Abel*, God embodies spiritual authority: to deride and defy him is therefore a natural, if daring, outlet for comedy, an outlet which Cain's wickedness permits the dramatist. Christ, in the Passion plays, on the contrary, though he is God as well as Man, is the victim of worldly authority: helpless, passive, resigned, his plight excites nothing but pity, which is increased for the thoughtful spectator by the paradox of his omnipotence (to which attention is drawn by the Jews' scornful invitation to work a miracle and come down from the cross). In a sense he directs his own martyrdom, as an incident in the York *Crucifixion* indicates:

> *3 Miles* Have done belyve, boy, and make the boune,
> And bende thi bakke unto this tree.

> *4 Miles* Byhalde, hymselffe has laide hym doune,
> In lengthe and breede as he schulde bee.

The Soldier is surprised: evidently his companion was speaking ironically and they expected to have to hold Christ down by force. But though the Crucifixion is part of the divine scheme for man's redemption, Christ's sufferings both in body and mind are stressed. It has been mentioned that the late Middle Ages stressed his bodily sufferings in order to move the hearer. In the Hegge Passion plays, Christ is beaten 'tyl he is alle blody', and though I do not know how this stage-direction was fulfilled it is clear that the effect was achieved.[16] The mockery is part of his mental suffering.

In their mockery the Jews are, of course, speaking 'in character', as Cain speaks in his irreverence, as Herod, Caiaphas and sometimes Pilate speak in their fury, as Noah's Wife speaks in her rebelliousness, as

---

[16] Neville Denny points out that late medieval artistic representations of the scene (for instance miniatures in Flemish Books of Hours that seem to have been influenced by the drama) invariably show Christ being *birched*, not whipped. It is a relatively easy matter, he goes on, to sprinkle birch-bunches with red dye; easier too to fake a flogging—and each stroke will bead and stripe the victim very convincingly with 'blood'.

G

Isaac speaks in his touching obedience. The medieval playwright's plot, and with it the outlines of character, were laid down for him in advance. Sometimes the story offered good opportunities for developing the characters in it, or for superimposing fresh ones upon it. One cannot imagine Abraham fitted with a comic servant in the plays where he takes Isaac to sacrifice, but it is an easy matter to give Cain a comic servant, as the Towneley dramatist and the York reviser found. Lamech, the blind archer who accidentally shoots and kills Cain, has in the Hegge *Noah* such another 'boy', a rude one who agrees that in his prime Lamech could have hit any mark—if it were half a mile broad and if he stood close to it. This boy guides his aim, and apparently his mistaking Cain for a beast in a bush is genuine. Nevertheless, when Lamech learns what he has done, he beats this 'stynkynge lurdeyn' to death with his bow, without any regrets (at 194, 'these to mennys deth' are the deaths of Abel and Cain, not of Cain and the boy). It is a curious incident. In the Towneley *Buffeting*, the Torturers have a servant appropriately called Froward, whom they send for the stool and the blindfolding cloth, and who grumbles that he gets all the work and bad wages; he then takes his part in buffeting Christ, saying that he will knock the scurf out of his hair: 'I can my hand uphefe and knop out the skalys.' It was in such areas that extension of the material was possible: Christ's own part is hardly expanded beyond what is found in the Gospels and the liturgical plays.

Whether such extension gets out of hand is a matter of critical opinion. Perhaps a case in point is the Towneley *Crucifixion*, when, during the usual stretching of Christ's limbs to fit the holes, the question arises whether each man is pulling his weight, and they each justify themselves by solo exhibitions of strength. I should myself say that the audience's attention is not really allowed to wander. Although in reading the play only the Torturers' dialogue is before our eyes, on the stage Christ suffers silently and centrally all the time, and the pathos is made clear, at suitable intervals, by his lament from the cross and by the long dialogue between the Virgin Mary and St. John. But this is a matter which must be decided for each play by each reader or, ideally, spectator.[17]

[17] The topic is further discussed by Waldo F. McNeir ('The Corpus Christi Passion Plays as Dramatic Art', *SP* 48 (1951), pp. 601-28), who maintains that there are two kinds of relief from extreme tension in these plays, comic distraction and escapist exaggeration, and Kolve (*PCC*), who stresses the

In general, in spite of some instances to the contrary, I think the medieval playwright handled his violence with discretion. It can, indeed, be argued that there is a kind of discretion even in the self-indulgence of the Towneley *Murder of Abel*. Abel's character, it is true, has been cavalierly treated by the dramatist, and Miss Prosser does not exaggerate in saying that he becomes 'a stuffed-shirt' and 'a pompous do-gooder'.[18] Doubtless this was very naughty of the dramatist, and a desertion of his didactic duty, especially as Abel is an acknowledged ante-type of Christ, and his death a prefiguring of the Passion. But no treatment of the story, even the serious and well-controlled one at Chester, can deeply involve the audience's emotions for Abel. Isaac (another ante-type of Christ in his obedience to his father's will) suffers long in mind; Christ himself suffers very long in mind and body; Abel suffers hardly at all—it is all over in a moment. Returning finally for a last look at the Massacre of the Innocents, with which we began, this is why all the business of distaffs and pot-ladles is so unsatisfactory. Every spectator, as I have said, will naturally pity the mothers, and it is unseemly to make their sorrow take the form of grotesque and comic violence. What is wanted is something more like the Virgin Mary at the foot of the cross.

---

formal nature of drama as 'play' or 'game', and also examines the character-ization of the tormentors as ignorant but human sinners who know not what they do.

[18] Prosser, *DR*, p. 78.

Note

Texts.
The texts used and referred to in this chapter are contained in Block, *LC*;
Eccles, *MP*; Furnivall, *DP*; and Norris, *CC*.

Scholarship and Criticism.
The standard and indispensable works of reference are Chambers, and Wickham, *EES*. Southern, *MTR*, is also invaluable to any student of medieval
staging.

Abbreviations.
SD—stage-direction (occurring immediately after the line-number cited)
PP I—Passion Play I
PP II—Passion Play II

IX

The Staging of the Hegge Plays

MARTIAL ROSE

I

THE HEGGE PLAYS, sometimes referred to as the N-town plays or *Ludus Coventriae*, and thought by several modern scholars to belong to Lincoln, comprise a cycle of 42 plays of approximately 11,390 lines in all. A proclamation spoken by three vexillators, or banner-bearers, gives notice of the plays as they are to be performed in successive pageants. There are, however, several discrepancies between this description of the plays and the texts themselves. The plays dealing with St. Anne, the mother of Mary, and those dealing with the Blessed Virgin herself are either not included in the Proclamation at all or are inadequately described. For instance, there is no mention of the Conception of Mary, the Visit to Elizabeth, the Purification or the Assumption of the Virgin. On the other hand, the Trial of Joseph and Mary and the Birth of Christ are described in the Proclamation each by a quatrain, whereas the regular verse form is a thirteen-line stanza. This change in the verse structure might well indicate that reference to these plays was made as a later interpolation within the original Proclamation. In the speech of Contemplacio at the beginning of Passion Play II, for instance, we are given to understand that the two Passion Plays were performed separately in succeeding years:

> The last ȝere we shewyd here how oure lord for love of man
> Cam to þe cety of jherusalem · mekely his deth to take . . .
> Now wolde we procede how he was browth þan
> be-forn Annas and cayphas · and syth beforn pylate   *then*
> And so forth in his passyon . . .

The conclusion that may be drawn from such discrepancies is that the Proclamation in its original form referred to a traditional Corpus Christi cycle of plays. There were subsequent expansions to the cycle, the most significant being the addition of the material relating to

St. Anne and the Virgin Mary. The Passion Plays were also radically refashioned, and played, it would seem, in alternate years. Consequently, evidence for staging derived from the Proclamation would be more applicable to a production of the cycle which antedates by some time the compilation of the manuscript (1468).

The Proclamation is a public advertisement of the plays. The three vexillators tell the citizens of N-town, 'gentyllys and yemanry',

> A sunday next yf þat we may
> At vj of þe belle we gynne oure play   (525–6)

Reference throughout is to performance on pageants—a term that had come to apply to 'show', 'play', 'mansion', and even 'stage' (in our modern sense) fairly indiscriminately, by this time, although no mention is made of trade-guild involvement. But the stanza that describes that part of the Passion Play in which the blind knight, Longeus, is made to thrust with a spear at Christ's side, begins

> we purpose to shewe in oure pleyn place.   (404)

This is the only indication within the Proclamation of an alternative playing area. Apart from this we might assume that the staging was undertaken on separate pageants, each being self-contained. Whether performance was given on movable pageants or in a fixed acting area, there are very many interesting details, relating to the staging contained in the Proclamation. Lucifer, 'þat Angell so gay', we are told, sits on God's throne, but when he is thrown into hell, 'he ffallyth a ffend ful blake'. This calls for a split-second costume change from angel of light to Gothic devil, a transformation that might have been effected by Lucifer casting aside his angel's robes, or having them torn from him by the other angels in his descent, to reveal his devil's garb underneath. A possible further reference to costume in the Proclamation, to Pilate's wife being 'coveryd with clothis al of þe best' (356), *may* suggest something of that lady's richness of dress, but more likely refers to the fabrics her bed is covered in. Both the Prologue of Demon which begins Passion Play I, and the Towneley *Judgment*, though, are full of references to the excesses of contemporary styles. The Damned Souls are traditionally the best-dressed in any Cycle play, and for Pilate's wife nothing-but-the-best would be highly appropriate for a bed-chamber encounter with the Devil.

The Proclamation also provides us with a few hints on staging

methods. The sacrifice of Isaac is to take place 'upon a hill' (87). Is the
hill part of the pageant, or is the hill the pageant itself, and 'the place',
the area in front of the pageant, the main acting space? Or should we
accept Glynne Wickham's suggestion that, as no movable pageant
would be large enough to contain both an acting area and 'a hill',
the pageant containing the hill was possibly placed behind a scaffold
stage which served as the main acting area?[1]

If we could answer these questions satisfactorily, we should know
better how to present the different *loca* required in such plays as the
Death of Herod, when the Devil takes Herod's soul to Hell; in the
Baptism, where we have the river Jordan, the Holy Ghost sent down
from heaven, and God the Father speaking in Heaven; in the Harrowing of Hell, when Anima Christi passes from Mount Calvary to Hell;
in the Journey to Emmaus when Cleophas and Luke 'to a castel go'
(465). In examining the plays we might be led to a greater understanding of how they were staged through the stage-directions, through
the dialogue, and through comparing what the Proclamation has to say
about the action of a play with the play itself. We shall look for any
indication of acting areas, of moving pageants or fixed stages, of stage
levels which might, for instance, distinguish 'a hill' from 'the place' or
'Hell's mouth', of the actor's movements within the play, of the continuity of playing between one play and another, and of the types of
costumes worn, and properties and stage-machinery used. For this
purpose, rather than deal with each of the 42 plays separately, it is more
convenient to discuss them in groups as follows:

The Creation to the Prophets
The Conception of Mary to the Purification
The Massacre of the Innocents to the Raising of Lazarus
Passion Play I to Doomsday.

II

The first is a fairly homogeneous group of Old Testament plays
whose action, with the exception of the Lamech episode in the *Noah*
play, is on the whole accurately described by the Proclamation. The
first two plays dealing with the creation of Heaven and the angels,
the Fall of Lucifer, and the Fall of Man, have a continuous action. The

---

[1] Wickham, *EES*, Vol. I, p. 173.

characters are God the Father, God the Son, and God the Holy Ghost, Lucifer, Good and Bad Angels, a choir of angels, the Seraphim and Cherubim, Adam and Eve. The references to the separate manifestations of the Trinity are clearly set out in the second stanza of the play. The Trinity appear together later in the cycle, having distinct functions, in the Parliament of Heaven, the Annunciation, and the Baptism. It is most likely that they would also all be present at the Assumption of the Virgin and at Doomsday. God the Holy Ghost appears as Anima Christi in Passion Play II at the moment Christ dies on the cross. In this first play of the cycle, therefore, we are introduced to the Trinity, as a trio of actors each subsequently having quite different and separate functions in the unfolding drama; but at the outset it is God the Father who controls the action.

The action begins before God has created Heaven. The Trinity walk in state in 'the place' (15) before Heaven, the stars, and the angels are created. Only then do they go up to God's throne, where God sits; and the creation of the stars and the heavens, of Lucifer and the angels, takes place during the third stanza, at the end of which the angels sing to God's glory and the Cherubim and Seraphim sing the Sanctus (SD 39). God must then leave his throne for the ensuing dissension to take place between the good and bad angels. Lucifer launches his revolt and sits on God's empty throne. There is no stage-direction for God's withdrawal, but the direction after line 364, 'Hic recedit deus . . .' might indicate that within Heaven there is a place for withdrawal, perhaps through a curtain behind God's throne, no doubt used by the other two persons of the Trinity when God the Father took his throne. When God returns he drives Lucifer to Hell and continues with his acts of creation. Once he has created Adam and Eve he leads them down from Heaven's 'hill' (240) to Paradise and returns himself to rest in Heaven. In Paradise Adam is absorbed in looking at and naming the fruit and flowers while Eve is being beguiled by Satan, an erect and beautiful beast, of course, till condemned by God to grovel on its belly. At their Fall God condemns Satan to be locked in Hell's lodge, where he shall never more lift the latch (315-16). The Seraphim drives Adam and Eve out of Paradise, and Eve mourns that the gates of Paradise are shut upon them (384). Satan too laments his Fall:

> and now I am cast to helle sty
> streyte out at hevyn gate.   (323-4)

Within the dialogue, therefore, there is evidence of separate *loca* representing Heaven, Paradise,[2] Hell, each with a gate moreover, Hell's gate with a lock on it—as Heaven's has too, on the evidence of *Doomsday*, 50. When Adam and Eve are expelled from Paradise, furthermore, Adam says:

> But let us walke forth to þe londe . . .   (404)

Clearly they are not wheeled out on a pageant-cart. Rather, as at the opening of the play God the Father had walked into the acting area, so at the end Adam and Eve walk off.

The next few plays in this first group begin with the actors walking into the acting area rather than being 'discovered' in any way, or being pushed on in a pageant-cart. They also walk off at the end, the Noah family excepted—apart from the dead, of course (Abel, and Cain, and Lamech's Boy in the *Death of Cain* insertion), who may be retrieved by devils, as in the Cornish cycle Old Testament sequences, and as Herod and his Knights are later in this play (*Death of Herod*, SD 232), and carried off triumphantly into Hell. Abraham and Isaac walk off happily together, with Abraham calling for God's blessing on all, 'whethyr we syttyn walk or stonde' (263), perhaps referring here to various systems of audience differentiation, in a way that recalls the East Anglian *Mankind* ('ye souerens þat sytt and ye brothern þat stonde ryght wppe'). Moses, having preached his sermon on the ten commandments, leaves in a like manner:

> my tale I have taught ȝow my wey now I goo.   (194)

In the *Noah* play there is some unusual stage movement. When Noah

---

[2] The profusion of fruit trees in Paradise might puzzle a modern stage, property manager. I doubt whether there were more than two property trees one of which is the forbidden tree; the other, as indicated by the text, might contain pepper, peonies, liquorice, apples, pears, rice, dates and figs. It is probably from this stage tree that Adam plucks the two fig leaves. Such multiple fruit-bearing stage trees are not uncommon in the Middle Ages. One such appears in stained glass to the great East window in York Minister, and another in the Account Book of the Norwich Grocers, who enacted the Fall of Man:

Apples and Figs	4d.
Oranges	10d.
3 lbs. Dates	1s.
1 stone Almonds	3d.
Paid for coloured thread to bind the flowers	2d.

is told by the angel to build a ship he withdraws with his family, and while he is presumably building his ship offstage there is enacted the drama of Lamech, the blind archer, who first, by mischance, kills Cain and then beats his boy to death with his bow. When Lamech withdraws, Noah and his family enter again, with the Ark, singing. The Ark may be on wheels, may be portable.[3] In any event, having put it in position, they get into it, and the dialogue continues as though the floods have already come and the water is lapping against the sides of the Ark. At the end of the play, after the dove has returned with the olive branch, the family, singing once more, carry or push their Ark out of the acting area.

Heaven features in all these early plays. In *Cain and Abel* (90) it is located above the place of the tything, with God in His throne overseeing all. In *Noah* too, God and His Angel are in Heaven. God listens to Noah's prayer and sends down His Angel to him. Similarly in the next play God does not speak directly to Abraham but sends down His Angel. Dramatically there is everything to be gained by having God seated on His throne on 'hevyn hille' throughout this play and, when Abraham's obedience has been put to the test, sending down His Angel at the critical moment to prevent the slaying of Isaac. The Proclamation indicates that a hill is the site of the intended sacrifice:

Vpon An hill full Ryff.   readily
(87)

In the *Moses* play another close relationship with Heaven seems to be indicated. When Moses sees the burning bush and approaches it God tells him to take off his shoes because he is about to walk on holy ground. God and Moses then meet, but this would not be in Heaven.

---

[3] The East Midlands play of *Mary Magdalene* (Furnivall, *DP*, pp. 53–136) contains references to a ship moving in and out of 'the place':

> Ett tunc navis venit In placeam   (1716)
> et tunc navis venit ad-circa placeam   (1879)
> Here goth the shep owt ofe the place   (1923)

Mary Magdalene was almost certainly played in the round with the audience seated on scaffolds which alternated with the acting pageants (cf. David L. Jeffrey's chapter above, p. 85–6). It is generally accepted that there are many staging similarities between this Digby play and the Passion Plays of the Hegge cycle, but in this instance the resemblance is to one of the early plays in the cycle.

God either comes down to earth or Moses stretches up to Heaven to receive the tablets.

The *Prophets* play, by contrast, calls for little in the way of staging versatility. It has an unusually large cast, comprising Jesse, thirteen Prophets and thirteen Kings. The prophecies prepare more for the advent of the Virgin than for Christ. Apart from Isaiah's introduction, Prophets and Kings give their one set speech and make way for the next. The last speech of the play indicates that all the Prophets and Kings are gathered together in 'the place' (132) where they ask for God's blessing on the audience before presumably departing, as ceremoniously as they must have come.

In considering this first group of the Hegge plays, it would seem from their verse structure and from their description in the Proclamation that they formed part of the original Corpus Christi cycle. There is the addition of the Lamech episode and, most likely, a rewriting of the *Cain and Abel* play. The stage-directions are throughout in Latin. The method of performance, however, does not seem to be that of the movable pageant type associated with the York plays. A variety of *loca* or acting areas is required. The 'hill'[4] is a prominent feature of most of the early plays, and in some it would appear that more than one 'hill' is required: for instance 'Heaven's hill' and the hill on which Cain and Abel offer up their tythes, or 'Heaven's hill' and the hill on which Abraham prepares to sacrifice Isaac (if 'heavyn hille' indeed means anything more than '*high* Heaven' or 'the Heaven *eminence*', like Heaven's 'towre' in the Marian plays that follow—nothing more than a raised or elevated 'scaffold' or 'mansion' being indicated). The Creation and the Fall of Man call for different *loca* for Heaven, Paradise, Earth and Hell, some of them on different levels. Yet repeatedly actors walk on the ground, 'the place', and it would seem that it is at this level that many of their entrances and exits are made. Noah's Ark

[4] Mounts and hills feature in a great number of medieval plays, and in virtually all of the Biblical and Passion plays. They provided a useful elevation and also a practical base or pedestal, one imagines (suitably reinforced), for the assorted trees, posts and crucifixes required by the action. According to medieval conventions of 'emblematic' decor they would have been stylized and miniaturized for the most part, structures some four or five feet square in base area and three or four feet high being matter-of-factly offered—and as matter-of-factly accepted—as Horeb, Olivet or Calvary. Other scenic units —temples, castle, cities, etc.—could be and frequently were presented according to the same convention.

is brought in and out of 'the place'. The twenty-seven characters in the *Prophets* could scarcely all be bunched together at the end of the play on a single pageant-stage, and King Amon, indeed, in the final speech of that play, says they are all in 'the place' (132). Cain uses the phrase 'strete and stage' (188), and so reinforces the suggestion that a major part of the action was performed at ground level. Whether this is borne out by the later plays, and what sight-line problems this might raise for the audience, are questions we must face later.

III

The second group of plays, from the Conception of Mary to the Purification, is characterized by the detailed treatment accorded to St. Anne and to the early life of the Virgin Mary. These plays are full of ritualistic action. The central place of performance is often within a temple, with the main action focused on or around the altar. In the *Conception of Mary*, because of Joachim's and Anna's barrenness, Joachim's offering is rejected, and he himself driven from the temple. The following play also takes place in the temple when Mary, as a girl of three, mounts the fifteen 'degrees' or steps to the altar. The *Betrothal of Mary*, which follows, depicts Joseph, reluctantly drawn to the altar, finding, much to his surprise, his wand sprouting with green shoots. *The Trial of Joseph and Mary* also has its action focused within the temple and on the altar, as does the *Purification* as well.

The miracle element is strong in this group of plays: Anna's conception of a child in her old age; the three-year-old Mary's discoursing most eloquently as he mounts her fifteen steps to the altar, on the needful preparation of the spirit if one aspires to kneel before God's throne; the blossoming of Joseph's wand; the truth-drink which leaves both Joseph and Mary unharmed, but which fills the head of one of their detractors with fire; the unseasonal fruiting and bending to Mary of the cherry tree; the withering of Salome's hand when she touches Mary, disbelieving her virginity.

The language of these plays is consonant with the more formal ritualistic content. It is more learned, Latinate, and complex, dealing with more abstract theological concepts, especially in Contemplacio's five prologues and in the *Parliament of Heaven*. The angels' singing is in Latin, and the Magnificat, sung by Mary and Elizabeth, two lines at a time, is written in Latin and English alternately. The stage-directions are sometimes in Latin and sometimes in English, and sometimes in a mixture of the two languages, as follows:

> hic osculet terram here xal comyn Allwey An Aungel with dyvers presentys goynge and comyng and inþe tyme þei xal synge in hefne þis hympne Jhesu corona virginum And After þer comyth A minister fro þe busschop with A present and seyth
>
> *Mary in the Temple* (259)

The above stage-direction indicates the use not only of more than one language, but also of more than one acting area. Mary has climbed the fifteen steps to the altar and now, after she has kissed the ground, angels continue to pass to and from Heaven with gifts for her, while in Heaven the choir sing their hymn. Heaven is located above the altar. God sits there on his throne and Mary and Joachim, in the temple, kneel to him (24, 40). Angels come down from Heaven to greet Mary on God's behalf (146) or to bring to her manna in a cup of gold (227). There is singing in Heaven on each of these occasions.

There is strong evidence within this group of plays to support the theory that, because of the unity of theme (St. Anne and the Virgin Mary), and the repeated use of the same acting areas (Heaven, the temple, the hill, the Joachim–Anne '*domus*', and 'the place'), they were all performed in a fixed area on some system of multiple stages. As part of such a 'simultaneous' setting, heaven is a 'tower' in which God is clearly visible to all sitting on his throne: 'In hevyn we may hym se . . . and to his towere he mote vs brynge'—Prologue of Contemplacio to the Conception of Mary (21, 24). Heaven is both spacious and stoutly built, for it houses not only God on his throne and the heavenly choir, but also the Son and the Holy Ghost (the *Annunciation*), and a fair company of angels who busily do God's bidding between Heaven and earth.[5] In the *Parliament of Heaven* the cast is increased by the three Virtues, Verita, Misericordia, Justicia, Pax and Gabriel. The *loca* or 'mansion' overlooks the altar to which Mary moves, in Mary in the Temple, and at which the bishop receives the white rods of David's kin.

The Annunciation provides us with the most spectacular linking of

[5] The Cornish *Creation of the World* seems to have called for a three- or four-storeyed structure, accommodating not only God but also nine separate orders of angels (one of them doubling as musicians) in some huge ten-chambered pyramid.

Heaven and earth, however. Gabriel has greeted Mary, and at her acceptance of his message, the conception takes place:

> here þe holy gost discendit with iij bemys to our lady. the
> sone of þe godhed nest with iij bemys · to þe holy gost · the   (next)
> fadyr godly with iij bemys to þe sone · And so entre All
> thre to here bosom · and Mary seyth
>
> (SD 292)

The Holy Ghost comes down to earth and is at Mary's level; the Son takes up a midway position between Heaven and earth, possibly on that same ramp or flight of steps which took the angels up and down from Heaven in *Mary in the Temple*; and God stays in Heaven. The Trinity each touch the other with three golden cords, or rods, linking Heaven and the room in Nazareth.[6] Both Mary's mansion and the Temple, therefore, must be contiguous with heaven.

For the majority of plays in this group, therefore, common staging elements are required: Heaven, a Temple, one or two mansions (Joachim's and Joseph's—the same structure could be used for each), and a journeying or acting area at ground level. At the end of the *Betrothal of Mary*, Joseph takes his wife and her three maidens to 'a lytyl praty hous' (459), and there he says he must leave her for nine months while he labours in a far country. This house would be the setting for the Salutation and Conception. It might also be changed into the 'house of haras', or stud-stable, in the Birth of Christ. The Citizen recommends this lodging, but Joseph does not think very much of it:

> In an hous þat is desolat with-outy Any wall
> Ffyer not wood non here is.
>
> (101–2)

The same mansion would also be used for the visit of the Shepherds and the Magi in the Adoration plays, of course. It could be used as well

---

6 Neville Denny, whose comments on and assistance with parts of this essay I should gratefully like to acknowledge, writes: 'Iconographical tradition suggests an alternative dramatization, simpler and in some ways more effective, with a Holy Ghost *dove* and even an infant Jesus (i.e. a *doll*) fixed to the rods or cords linking God the Father and the Virgin's breast. See the innumerable treatments of the Annunciation in late medieval and early Renaissance art for the dove-and-rods convention. For the dove and miniscule Jesus see, for example, the *Annunciation* of the Master of the Retable of the Reyes Catolicos.'

for Elizabeth's house in the *Visit to Elizabeth*, although the probability is that another opposing mansion was used. This play, which moves on continuously from Joseph's Return, begins with Joseph and Mary making a 52-mile journey to 'Montana' in the land of Judah. Mary has some astringent things to say about the evils of long pilgrimages lightly undertaken, and urges haste. Joseph, unexpectedly, agrees.

> Amen Amen and evyrmore
> lo wyff lo how starkly I go be fore.
>> (et sic transiet circa placeam)
>> (22)

As they both journey round the 'place', Contemplacio speaks twenty lines, by which time they have arrived at Elizabeth's house. Joseph offers to call Elizabeth out, but Mary prefers to enter the house. At the end of the play Mary and Joseph return home, and Elizabeth and Zachariah go to the Temple.

The *Trial of Joseph and Mary* begins with the stage-direction:

> hic intrabit pagetum de purgacione Marie et   *'pageant'*
> Joseph   hic dicit primus detractor

In the Summoner's Prologue to this play, the audience is asked to make room for the Bishop to come and sit in the court. It may be that a Purgation pageant is wheeled or carried into the centre of the 'place', and the performance given within or upon it. At 72 the Bishop takes his place there, it seems, seated between two Doctors of the Law. Joseph is commanded to drink from 'þe botel of goddys vengeauns' and to walk round the altar seven times, however ('here is þis place þis Awtere abowth'—206). Mary has to do the same, and so has the First Detractor. This extensive walking round the altar would seem to demand more space than would normally be available on a pageant-cart. Is it the pageant itself that they circle? A central position for the Trial 'pageant' would correspond to the use of the oratory or council-house in Passion Play II, where the council-house serves as Pilate's judgment-seat (that worthy flanked moreover by two 'assessors', Caiaphas and Annas, just as the Bishop is here). Similarly, in the *Adoration of the Magi* we have as acting stations not only the stable (possibly Joseph and Mary's earlier 'mansion' the 'lytyl praty hous'), and a 'hill' (291 possibly an emblematic 'Mount' some three feet high, or just a raised place, 'scaffold' or wagon) on which the Kings fall asleep, but also Herod's palace, 'þe castel rownde' (129), which might again suggest a central positioning, as in *The Castle of Perseverance*. It would seem more likely that both *loca*—Trial 'pageant' and 'castle round'—were positioned on the periphery of the 'place', however, leaving the 'awtere' (and Temple?) to occupy the centre as it had for so many of the previous plays and must for the next (the Purification) as well.

For this group of plays, therefore, we seem to have a staging system of 'simultaneous mansions' operating once more, fronting, or embracing, or surrounding a ground-level acting area, the 'place'. Somewhere in this 'place', no doubt centrally sited (in the 'myd place' —SD PP I, 125), was a Temple, possibly just a dome or spire or tower on four slender legs (so as not to interfere too much with the sightlines) containing an altar, perhaps elevated on a low dais. The fixed mansions demanded by the action are Heaven, two 'houses', a 'hill', Herod's 'castel' or 'dwellynge', and possibly a sixth scaffold to serve as the Purgation 'pageant' (alternatively, as the stage-direction seems to suggest, this element was wheeled or carried into position somewhere in the 'place' at the start of the Trial play).

IV

The third group of plays, from the *Massacre of the Innocents* to the *Raising of Lazarus*, has close links with the previous group. The Temple that featured so regularly in the Marian plays is the main setting for Christ and the Doctors and would be used for the second Temptation as well ('hic ascendit deus [i.e. Jesus] pinnaculum templi . . .'—SD 113). The *Adoration of the Magi*, the *Massacre of the Innocents* and the *Death of Herod* have further acting areas in common. The Seneschal in the *Adoration of the Magi* leaves from Herod's 'castle' (or 'high hall' or 'dwellynge'—probably some fairly simple or emblematic mansion or *domus* is being referred to, not an ornate replica of a castle or palace), to 'walke . . . on wolde' (almost certainly the 'place'), where he meets the Kings—under a tree moreover. He invites them to follow after him, 'vpon þhis grownde', to meet Herod, and by the next stanza is reporting their coming to the King:

> Sere kyng in trone
> here comyth a-none

> by strete and stone
> kynges thre.
>
> (135-8)

Mention has already been made of Cain's use of the phrase 'strete and stage' (188). This particular reference in a Herod play calls to mind the stage-direction in the Coventry play of the Shearmen and Taylors:

> Here Erode ragis in the pagond and in the strete also.

Street and stage must be different acting areas in the Hegge plays as they would have been in the performance of the Coventry plays. The Magi enter the 'street' or the 'place' on horseback to be conducted to the 'castle round' by Herod's officer. In the *Raising of Lazarus* 'street' is referred to again, when Martha, moving from the *domus* in which Lazarus has died, says.

> I xal go forth in þe strete
> to mete with jhesu if þat I may
>
> (267-8)

All internal evidence points to the 'street' as being at ground level, below the level of the *domus*, and in the 'place' (when Jesus meets Martha there a little later he asks her to go and bring her sister to 'þis place'). Lazarus' tomb would also seem to be situated at ground level, in the 'place' somewhere, possibly in the space beneath some raised 'mansion' (wagon or scaffold—possibly Heaven itself) but apparently not the Bethany *domus* where he has died. After his death he is carried by the four Consolators to his burial-place, an area referred to as a 'cave' (144, 165) or 'pit' (140). The grave is 'shut' with a large stone (163).

Within the Hegge plays there are three burials and resurrections: Lazarus, Jesus, the Virgin. From the similarity of the stage-directions and from the references within the dialogue it is probable that each burial and resurrection was staged more or less in the same way. Certainly, Lazarus' resurrection, visually and typologically, must be made to foreshadow Christ's.

The *loca* or mansions demanded by this group of plays, then, include the Temple; a 'castle'; a sepulchre-cave; a hill (for the Temptation—153; for the Magi play—291; possibly for the Seneschal's 'brown bank'); and a bed-chamber (for the consecutive plays of the *Woman Taken in Adultery* and the *Raising of Lazarus*)—apart from the 'place' itself as an acting area. Heaven and Hell also feature in several of the plays, both of them in the *Death of Herod* (where Death twice refers to himself as sent by God[7] and where after Death has struck, Herod and his Knights are carried off to Hell by devils), and Heaven, with its choir of angels, in the *Temptation* (where the angels sing a Gloria—195) and in the *Purification* (where they sing the Nunc Dimittis that is only spoken in the other versions of the play, as in the Biblical source). Heaven also plays a part in the Baptism. The Proclamation points to the appearance of the Trinity in this play, and indicates the separate functions that they undertake. The stage-directions bear this out:

> Spiritus sanctus hic descendat super ipsum [i.e. as a dove] et deus
> pater celestis dicet in celo . . .   (*SD* 91)

The baptism itself probably takes place in the temple structure (Jesus climbs up to John to receive it—*SD*39); the dove must descend mechanically from somewhere, either from Heaven or from the Temple's roof; the baptism must take place in contiguity with Heaven).

A staging situation is indicated, in other words, very similar to that indicated for the first two groups of plays: a fairly extensive 'place' (capable of accommodating three or four horses, riders in the saddle, however briefly) overlooked by a row or ring or crescent of separate mansions, some sort of larger structure—but surely not so solid or elaborate as to interfere with the sight-lines—at ground level before them in the 'place', either in the centre or in some sort of close and special relationship to Heaven.

V

The last group of plays comprises the two Passion plays, the *Announcement to the Three Maries*, the *Appearance to Mary Magdalene*, the *Appearance on the Way to Emmaus*, the *Ascension*, the *Day of*

---

[7] There is a great similarity between this Death and the Death in *The Castle of Perseverance* (*MP*, pp. 85–6), where the figure is also presented as God's messenger, speaking in a thirteen-line stanza beginning with the same cry 'OW', and giving the death stroke with his lance (2808). A grim theatrical irony invests Death's taking up his position above and behind a Herod vainglorious in his paramountcy and invincibility ('ffor now my fo is ded and prendyd as a padde [i.e. stuck like a toad] above me is no kynge on grownde here on gerth'—211–12).

Pentecost, the *Assumption of the Virgin*, and *Doomsday*. By 1468 it would appear that the two Passion plays were not acted, or not always acted, together in the same year. Nevertheless the stage presentation of each of the Passion plays is similar, and the plays that complete the cycle rely on many of the same staging elements. Although in the manucript the *Assumption of the Virgin* is written in different handwriting from the rest of the cycle, and no mention is made of it within the Proclamation, it is clearly written for a fixed acting area, and uses many of the devices required by this last group of plays: a burial and a resurrection; miraculous and sudden appearances; stage clouds for wafting characters in and out of the main acting area; regular access from heaven to earth which can be used by a dozen or more characters.

In comparison with the other medieval cycles which were played from the Creation to the Judgment as a continuous performance, there is no reason, dramatically, why the Hegge plays should not have been treated similarly. It is true that the Chester plays were spread over the first three days of Whit week, and the Norwich plays were performed on the Monday and Tuesday of Pentecost week, but here the evidence is that the plays in their entirety were not performed within the same year. We have no certain knowledge how much of the Hegge cycle was performed continuously in any one year. According to the Proclamation all the plays therein listed were to be performed 'A Sunday next'. The Prologue to Passion Play II is here at odds with the Proclamation. We must assume that the earlier Corpus Christi play was acted out *in toto*, and that subsequently different arrangements obtained which included the alternation in consecutive years of the Passion Plays; but we cannot be sure what comprised the rest of the programme. What we can be sure of, however, is that, if the performance ended with the completion of Passion Play I, or moved from Passion Play I, omitting Passion Play II, to the *Announcement to the Three Maries*, the audience would have been left with a sharp sense of anticlimax. Passion Play I moves with ineluctable power and intensity through the conspiracy to the capture of Christ. To break off the drama at this point would be acutely frustrating. I should like to think that at some stage the two Passion plays were performed consecutively on the same day, and that they were marvellously linked together by that stage-direction which follows Herod's introductory scene at the opening of Passion Play II:

here xal A massanger com in-to þe place rennyng and criyng
Tydyngs tydyngs · and so round Abowth þe place, jhesus of nazareth
is take   Jesus of nazareth is take, and forth-with heylyng þe prynces
þus seyng

(69)

No modern paper-boy could bring more zest to the late-night news.

The stage-directions of this last group of plays contain a rare fund
of information about medieval stagecraft. Some are written in English,
some in Latin. In the two Passion plays the directions are often long
and detailed, describing the costumes worn, their colour, the stage
properties, the stage movement (as illustrated by the last quotation),
the stage business (such as Pilate's pretended writing on the tablet he
places over Christ's head on the cross—much as God must have pretended to write on the tablets of stone, 'with my ffynger'—39, in
the *Moses* play), the setting with references to the use of scaffolds, the
oratory in the centre of 'the place', and the use of curtains. The longer
directions are in English, some of the shorter are in Latin, some are
mixed. For instance, when Annas is inflaming the crowd against Jesus
and urging Pilate to heed the people's feelings:

> *Annas* We kan tell þe tyme where and whan
> þat many a thowsand turnyd hath he
> As All þis pepyll record weyl kan
> from hens in-to þe lond of galyle
>
> et clamabunt ʒa . ʒa . ʒa.
> (*PP* I, 321–4)

Here is the demagogue eliciting the mob-response. Time and again the
movement of the crowd and the crowd's reactions are powerfully
described within the stage-directions. Apart from one brief direction
in English in the *Announcement to the Three Maries*, all the stage-
directions following the Passion plays are in Latin.

From both the dialogue and the stage-directions of the Passion plays
we also derive a vivid picture of the costumes worn by the audience
and the players. The Prologue of Demon (*PP* I, 69–108) gives almost
as full a description of the contemporary fashions as Titivillus's speech
in the Towneley *Judgment* (255–367). Both cycles stress that high
fashion is the 'primrose path to the everlasting bonfire'. The hazards
of young men having long hair that falls below their collar sounds
uncomfortably modern:

With syde lokkys I schrewe þin here, to þi colere hangyng down
to herborwe qweke bestys þat tekele men onyth.

(PP I, Prologue of the Demon, 85-6)

The first long stage-direction in Passion Play I spells out the detail that
should be given to the costuming of the characters, particularly those
who will be pitched into hell's flames:

Here xal annas shewyn hym-self in his stage be-seyn after [*arranged
as*] a busschop of þe hoold lawe in a skarlet gowne and ouer þat a
blew tabbard furryd with whyte and a mytere on his hed after þe
hoold lawe · ij doctorys stondyng by hym in furryd hodys and on
be-forn hem with his staff of A-stat and eche of hem on here hedys
a furryd cappe with a gret knop in þe crowne and on stondyng
be-forn as a sarazyn þe wich xal be his masangere, Annas þus
seyng . . .

(PP I, Prologue of John the Baptist, SD 40)

When Caiaphas appears he is dressed as Annas, with a scarlet gown,
but his tabard is red furred with white. His two counsellors are dressed
as those of Annas, with furred hoods and caps. The red and blue tabards,
then, sharply distinguish the two high priests. Rewfyn and Leyon,
their henchmen, make their appearance (80) in furred tabards and
furred hoods about their necks. In contrast to this colour and richness
of array, Jesus and all his disciples are dressed alike, probably in hand-
woven, un-dyed natural wool—i.e. greyish-white. Indeed, it is because
of their indistinguishable dress that Judas, in this play, offers to identify
Jesus to the conspirators by kissing him:

Leyon Ʒa be ware of þat for ony thynge
for o dyscypil is lyche þi mayster in all parayl
An ȝe go lyche in All clothyng
So myth we of oure purpose fayl.

(PP I, 642-5)

In sharp contrast too with their judges' costumes is that of the prisoners
at the bar:

here þei xal brynge barabas to þe barre and jhesu and ij þewys
[*thieves*] in here shertys bare leggyd and jhesus standyng at þe barre
be-twyx them and annas and cayphas xal gon in to þe cowncelle
hous qwan [*when*] pylat syttyth.

(PP II, 635)

After Jesus has been buffeted a white cloth is cast over him, and he is led about 'the place' (*PP* II, 405). When he has been scourged a cloth of purple silk is put on him, and he is thrust onto a stool and mocked as king (*PP* II, 667). Some of the conspirators who arrest Jesus in the garden at night are dressed in armour.

> here jhesus with his dyscipulis goth in-to þe place and þer xal come in A x personys weyl be-seen [*arrayed*] in white [i.e. silver] Arneys and breganderys and some dysgysed in odyr garmentys with swerdys gleyvys [*broad-swords*] and other straunge wepone as cressettys with feyr and lanternys and torchis lyth and judas formest of Al conveyng hem to jhesu be contenawns.
>
> (*PP* I, *SD* 972)

It all suggests a striking theatrical effect—agitation, torchlight, swooping shadows, fire flashing off armour.

Earlier in this essay attention was drawn to the rapid costume change which was required to transform Lucifer into Satan. In Doomsday many such changes are called for, but this time from wretchedness to a state of bright redemption. When the dead rise from their graves (*subtus terram*, 26) they come, as Death appeared in the Herod play, as skeletons, gnawed about by worms. But they are transformed before they enter heaven:

> *Deus* All þo ffowle wyrmys ffrom ʒow ffalle   *foul worms*
>   With my ryght hand I blysse ʒou here
>   my blyssynge burnyschith ʒou as bryght as berall
>   As crystall clene it clensyth ʒou clere
>   All ffylth ffrom ʒou ffade
>   Petyr to hevyn ʒatys þou wende and goo
>   þe lokkys þou losyn and hem vndo
>   my blyssyd childeryn þou brynge me to
>   here hertys for to glade.
>
> (44–52)

As Lucifer shed his Angel's robe to reveal his Satanic form, so most likely the risen dead, who are blessed by God, put on their brightness by donning a cloak or overmantle and move up towards the gates of heaven which Peter is unlocking with his key. The damned souls, unlike their brethren in the Towneley *Judgment* who are resplendently dressed, are driven to hell in all their skeletal bareness, and among them are the personifications of the seven deadly sins, each of which has his cardinal sin written on his forehead in black letters (76, 77, 92).

It is to be regretted that the manuscript does not contain the end of this play.

VI

The action of this last part of the cycle is swift and compelling. We are never the victims of the longueurs of medieval prolixity. Both Passion Plays move briskly to their respective climaxes: the capture of Jesus by night, and the Crucifixion. In the earlier part the Magi and Herod had made their entries on horseback. Here Jesus makes his entry into Jerusalem riding on an ass. The text furnishes us with full details. Jesus tells his disciples to 'Go to yon castel' to fetch for him an ass which they find tethered with a foal (PP I, 183–95). Jesus then rides out of 'the place', leaving Peter and John preaching to the people. When Jesus returns to 'the place' it is for his triumphal entry into Jerusalem. He is still riding the ass and is greeted by the burgesses and children as they would have greeted their fifteenth-century monarch coming to the gates of their city. Sir Walter Ralegh was not the first subject to cast his cloak on the ground for his monarch to walk on.

> here þe iiij cetesynys [citizens] makyn hem redy for to mete with oure lord goyng barfot and barelegged and in here shyrtys savyng þei xal haue here gownys cast A-bouth theme and qwan þei seen oure lorde þei xal sprede þer clothis be-forn hyme and he xal lyth [alight] and go þer upone and þei xal falle downe up-on þer knes alle atonys . . . (PP I, SD 285)

Jesus dismounts from his ass to walk upon the garments that are spread before him as a sign of the people's subjection. He is then met by a group of children who cast flowers before him and sing his praise (PP I, SD 289). As Jesus is greeted by the citizens as their king, so in Pilate's eyes does he continue to be regarded as a king. Although Pilate gives the most precise instructions concerning the scourging and the Crucifixion (PP II, 658–75), he has taken the precaution of publicly dissociating himself from the responsibility by literally washing his hands of the affair (PP II, 620–23). But he insists that only men of gentle birth should handle Jesus:

> þat þer be no man   xal towch ʒour kyng
> but yf he be knyght   or jentylman born.

How this contrasts with the treatment of the two thieves who are crucified by 'the simple men', who are the poor commoners pressed into this service!

Pilate's final acknowledgment of Christ's kingship is written into one of the most fascinating stage-directions in the whole of the manuscript:

> here xal pylat Askyn penne and inke and A tabyl xal be take hym wretyn A-fore [*written out beforehand*] hic est jhesus nazarenus rex judeorum.
> and he xal make hym to wryte and þan gon up on A leddere and settyn þe tabyl abovyn crystys hed and þan cayphas xal makyn hym to redyn and seyn

>   (*PP* II, *SD* 853)

Clearly the writing on the tablet was large and important for all to see. It could not be left to the actor playing Pilate to write under the pressure of the dramatic action. He makes as if he is writing the inscription, mounts the ladder, and places the tablet above Christ's head for all to see. Ladders are used against the cross by Joseph or Arimathea and Nicodemus for the Deposition. This use of ladders emphasizes the height of the cross, which by Pilate's orders is set high

> on þe mownth of calverye þat men may sen.
>   (*PP* II, 675)

The appearance of Anima Christi to harrow Hell, while Christ in the flesh still hangs from the cross, is a unique feature of the Hegge Plays, though some such treatment featured in the Cornish cycle too. Theologically it is correct. Dramatically most other cycles interpose other scenes between the Crucifixion and the Harrowing. Here it would seem logical that the Holy Ghost, who has made so many previous appearances within the cycle, should take the part of Anima Christi. It is by no means unusual in medieval drama for body and soul to be played by different actors. Indeed, this is probably what happens again in this cycle in the *Assumption of the Virgin*, when, on her death, Mary's soul goes from her body to the 'bosom of God':

> hic exiet anima marie de corpore in sinu dei.

>   (*SD* 301)

Mary's body is then buried elsewhere. Such a division occurs also in the *Castle of Perseverance*. When Humanum Genus dies his Anima is tugged between the Good and Bad Angels. The stage-plan contains this note:

> Mankyndeis bed schal be vndyr þe castel and þer schal þe sowle lye vndyr þe bed tyl he schal ryse and pleye.

The 'castel' was situated in the middle of 'the place'. The actor playing Anima, a character which appears at the end of the play, would have had to wait there some 3,000 lines before revealing himself. The notion of the Soul coming from under the bed would certainly be acceptable in the staging of the Assumption. The Soul emerging from a hiding place in the centre of the acting area might be applicable to the scenes in which Anima Christi appears.

The council-house or oratory, sited in the middle of 'the place', is a focal point of much of the drama in both Passion Plays. The last stated use of it in Passion Play II is when the prisoners are brought to the bar, and Pilate, Annas and Caiaphas take their seats within the council-house (SD 635). At this stage Passion Play II has a further thousand lines to run, and it is extremely unlikely that this focal area would remain unused. It is probable that the burial of Christ, the Guarding of the Sepulchre, and the Resurrection were played centrally. The council-house was raised from ground level. When Judas leaves Jesus at the Last Supper (PP I, 589) he goes into the place and moves towards the council-house and is helped into it 'by the hand' (615). There is some indication also that the burial of both Lazarus and the Virgin Mary was carried out in this central position, and this would certainly be an appropriate and large enough area from which the dead might rise at Doomsday. The reference on the stage-plan of the Castle of Perseverance to the hiding-place of 'þe sowle' might strengthen this suggestion. Hiding place there must be for, just before the Resurrection of Christ, Anima Christi goes towards the sepulchre saying:

> now wele I rysyn flesch and felle   *skin*
> þat rent was for ȝour sake
> myn owyn body þat hynge on rode
> And be þe jewys nevyr so wode   '*mad*', *enraged*
> It xal a-ryse both flesche and blode
> my body now wyl I take.
>
> Tunc transiet anima christi ad resuscitandum corpus quo reuscitato dicat Jhesus
>
> (PP II, 1410–15)

Anima Christi must conceal himself near the tomb or beneath the tomb.
At this point the actor playing Jesus lifts the stone covering the tomb,
or this is lifted by two Angels, so breaking the seals that Pilate had
affixed to the four corners of the sepulchre, and rises flesh and fell.

Throughout this cycle there are very many references to the angels
singing in heaven. In the *Assumption* we hear the playing of citherns
(*SD* 90) and organs (*SD* 285, 493), when God or His Angels move
between Heaven and earth. Hardin Craig is of the opinion that the
mention of organs in this play points to performance within a church.[8]
Portable organs could well have been used for outdoor performances,
though. Heavenly music marks the harmony of those moments when
Heaven and earth are in accord. Cacophony is the Devil's sound.
Juxtaposition of the two occurs in the Temptation, when the frustration
at his failure to lure Jesus into any temptation causes Satan to break
wind, but causes the Angels to sing a Gloria. The fearful farting of a
frustrated fiend has provided some of the comedy for the Creation
(81, 355). Any actor who has performed out of doors will know the
difficulty of making the voice carry. The medieval devices for making
Satan's breaking of wind carry are set out at the beginning of the
Castle of Perseverance:

> and he þat schal pley belyal loke þat he haue gunnepowdyr bren-
> nynge In pypys in hys handys and in hys ars whanne he gothe to
> batayl.

(Stage-plan)

Throughout the two Passion plays the pace and continuity of the
action is dependent on the variety and flexibility of the acting areas,
and there is an impressive number of distinct acting areas. There is
Heaven (944), the central Temple-cum-oratory, which in Passion
Play II becomes the moot-hall or council-house,[9] and then possibly a
sepulchre. There are the (three?) scaffolds for Annas and Caiaphas,

---

[8] Craig, *ERD*, p. 252.

[9] The 'council-house' reverts to its ecclesiastical role again for the 'temple'
in which Mary sojourns briefly as the Crucifixion approaches its harrowing
climax (*SD* 962). 'The dramatic motivation for removing her from the
tableau at the foot of the cross seems to me rooted in a sense of religious
decorum prompting the clearing of so venerable a figure from the arena before
the pandemonium and tumbling about that must accompany the earthquake
at Christ's death. She returns almost immediately for the Deposition (*SD*
1139).' (ND)

Herod, and Pilate. There are also the 'castle' or mansion against which the ass and the foal are tethered; the Last Supper room (possibly doubling as Pilate's Wife's bed-chamber); a hill, Mount Olivet, with its garden below (908); another hill, Mount Calvary (possibly the same structure), which bears the weight of a cross at least ten feet high, and that cross so firmly positioned that it not only supports the body of Christ but also the two ladders set against it and the weight of Joseph of Arimathea and Nicodemus on top of those ladders (1139).

A similar fluency of movement is found in the *Assumption*. There is not only the miraculous bringing of the Apostles to Mary's death-bed, with St. John coming in a single cloud (165), and St. Peter and another arriving in a double cloud (257), but also the extensive movement of God and His Angels from Heaven to earth and back again to Heaven:

> hic dissendet dominus cum omni celesti curia et dicet
>
> (SD 283)

There is also the burial of Mary, the release of her Soul, followed as in Christ's Resurrection by the Soul returning to the body for the physical resurrection. The acting area for this sequence must surely be in the middle of the 'place'. Many actors are required for this play: the Apostles, the host of heaven, the heavenly choir, Mary, the princes, and the demons. The total cast could not have been much less than fifty actors.

An even greater number would have been required for the two Passion Plays, in which the drama depends so extensively on crowd participation, crowd movement and crowd response. The dramatist is clear in his intention. The citizens' royal welcome of Jesus to the gates of Jerusalem soon changes to the irrationality and brutality of mob-violence:

> here þe jewys lede cryst outh of þe place with gret cry and noyse some drawyng cryst forward and some backwarde and so ledyng forth with here weponys A-lofte and lytys brennyng.
>
> (SD 1040)

The weapons and the lights held aloft, the swirling movement of the crowd, and the great noise, are stage effects, visual and aural, which no producer should fail to observe. The crowd's excited reaction sweeps the audience along with it. Caiaphas can whip the crowd to the frenzied response he requires:

> *Caiaphas* Thynk ʒe not he is worthy to dey.
>   (et clamabunt omnes)
>   ys. ys. ys. All we seye he is worthy to dey
>   ʒa. ʒa. ʒa.

It is the crowd's response to the Doctors' demand for Christ's death that sways Pilate against his better judgment.

> *2nd Doctore* Sere we wyl All,   þat he xal be put upon þe crosse.
>   (et clamabunt omnes voce magna dicentes ʒa. ʒa. ʒa.)

So large a cast can be reasonably contained in a flexible acting area. The crowd's main acting area is 'the place', while the chief characters move from oratory through or round 'the place' to the scaffolds and mansions featuring in the action. There are curtains around the oratory and around some of the scaffolds. When, for instance, Christ enters with his disciples into the house where he is to eat the Last Supper, a curtain is closed on that scaffold but another opened on the oratory:

> in the mene tyme þe cownsel hous
> beforn-seyd xal sodeynly onclose
> schewing þe buschopys prestys and jewgys syttyng in here
> Astat lyche as it were a convocavyone . . .
>
>   (*PP* I, *SD* 397)

There would certainly be a curtain in front of Herod's scaffold (*PP* II, *SD* 20, 356). It is a helpful device with which to present a set-piece: Herod in estate with all the Jews kneeling, except Annas and Caiaphas (*SD* 356); Jesus seated at table with his disciples; or Jesus at the beginning of the Ascension, already attached to his cloud-harness, with the disciples all about him, and two Angels awaiting him in heaven. Pilate's Wife, 'þe corteyn drawyn as she lyth in bedde', is a ready victim for the stealthy Devil (*PP* II, 522).

In conclusion, the 'simultaneous mansions' staging method, which it has long been agreed was the mode of presentation of the two Passion plays, was most likely the method adopted for the presentation of the whole of the Hegge plays. Throughout there is a consistent requirement for the use of 'the place'. In the middle of 'the place', moreover, there are frequent occasions when some additional mansion or element is indicated as the focal point of the drama. In the Passion Plays this is the temple-oratory, which also doubles as a 'council-house'. It could well serve as the sepulchre in addition (as it might have done in the Lazarus play, too, in the *Assumption of the Virgin* and for the dead at *Doomsday*).

The emphasis seems generally to be on drama in the round. A physical reconstruction of the staging of the Hegge plays might well approximate very closely to the staging of the Cornish plays and to Richard Southern's interpretation of the staging of *The Castle of Perseverance*. The audience would be accommodated either on tiered seating erected between the acting scaffolds, together forming a large circle facing inward to the 'place', or fronting a row or crescent of 'mansions' (as in the Valenciennes Passion play illustrations) across a similar expanse of 'place'. The scaffolds or mansions would be curtained in front, some of them—Heaven, Hell, possibly the Temple—more spectacularly presented than others and (Heaven and Hell) permanently associated with a particular presence or function in the action, others serving a multiple purpose. Part of the audience could possibly be accommodated in the 'place' itself, as Richard Southern believes to have been the case with *The Castle of Perseverance*, their movement and deployment controlled by stewards according to the needs and movements of actors in the 'place'. The gentlefolk and their wives, at any rate, would be seated on special scaffolds or on tiered seating, wherever any groundlings might be massed. (A class range of some kind is suggested by the various Prologues, which at one time direct the menials to doff their hoods and at another defer to the presence of princes in the audience.)

Contemplacio refers to the audience as 'þis congragacion', and the fifteenth-century audience, witnessing these religious plays, would indeed have thought of themselves as a congregation, whether the plays were performed against the West front of a great cathedral or some distance from it. The unity of the Passion Plays, and the uniformity of the staging methods discernible throughout, argue a centrally-organized system of production, rather than a dispersed system in which different trade-guilds were responsible for each separate play in the mystery cycle. I strongly support the theory that the responsibility for staging these plays rested with a religious guild. We should all very much like to know the East Midlands or Norfolk town (if indeed it was not Lincoln) in which such a guild operated, so that local records might help illuminate the many remaining mysteries attendant upon our full understanding of the origin and the staging of the Hegge Plays.

Note

Texts

Texts used and referred to in this chapter are to be found in Eccles, *MP*; Furnivall, *DP*; Shakespeare, *Works; Studies in English Faust Literature: I—The English Wagner Book*, ed. Alfred E. Richards (Berlin, 1907).

Scholarship and Criticism.

Chambers (*MS* and *ES*) and Wickham (*EES*) provide the standard commentaries on medieval and Renaissance English staging and theatre design. Other basic works are John Cranford Adams, *The Globe Playhouse* (Cambridge, Mass., 1942) and C. Walter Hodges, *The Globe Restored* (New York, 1953; rev'd 2nd edn., London, 1968).

X

Medieval Rounds and Wooden O's: The Medieval Heritage of the Elizabethan Theatre

JOHN R. ELLIOTT, Jr.

I

OF ALL the discoveries that have been made in recent years about medieval plays, the most important has been the discovery that they are plays for the stage. The old myth that mysteries and moralities were little better than crude mimings, clumsily acted by Bottom the Weaver on rickety hay-carts, has happily vanished from our textbooks. In its place has come the realization that these were exciting and sophisticated pieces of theatre, as skilfully suited to the kinds of stages for which they were written as were the plays of Marlowe and Shakespeare. Two works of scholarship in particular have aided in this realization. In *The Medieval Theatre in the Round* (1957) Richard Southern showed how intricate and absorbing a performance might have been in such a theatre as is depicted in the manuscript of *The Castle of Perseverance*, with its complex arrangement of mansions, platforms, and scenic emblems. And in *Early English Stages* (1959) Glynne Wickham documented the existence of an exciting variety of medieval staging methods, from the simple booth-stage and pageant-wagon, to the splendidly ornate theatres erected for royal tournaments and entertainments, and the Gothic magnificence of the Valenciennes Passion play stage. Modern revivals of a number of medieval plays before enthusiastic audiences have confirmed the judgment of the scholars, notably the productions of the York Cycle by E. Martin Browne at York and, more recently, the Cornish Cycle by Neville Denny at Piran Round in Cornwall.

The rediscovery of the medieval stage has already had important consequences on our understanding of the whole course of English theatrical history. It is, for example, becoming increasingly hard to think of the medieval theatre as something that had to be cleared away before the splendours of the Elizabethan stage could come into being. Far from springing full-blown from the mind of James Burbage in 1576, the Elizabethan public theatre, in its design and its stagecraft, shows a clear ancestry reaching back to the medieval rounds and playing-places. As Glynne Wickham has suggested, the dividing line between two eras of theatrical history is to be drawn, not between the Globe and the pageant-wagon, but between the Globe and the new Stuart Court theatres that followed it, paving the way for the even more radically different Restoration playhouses. As Wickham writes:

> Shakespeare's Globe and all other playhouses resembling it in architectural design are theatres which provide permanent homes for a stagecraft based on representation by formal symbols; the theatre of the Stuart Court Mask and the Restoration public playhouse has rejected this form of representation and is groping its way, however fitfully, towards the naturalism of actuality. From the Globe one can look backwards over the centuries and, in the *sepulchrum* of the liturgical *quem quaeritis* and in the *sedes* of later ceremonies, trace the beginnings of its stage conventions; but one cannot look forward. Its stage conventions do not develop; they are superseded.[1]

It is likely that in the future we shall 'look backwards' more and more to what is known about the medieval stage in order to illuminate what is obscure about the stage practice of Shakespeare and Marlowe. Here I simply wish to suggest a few of the ways in which this may be done. For the sake of brevity I will confine myself to an examination of a single type of staging problem that occurs in a number of different plays performed in the public playhouses during the late 1580s and 1590s.

By far the most numerous group of plays produced on the stages of the Elizabethan public theatres during these two decades were the history plays. This type of play has commonly been described as an Elizabethan invention, the product of Tudor nationalism and the Armada scare. History plays, however, in the form of the Scriptural cycles, had been popular in England for centuries before, and it seems clear that the secular history play of the Elizabethans was a direct

---

[1] Wickham, *EES*, Vol. II, Part 1, pp. 4–5.

offshoot of the traditional English taste for historical drama, coming into being only when the Scriptural histories of the Middle Ages ran foul of the Reformation censors. A glance at the chronological listings of play-titles from the 1530s to the 1590s in Harbage and Schoenbaum's *Annals of English Drama* confirms this judgment. During the decades of the 1530s and 40s, for example, Scriptural plays continued to be the dominant form of historical drama in England, despite the shifts in religious doctrine. For the 1530s we find, in addition to the ongoing performances of the medieval cycles, nineteen new plays on Scriptural subjects (most of them by John Bale), while only two are drawn from English history—both of them with a religious emphasis (Bale's *King John* and *Becket*). For the 1540s the proportions are even more one-sided: thirteen new Scriptural histories, by a variety of authors, and not a single play based on either English or classical history. In the 1550s—a decade of persistent censorship of controversial plays on politics and religion—we find few examples of either type: three new plays on Scriptural subjects (Udall's *Jacob and Essau*, Foxe's *Christus Triumphans*, and Wager's *Mary Magdalene*), none on secular historical subjects. In the 1560s, which saw the formation of a consistent government policy against religious drama, the balance begins to draw closer: four new Scriptural plays are listed (none of which have survived) and two on secular subjects. By the 1570s, which saw the final rooting-out of the traditional Scriptural plays in the north, the balance has definitely begun to swing to the other side: the figures are seven secular histories for one Scriptural play (written in Scotland). In the last two decades of the century the secular history play emerges triumphant. The figures for the 1580s are 20 : 2 in favour of the secular plays, both Scriptural plays being on Old Testament subjects. For the 1590s the ratio is an overwhelming 80 : 4, all the Scriptural plays again being on Old Testament subjects, with the single intriguing exception of a lost play on *Pontius Pilate*, possibly written by Dekker. The situation may be summarized in the table on p. 226.

It is clear from the inverse ratio shown by the chart that the Elizabethan history play did not suddenly spring into being, *sui generis*, in the last two decades of the century. Rather, it emerged gradually as a replacement for the traditional Biblical drama of the Middle Ages, coming into its own only when its illustrious ancestor had been formally laid to rest. We may surmise from this that, in some way that has as yet gone unnoticed, these plays continued to satisfy the same

'History' Plays: 1530–1600

	Scriptural Plays		Secular Plays	
	Number	Percentage of total 'History' Plays	Number	Percentage of total 'History' Plays
1530–40	19	90	2	10
1540–50	13	100	0	0
1550–60	3	100	0	0
1560–70	4	67	2	33
1570–80	1	13	7	87
1580–90	2	10	20	90
1590–1600	4	5	80	95

theatrical tastes which had once been catered for by 'miracles' and moralities. An idea of what these tastes were may be gleaned from the surviving description of the Passion Play performed at Valenciennes in northern France in 1547, which shows us more clearly than any surviving English document the mixture of piety and spectacle that went into such productions during the sixteenth century. As reported in D'Outreman's *Histoire de la Ville . . . de Valentiennes*, the spectators on that occasion witnessed:

> . . . strange things, full of wonder: the devices used for Paradise and Hell were altogether marvellous and capable of seeming to the audience like enchantments. There one could see Verity and the Angels and various other characters descending from on high, sometimes visible, at other times invisible, then suddenly becoming visible again. Lucifer rose out of Hell without anyone knowing how, riding on a dragon. Joseph's wand, from being dry and sterile, suddenly threw forth fruit and flowers; the souls of Herod and Judas were carried off into the air by devils; devils were expelled from bodies; afflicted persons were cured, all in a most wondrous manner. Here Jesus Christ was raised aloft by the devil, who crept the length of a wall more than forty feet high: there he became invisible: then he was transfigured on Mount Tabor. One could see water changed into wine, but so mysteriously that one could not believe it, and more than a hundred people in the audience wanted to taste this wine; the five loaves and two fishes were similarly multiplied and distributed to more than a thousand people: and yet there were twelve baskets left over. The fig-tree condemned by our Lord appeared dry and its leaves faded in an instant. The eclipse, the earth-

quake, the shattering of the rocks and the other miracles that occurred at the death of our Saviour were represented by yet new marvels.[2]

It is little wonder that such theatrical legerdemain continued to hold the attention of audiences long after the theology it served had theoretically been undermined by the new learning. Clearly any plays hoping to replace the Scriptural cycles in popular appeal would be obliged to match the scenic splendour of their predecessors. Moreover, it is precisely in their attempts to do so that we should expect to find evidence of the continuing influence of the older staging methods. The nearest equivalents in Elizabethan history plays of the flying machines, Hell-mouths, and miraculous *trompe-l'œils* of the Scriptural cycles were the battle scenes. Here the playwright had all the opportunity he needed to fill his stage with action and spectacle. A look at some of the staging requirements of battle scenes written during the 1580s and 90s suggests that when he did so, he had little hesitation in drawing upon the theatrical lessons of the past.

II

In Act I, scene 4 of Shakespeare's 1 *Henry VI*, for example, the English army lays siege to Orleans. The first characters to appear are, according to the Folio stage-directions, '*the Master Gunner of Orleance, and his boy*'. The Gunner tells the Boy that the English are 'in the suburbs close intrench'd', and calls his attention to 'yonder tower' from which the enemy is able to 'overpeer the city'. Together they place 'a piece of ordnance 'gainst' this tower and 'watch' for movements there. Salisbury and Talbot, the English captains, then enter, with other lords, '*on the Turrets*'. Salisbury tells his companions how he has been able to spy on the French 'through this secret grate' and invites them all to 'look in' in order to advise him on the best place to attack. As they are describing what they see ('the north gate', 'the bulwark of the bridge'), the French Boy produces a 'linstock', touches off his 'ordnance', and Salisbury is killed. Shakespeare's stage-direction reads: '*Here they shot, and Salisbury falls downe.*' A Messenger then arrives to

[2] D'Outreman, *Histoire de la Ville et comte de Valentiennes* (1639, p. 396; quoted by Élie Konigson, *La Représentation d'un mystère de la Passion à Valenciennes en 1547*, Éditions du Centre National de la Recherche Scientifique (Paris, 1969), p. 23 (my translation).

announce the approach of Joan La Pucelle towards the city to raise
the siege and the English make their exit.

So far in this scene we have a series of actions requiring, first, a
'tower' or 'turret' with a 'grate'; and, second, the walls of the city,
containing a 'gate' and at least one piece of 'ordnance', at some
distance from the 'tower'. The scenes that follow give further details
about these structures and how they are to be used. In the next scene,
Act I, scene 5, for example, a skirmish is fought before the gates of the
city, at first inconclusively. The stage-direction reads: '*Here an Alarum
againe, and Talbot pursueth the Dolphin, and driveth him: Then enter
Joane de Puzel, driving Englishmen before her.*' Talbot and Joan fight,
then there is an Alarum, the English retreat 'into [their] trenches',
and Joan '*enters the Towne with Souldiers*', only to appear a few lines
later 'on the Walls', where she plants her banners. At the beginning
of Act II a Sergeant places two Sentinels on guard, ordering them to
report 'any noise or soldier you perceive / Near to the walls'. Talbot
and his men then enter, '*with scaling Ladders*', Talbot urging his soldiers
to 'scale the flinty bulwarks'. The dialogue that follows makes it
clear that the English place their ladders in at least three different
positions along the walls:

> *Bedford*   Ascend, brave Talbot; we will follow thee.
>
> *Talbot*   Not all together. Better far, I guess,
>   That we do make our entrance several ways;
>   That, if it chance the one of us do fail,
>   The other yet may rise against their force.
>
> *Bedford*   Agreed. I'll to yond corner.
>
> *Burgundy*   And I to this.
>
> *Talbot*   And here will Talbot mount, or make his grave.
>
>   (II. 1. 28–34)

The walls of Orleans having been scaled, the sentinels are taken by
surprise and '*leape ore the walls in their shirts*'. As the English take the
city, the banqueting nobles, now roused from their beds '*halfe ready
and halfe unready*', also make their escape by 'leap[ing] o're the Walls',
then reappear by '*severall wayes*' to take 'refuge in the field'. As they
attempt to regroup their forces, an English soldier enters crying
'A Talbot! A Talbot!' and the French flee, 'leaving their clothes
behind'. The sequence ends with the English marching triumphantly

through the streets of Orleans to 'the market-place, / The middle centre of this cursed town', bearing the body of Salisbury for burial 'within their chiefest temple'. Orleans is taken.

What sort of a theatre, we may ask, is needed in order to stage this scene, and with what equipment at its disposal? Evidently we are dealing here with something more than 'poetic drama'. Shakespeare's verse may do much to stimulate our imagination, but it cannot fire a cannon, leap over walls, or scale a fortress. These things must be done by actors and they cannot be done without considerable help from what we would now call the set-designer, not to mention the special-effects man. If we turn to the conventional reconstructions of 'the Elizabethan stage', such as those hypothesized by John Cranford Adams or C. Walter Hodges, however, we shall be largely at a loss to know how Shakespeare's scenic requirements might have been met. In these reconstructions we have a bare platform, surrounded on three sides by a 'pit' full of 'groundlings', and backed by a tiring-house façade containing a curtained inner stage, an upper gallery, and (in Adams's version) two bay windows. The trouble with this theatre is not that it lacks sufficient space and variety of scenic locale to stage a scene like the siege of Orleans, but that it lacks the right space and variety. We may, if we try, visualize the French sentries jumping from the balcony to the fore-stage, but we shall then have to account for the peculiarity in the following scene of the English entering the 'middle centre' of the city whose forward walls they have just scaled at the rear of the stage. We can also, if we try even harder, imagine the French boy applying his linstock to a cannon sticking out of one bay window and firing it across at Salisbury in the other bay window, but we shall not in that case have anything that looks conceivably like a turret, much less a 'secret grate'. There is, in any case, grave doubt whether Adams's 'bay windows' ever existed in the Elizabethan theatre: according to recent investigations they appear—along with many other features of the Adams and Hodges reconstructions—to have originated no earlier than the Georgian theatres of the eighteenth century.[3]

[3] See Richard Hosley, 'The Origins of the So-called Elizabethan Multiple Stage', *The Drama Review* XII (1968), pp. 28–50. Wickham concludes that 'evidence of a factual kind to substantiate the idea that the galleries of the early playhouses ever accommodated . . . battle scenes is non-existent' (Wickham, *EES*, Vol. II, Part I, p. 321).

If even the most fanciful modern reconstructions of Shakespeare's theatre fail to meet the staging requirements of the Siege of Orleans, the contemporary rendering of this theatre contained in the famous Swan drawing raises even more questions. There we have a bare stage running flush against the tiring-house wall, without benefit of inner stage or alcove of any sort, with the exception of two doors leading to the interior of the tiring-house (see Plate 8). Above it is a gallery divided into six compartments, none of which, if we can believe De Witt's proportions, is wide enough to accommodate more than two people standing or sitting side-by-side at a time. The drawing, moreover, shows each of these compartments filled with spectators rather than with actors, who are shown only on the stage below. While the spectators might possibly have been cleared from the gallery for its use on special occasions as an acting area, the same objections apply as to Hodges's and Adams's galleries: there is no scenic localization, and little possibility of imitating a cannon-shot fired from one compartment to another, as all six compartments are on a flat plane against the tiring-house wall.

Clearly something else is needed on this stage in order to perform such a scene as the Siege of Orleans, something that was not a permanent part of the architecture of the theatre. What this 'something' was becomes clear as soon as we look back at the methods by which siege scenes had traditionally been staged in the pre-Shakespearian theatre. Such scenes in medieval entertainments were both frequent and spectacular. Whether they occurred in plays, tournaments, or commemorative re-enactments of actual sieges made little difference in the manner of their staging. As Wickham has shown, portable scenic furniture, generally made of wooden frames covered with canvas and painted to resemble stone or brick, served for castles, towers, city walls, trenches, and any other military architecture that might be needed for the entertainment. One of the most detailed descriptions of a medieval mock-siege comes from the court of Charles V of France, where in 1378 a play on *The Siege of Jerusalem* was given before an audience of 800 knights in the King's banquet hall. A ship full of men was wheeled into the hall up to a large platform. On the other side appeared the 'city of Jerusalem', replete with Saracen minarets, 'battlements, walls and towers'—one of which was so high 'that the men on the top nearly reached the beams of the hall'. Along the walls the Saracens gathered, 'equipped for battle in defence of the city'. The ship then drew up to the side of the city, the Crusaders disembarked and scaled the walls with scaling-ladders. (A chronicler remarked that it was 'very amusing' when some of them fell down.) After throwing the Saracens over the walls, the Crusaders retired, the 'entremés' (pageants) were wheeled out of the hall, and the banquet proceeded.[4]

A commemorative re-enactment, accomplished by much the same methods, was also performed in the city of Orleans itself. Called 'The Siege of Orleans' and referred to as a *'mistère'*, it was produced annually during the years 1435–70 on the anniversary of the actual siege on 8 May 1429, to commemorate the liberation of the city from the 'goddams' (*'godons'*)—Joan of Arc's contemptuous name for the English. City records report payments for building platforms and towers; stage-directions indicate not only that great battles were to be fought but that parts of the town were to go up in flames. Despite the secular nature of the subject, use was found for a Paradise mansion presumably left over from a previously performed Biblical play.[5] Even more like Shakespeare's scene was a mock-siege held in Zaragoza in 1414 which involved two castles, the men inside using siege-engines to fire missiles into a 'town' constructed of wood (the missiles were made of leather stuffed with wadding and were said to be 'as big as a boy's head').[6]

Siege scenes in dramatic entertainments undoubtedly originated in commemorative mock-sieges like those at Orleans and Zaragoza, and from them derived their high degree of realism. It is doubtful whether any theatrical siege-mansion ever attained the grandeur of the one described by Froissart in a re-enactment of *The Siege of Troy* at Paris in 1389. There the city of Troy was represented by 'a castle built on a square frame, forty foot high and twenty foot square; it had four

---

[4] Wickham, *EES*, Vol. I, p. 213. The manuscript illumination depicting this play has been reproduced in L. H. Loomis, 'Secular Dramatics in the Royal Palace, Paris, 1378, 1389, and Chaucer's "Tregetoures"', *Speculum* XXXIII (1958), pp. 242–55, and (in colour) in Bamber Gascoigne, *World Theatre* (London, 1968), Plate XI.

[5] Gustave Cohen, *Etudes d'Histoire du Théâtre en France au Moyen Age et la Renaissance* (Paris, 1956), pp. 181–200. The text has been published by F. Guessard and E. de Certain, eds., *Le Mistère du Siége d'Orléans* (Paris, 1862). I am indebted to Mr. Max Harris for calling this reference to my attention.

[6] N. D. Shergold, *A History of the Spanish Stage* (Oxford, 1967), pp. 116–117, quoting from MS. Esp. 104 in the Bibliothèque Nationale.

towers, one on each corner, and another, higher tower placed in the middle . . . and this castle moved on four wheels, subtly concealed within'.[7] But even in popular English religious drama sieges could be staged with a high degree of authenticity. The ground-plan for *The Castle of Perseverance*, for example, shows a two-storey, three-dimensional, crenellated tower in the middle of the round, capable of holding the weight of several actors at a time. The text of the play describes the castle as being 'high' (1803, 1818) and made of 'stone' (2042). The fact that it is three times referred to as a 'castel town' (2015, 2157, 2316) and once as having a 'wall' (2030) may indicate that in addition to the castle itself there was a walled rampart surrounding it, like the scenic units used in the French sieges of Jerusalem, Troy and Orleans. (Shrift pointedly assures Mankind that it is 'stronger than any castle in France'.) During the siege of the Castle of Perseverance at least eight different characters are stationed on its tower at once—the Seven Virtues and Mankind. They are attacked by the Seven Deadly Sins, who employ the familiar tactics of besieging armies. The stage-directions inform us that Belial carries barrels of gunpowder, Anger wields a cross-bow, Flesh brandishes a 'schot' and 'slynge', while Gluttony, Lechery and Sloth all bear lances with which they hope to skewer one of the holy ladies. At least one of the attackers, Flesh, approaches the castle on horseback (1940). When Gluttony reaches the castle, he sets fire to the gunpowder in an effort to smoke the defenders out. Sloth attempts to dry up the moat surrounding the castle by shovelling out the water with his spade (2329).[8] While scaling-ladders are not mentioned by name, the dialogue indicates that the attackers attempt to 'come alofte' (2142), and physical contact between the siegers and the besieged clearly takes place. A stage-direction reads 'Here they will fight for a long time' ('*Tunc pugnabunt diu*'), after which Pride complains that 'I am beaten in the head'. While the purely symbolic missiles which the Virtues hurl at the attackers may appear to diminish the physical realism of the scene, the effect on the besiegers is rendered painfully enough, and the defenders' aim is none too decorous. Anger complains that he is 'beaten black and blue'

[7] Quoted and translated by Wickham, *EES*, Vol. I, pp. 213–14.

[8] On the probable existence of a moat surrounding the castle, see Natalie Crohn Schmitt, 'Was There a Medieval Theatre in the Round?', *Theatre Notebook* XXIII (1969), pp. 130–42 and XXIV (1969), pp. 18–24, challenging Southern's assumption that the moat was outside the banks of the theatre.

by Patience's roses (2220), Chastity empties a bucket of water on Lechery's head, and Industry's flying beads cause Sloth to cry out for water 'where I may my ballokys bathe' (2388, 2403). The strength of the invisible grace of God is made all the more graphic to the audience for its success in withstanding the visible weapons of Sin.

Mock-sieges of the kind employed so entertainingly in *The Castle of Perseverance* continued to be performed in much the same way, both inside and outside the theatre, throughout the sixteenth century. Court masks and tournaments provided the most usual setting. A secularized version of *The Castle of Perseverance* siege, for example, was staged as a compliment to Queen Elizabeth at Whitehall in 1581, in which the 'Foster Children of Desire' attempted to scale the 'Fortress of Beauty'. The besiegers entered the tilt-yard in a portable trench, constructed from 'a frame of wood, which was covered with canvas, and painted outwardly in such excellent order, as if it had bene very naturall earth or moulde, and carried the name of a Rowling trench, which went on wheeles, which way soever the persons within did drive it'. On top of this contraption were 'two cannons of wood', painted to resemble 'two fayre fielde pieces of ordinances'. When they had emerged from their 'trench', the besiegers produced 'pretie scaling-ladders' and proceeded to throw 'floures and such fansies against the wals, with all such devises as might seeme fit shot for Desire'.[9] A similar entertainment staged at Warwick in 1572 involved a pair of castles which 'shot' at each other in much the same way that Shakespeare specifies in *Henry VI*.

> There was devised a fort made of slender tymber coverid with canvas. In this fort were appointid divers persons to serve as soldiers, some others appointid to caste out fire-woorks, as squibbes and balles of fyre. Against that fort was another castlewise prepared of like strength . . . Between thies forts or against them were placid certen battering-pieces, to the nomber of twelve or fourteen, brought from London, and twelve faire chambers or mortyr-pieces, brought also from the Towre . . . Thies pieces and chambers were by traines [i.e. fuses] fyred, and so made a great noise as though it had bene a sore assault . . . they in the fort shoting agayn, and casting out divers fyers . . .[10]

[9] John Nichols, *The Progresses and Public Processions of Queen Elizabeth* (London, 1823), Vol. II, pp. 315, 319.

[10] *Ibid.*, Vol. I, p. 319.

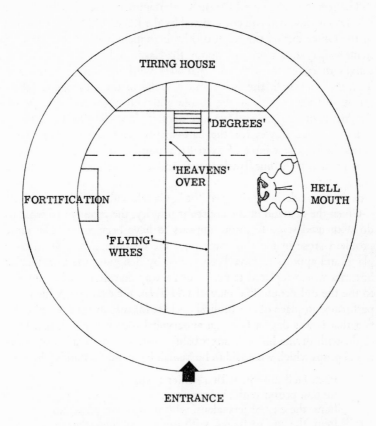

TIRING HOUSE

'DEGREES'

'HEAVENS'
OVER

FORTIFICATION

HELL
MOUTH

'FLYING'
WIRES

ENTRANCE

Fig. 5 (opposite). Neville Denny's reconstruction of an Elizabethan playhouse as it might have been prepared for a production of Wagner's *Death of Faustus*. Angels, according to this concept, could have been 'flown' on cables anchored to principal beams and strung across the pit, and a 'Heavens' cloth hung across a section of it. Scenic units of the kind depicted would be prefabricated and collapsible, though the *Wagner Book* seems to call for their location at either side of a platform stage, not confronting each other across an otherwise bare *platea*.

Fig. 6 (above). Plan of an Elizabethan playhouse as it might have been prepared for a production of Wagner's *Death of Faustus* (Neville Denny's reconstruction).

The scenic devices used for such entertainments were, as Wickham has shown, designed and constructed by the Revels Office. The records of the Office during the reign of Elizabeth include payments for such items as 'payntars workinge uppon the Castle and lynen drappars ffor canvas to cover yt with all', 'payntars workinge divers Cities and Townes', 'a castell, the Rock and churche in the Castle, the pillers Arcatrye frize cornish & the Roofe gilt with golde and ffine silver, the Armes of England and ffraunce upon it', 'a scalling Ladder', 'ffurre poles to make Rayles for the battlements', and, for plays given at court during the winter of 1580–81, a number of 'citties' (including 'one great citty'), four 'battlements', and a 'pallace'. As far as military architecture goes, the most intriguing item in the Revels accounts is a payment made in April 1581, for 'a Castell with ye falling sydes'.[11]

Given the demand of the court for novelty, the problem of what to do with used stage furniture appears to have been acute. The same problem arose in the provinces with the dissolution of the miracle plays, and appears to have been solved by designing the new secular histories which replaced them in such a way that they could continue to use the old props. The play of *Old Tobit*, for example, which was performed in place of the Biblical cycle at Lincoln in 1564, despite the fact that it was drawn from an apocryphal romance which had little to do with divine history, improbably made use of an array of traditional props which were said to be 'remaining in St. Swithin's Church':

> First, Hell mouth, with a nether chap.
> Item, a prison with a covering . . .
> Item, the city of Jerusalem, with towers and pinacles.
> Item, the city of Rages, with towers and pinnacles.
> Item, the city of Nineveh.
> Item, the King's palace of Nineveh . . .
> Item, a firmament, with a fiery cloud and a double cloud.[12]

It is likely that *The Destruction of Jerusalem*, performed in Coventry in place of the normal cycle in 1584, made similar use of Coventry's scenic treasures. Wickham has suggested that the solution of the Revels Office to this problem was to give or sell its cast-off furniture

[11] Albert Feuillerat, ed., *Documents relating to the Office of the Revels in the time of Queen Elizabeth* (Louvain, 1908), pp. 116, 117, 158, 307, 327, 336 and 345.

[12] This is only a partial list. The full inventory is given in Wickham, *EES*, Vol. I, p. 246.

to the professional acting companies. However they got them, we know from Henslowe's Inventory that the public companies were well supplied with structures of the sort that we have been describing, many of them identical to those listed in the Revels accounts. In 1598, for example, Henslowe reported that the Admiral's Men possessed, among other things, a rock, a cage, a tomb, a Hell-mouth, a 'payer of stayers for Fayeton', 'the sittie of Rome', and a 'Whell and Frame in the Sege of London'.[13]

III

How, and how much, these properties were used on the Elizabethan stage is uncertain. One surviving document, however, graphically describes not only what Elizabethan stage-structures looked like but how they may have been used in actual performance. This is the so-called 'English Wagner Book' of 1594.[14] The 'English Wagner Book' is an anonymous series of tales about the adventures of Wagner, Faustus's servant, after the death of his master. In Chapter 8, Wagner shows off his magical powers by 'staging' the 'Tragedy of Doctor Faustus . . . in the ayre, acted in the presence of a thousand people of Wittenberg'. The performance takes place on a fine spring day when the people of Wittenberg are gathered in a 'meadow' near the River Elbe 'to behold certaine matches for the Garland who could drinke most, and also to see a match shotte at a pair of Buts with Harquebushiers'. In place of this contest, Wagner unexpectedly produces a stage-play enacted in an 'excellent faire Theator' in the sky. Apparition or not, the account of the play that follows, the author assures us, contains nothing but what 'in the like houses either use or necessity makes common'. The description of the theatre comes first:

> On a sodaine there was seene a maruailous bright and glorious Raynebow, spreading the wide armes ouer the wide World, and streight was there hard a noise of Trumpets, soundinge a short florish, and then another, and by and by another all alike short, at the which the assembly was wonderously affeard, and listned, desirous to see the effect of this wonder and straunge miracle, some of them fell to their *Aue maries* lustely, thinkinge that the vniuersall Doome had been at that instant, as thus they behold with admiration,

[13] *Henslowe's Diary*, ed. R. A. Foakes and R. T. Rickert (Cambridge, 1961), pp. 319–20.
[14] '*The Second Report of Dr. J. Faustus with the end of Wagner's Life*', Stationer's Register 1594 (Bodelian, Douce MM 475).

they might distinctly perceiue a goodlye Stage to be reard (shining
to sight like the bright burnish golde) vppon many a faire Pillar
of clearest Cristall, whose feete rested vppon the Arch of the broad
Rayne bow; therein was the high Throne wherein the King should
sit, and that prowdly placed with two and twenty degrees to the
top, and round about curious wrought chaires for diuerse other
Potentates, there might you see the ground-worke at the one end of
the Stage whereout the personated dieuls should enter in their fiery
ornaments, made like the broad wide mouth of an huge Dragon,
which with continuall armies of smoake and flame breathed forth
his angry stomackes rage, round about the eies grew haires not so
horrible as men call brissels, but more horrible as long and stiffe
speares, the teeth of this Hels mouth far out stretching, and such as
a man might well call monstrous, and more then a man can by
wordes signifie: to be short his hew of that colour which to himself
means sorrow, & to others ministers like passion: a thicke lampe
blacke, blacker than any paint, any Hell, blacker then it owne selfe.
At the other end in opposition was seene the place where in the
bloudlesse skirmishes are so often perfourmed on the Stage, the Wals
(not so pleasaunt as old wiues would haue their tales addorned with)
of Pasty crust, but Iron attempered with the most firme steel, which
being brightly filed shone as beautifully ouer the whole place as the
Pale shininge Cynthia, enuironed with high and stately Turrets of
the like mettall and beautye, and hereat many in-gates and out-gates:
out of each side lay the bended Ordinaunce, shewing at their wide
hollowes the crueltye of death: out of sundry loopes many large
Banners and Streamers were pendant, brieflye nothing was there
wanting that might make it a faire Castle. There might you see to
be short the Gibbet, the Posts, the Ladders, the tiring house, there
euery thing which in the like houses either vse or necessity makes
common. Now aboue all was there the gay Clowdes *Vsque quaque*
adorned with the heauenly firmament, and often spotted with
golden teares which men call Stars. There was liuely portrayed the
whole Imperiall Army of the faire heauenly inhabitauntes, the bright
Angels, and such whose names to declare in so vile a matter were too
impious and sacrilegious. They were so naturally done that you
would haue sworne it had beene Heauen it self or the Epitome of it,
or some second Heauen, and a new Heauen it was, from thence
like dewy drops wherein the Sun layes his golden shine, making
them to appeare like small golden teares, the sweete odours and
comforting liquor streamde, and seemde alwaies to raine from thence
but they neuer fell, but kept a beaten path from downe on high

wherein the descending Angell might reioyce. I should be too long if I should expresse this rare Stage, especially in such sort and such like words as the like occasion in a more worthy subject would require, but of necessity we must barely apply our descriptions to the nature of the whole History.

So much of the passage was quoted by Chambers,[15] who cautioned that it may only have been a 'fantasy'. There is, however, nothing in the 'Wagner Book' description that cannot be paralleled in the Revels accounts or Henslowe's Inventory. The throne placed at the top of a flight of stairs ('degrees') recalls Henslowe's entry for 'i payer of stayers for Fayeton'. Hell-mouths, walls with 'high and stately turrets', and 'bended Ordinaunce' are common entries in both the Revels accounts and the list of properties belonging to the Admiral's Men. As for the 'Gibbet', we know that Henslowe employed one for a play called *Absalom* in 1602, the entry in his Diary reading: 'pd. for poleyes & worckmanshipp for to hange absalome . . . xiiiid.' Ladders, i.e. scaling-ladders, have been mentioned above in connection with the Revels accounts. The description of 'the heavenly firmament, spotted with golden tears', may be compared with Hamlet's reference to the Heavens as 'this brave o'erhanging firmament, this majestical roof . . . fretted with golden fire'. Even the 'rainbow', which appears to be a purely imaginary detail, is listed as a property by Henslowe.[16]

The remainder of the passage—which Chambers failed to quote—tells us how the actors used this impressive scenery in their play. It will perhaps not come as a surprise to discover that the principal action of the play is a siege:

But now this excellent faire Theator erected, immediatly after the third sound of the Trumpets, there entreth in the Prologue attired in a blacke vesture, and making his three obeysances, began to shew the argument of that Scenicall Tragedy, but because it was so far off they could not vnderstand the wordes, and hauing thrice bowed himselfe to the high Throne, presently vanished. Then out of this representaunce of Hels mouth, issued out whole Armies of fiery flames, and moste thicke foggy smoakes, after which entred in a great batell of footemen Diuels, all armed after the best fashion with pike &c, marching after the stroake of the couragious Drum, who girded about laid siege to this faire Castle, on whose Wals after the summons *Faustus* presented himselfe vppon the battelments, armed

15 *ES*, Vol. III, p. 71.
16 *Henslowe's Diary*, p. 320. The entry for 'Absolome' occurs on p. 217

with a great number of Crosses, pen and incke hornes, charmes, characters, seales, periapts &c. who after sharpe words defied the whole assembly, seeming to speake earnestly in his owne defence, and as they were ready to reare the Ladders, and *Faustus* hadde begun to prepare for the counterbattery, determining to throw downe vppon the assemblies heads so many heauy charmes and coniurations, that they should fall downe halfe way from the ascendant, whilst these things began to waxe whot from the afore-sayd Heauen, there descended a Legion of bright Angels ridinge vppon milke white Chariots, drawn with the like white steeds, who with celestiall diuine melody came into the Towre, to the intent to fight for the Doctor against his furious enemies, but he wanting pay-money, and voide in deede of all good thoughts not able to abide their most blessed presence sent them away, and they returned from whence they came, sorrowfully lamenting his most wilful obstinacy, whilst he had all be nointed the Wals with holy Water, and painted with Bloud many a crimson Crosse. At length the Alarme was giuen, and the Ladders cleaude to the Wals, vp the assaylants climbde, vppe they lifted their fearefull weapons. *Faustus* not able (destitute of helpe) to withstand them was taken prisoner, and his towre down rased to the earth, with whose fall both the large Heauen and World shooke and quaked mightely, whom when they had fettered they left ther, they marching out and the forenamed Chaires were presently occupied with all the Imperiall rulers of Hell, who clothed in their holyday apparel sat there to giue Judgement vppon this willfull *Faustus*, whom two Hangmans of Hell vnloosed, and there in presence of them all the great diuell afore his chiefe peeres, first stamping with his angry foote, and then shaking his great bushe of hair, that therewith he made the neare places and the most proud Diuels courages to tremble, and with his fire burnt scepter, and his like coloured Crown, all of gold, setting one arme by his side, and the other vppon the pummell of his Chaire, shooke a prettye space with such angry fury, that the flames which pro-ceeded from his frightful eyes did dim the sight of the Witteber[ger]s beeloe.

None of the actions involved here—with the possible exception of the descent of the angels in chariots drawn by 'Milkewhite steeds'—would have been difficult to execute on the stage that the author has described, or in any large-scale European theatre of the previous two hundred years. The razing of Faustus's castle, for example, might have been accomplished by some such device as 'the Castle with ye falling sydes' mentioned in the Revels accounts. Even the angelic descent requires no more complicated flying machinery than that used at Valenciennes in 1547, or than is called for in the manuscript of the York cycle. As for the siege of Dr. Faustus's castle by his 'furious' enemies, it follows the familiar pattern of dramatic mock-sieges reaching back to *The Castle of Perseverance* and beyond.

At this point in the narrative the author inserts a long digression about a young virgin in the audience who fell into a swoon at the sight of the Devil, and about the miraculous cure devised for her by a Doctor. During this digression the author seems to forget that the performance is taking place in the air and to conceive of it instead as taking place in an ordinary outdoor round playing-place. Upon the recovery of the girl he describes how her parents determined to 'cause to be unaccesable the place wherein their daughter was thus scared' and proceeded to 'compass it with a high wall' and to 'overthrow the banckes'. The author then returns to his description of the performance, which ends with Faustus jumping 'down headlong of the stage' pursued by 'the whole company'. Actors and stage both vanish, and the audience make their way fearfully home.

IV

With the help of the 'Wagner Book' description we may now suggest the methods by which siege and battle scenes appear to have been carried out on the Elizabethan stage at least as late as 1594. Portable scenic furniture, moving on wheels, served to represent castles, towers, city walls, or trenches. The units were three-dimensional and capable of withstanding the weight of several actors. They were made, as Wickham has shown in considerable detail, by wrapping canvas around a wooden frame, painting the canvas in position, then dismantling the whole assembly for transport or storage—the same method which we know had been used to construct the mansions of the medieval miracle plays and moralities in previous centuries.[17] In performance, assaults on these mansions could be made by means of scaling-ladders; 'ordinance' could be placed on top of turrets or walls and fired; 'falling sides' could reveal the interior of a town or castle once it had been captured or destroyed; and the whole unit could be removed once the scene was over to make room for the next scenic

[17] See Wickham, *EES*, Vol. I, 174–5 and 282–9.

locale that might be needed. The figures furnished by the Revels accounts indicate that several such units may often have been used in a single play. At Christmas time in 1582–3, for example, the Office furnished six plays with thirteen scenic units covering in total an area of some 2,800 square feet per play—or more than twice the floor space available in any Tudor banquet hall or Elizabethan public stage. Clearly all these units cannot have been on stage at any one time.[18]

The staging of Shakespeare's Siege of Orleans appears to fall clearly within this tradition. Two mansions are required for the scene, one for the 'walls' of the city and one for the 'turret' in the suburbs, since action occurs simultaneously in both these locales. The walls, we may surmise, were painted to look like flint-stone ('Let us resolve to scale their flinty bulwarks'), and they were positioned close enough to the front of the platform-stage for the French sentries to make their escape by jumping off the back as the English attacked from the front. At least two corners of the walls were visible to the audience, possibly three ('I'll to yond corner', 'I to this', 'And here will Talbot mount'), and at least two gates are visible, for Gargrave proposes to aim his gun at 'the north gate, for there stand lords', and Glansdale to aim his at 'the bulwark of the bridge'. One of the gates must have been operable, to admit Joan la Pucelle into the city. Once it was captured by the English, the walls were possibly let down to reveal 'the middle centre of this cursed town'. Whether the same unit was later used for the scenes requiring the cities of Rouen, Bordeaux and Angiers, or whether separate units were available for each, we cannot tell. It is worth noting that the Lincoln *Old Tobit* had separate mansions for the cities of Jerusalem, Rages and Nineveh; but the public playhouses may have exercised greater economy than this.

As for the 'turret' occupied by the English army, we may surmise that it was high enough to 'overpeer the city' and that it contained a 'grate' by which the English could do so. The grate may have exploded by means of a fuse when the French boy touched his 'linstock' to the 'ordnance', or an actual missile may have been fired from the walls to the turret—a city proclamation in 1574 complained that 'soundry slaughters and mayhemminges of the Quenes Subjectes have happened . . . by engynes, weapons, and pouder used in plaies'.[19]

---

[18] For the figures, see Wickham, *EES*, Vol. II, Part 1, p. 288.

[19] William Archer and W. J. Lawrence, 'The Playhouse', in *Shakespeare's England*, ed. Walter Raleigh (Oxford, 1916), Vol. II, p. 284.

Whether the 'trenches' referred to by Talbot were also a part of the siege-scenery, somewhere in the vicinity of the turret, or simply to be imagined offstage, must remain conjectural.

On the matter of precisely where these scenic units were placed in the theatre we can be less certain. The evidence of the 'English Wagner Book' indicates that when two scenic units were required for the same scene (in its case, Hellmouth and a castle), they were placed at opposite 'ends' of the stage. ('There might you see the ground-worke *at the one end* of the Stage whereout the personated divels should enter . . . *at the other end in opposition* was seene the place where in the bloudless skirmishes are so often performed on the Stage.') Yet we may wonder whether this positioning would serve Shakespeare's purposes in *Henry VI*. The dimensions of the platform-stage of the public playhouses have been reckoned at approximately 25 by 45 feet, or 1,125 square feet. A turret and a city wall large enough to accommodate the number of actors specified by Shakespeare must have taken up at least a third of this space, if not more.[20] Whether sufficient room would have been left on the platform for the numerous skirmishes and mêlées between the English and French armies is problematical. The French are said, in a stage-direction, to suffer 'great loss', implying a sizable number of actors in these scenes. In addition we may observe that, even if enough space were left on the stage, placing the mansions at opposite ends of the platform does not furnish the right *kind* of space for the action that Shakespeare has conceived. The turret is described as being 'in the suburbs', not a few paces away. The French must enter the city gates but then make an exit from the rear when they are surprised by the English scalers. The English must make their ascent in at least three different places along the wall, which implies that the long side of the wall must face outward, towards the audience, rather than sideways, towards the opposite 'end' of the stage. Most importantly, the triumphal procession of the English, if it is to take place 'in the middle centre' of the town, must not be shunted off incongruously to the extreme side of the stage.

A possible explanation of these difficulties is that one of the scenic units—probably the turret—was placed in the yard, or 'pit'. Such an arrangement would obviate most if not all of the difficulties involved in stationing the 'mansions' on opposite ends of the stage, and leave

[20] See the sample figures on the dimensions of scenic units given by Wickham, *EES*, Vol. II, Part 1, pp. 288–9.

plenty of room for skirmishing. It would also, we may note, bring the Elizabethan theatre into approximate conformity with the ground-plan of *The Castle of Perseverance*—a round arena with a scaffold on the perimeter, a neutral '*platea*' in front of it (De Witt's name for the pit is, significantly, '*planities*', or 'plain'), and, in the centre, a scenic emblem riveting the attention of the audience.

We are, of course, conditioned to thinking of the yard as an area for spectators only, chiefly by reason of Hamlet's famous reference to the 'groundlings'. De Witt's drawing of the Swan, however, shows no spectators in the yard, though they are shown in the gallery above the stage. Hamlet's remark gives no indication that the 'ground-lings' stood in the yard, only that they stood. They may equally well have stood, as F. E. Halliday has suggested, at ground level beneath the galleries, at the rear of the house.[21] No definite indication that spectators actually occupied the yard exists before 1609, when Dekker described the unmannerly crew who took pleasure in jeering at the actors at close range ('Neither are you to be hunted from there [i.e. the stage] though the Scar-crows in the yard hoot at you'). At what point between 1576 and 1609 the practice of placing spectators in the yard became usual we cannot know for sure. If, as Wickham has concluded, Burbage's procedure in building the Theatre was simply to place a traditional booth-stage within a circular arena, modelled on the bull and bear-baiting pits, it is not unreasonable to suppose that he would have perpetuated the medieval practice of using the entire space of the arena—or as much of it as he profitably could—as his acting area. That this was the traditional style of medieval theatre in the round is verified by the surviving pictorial evidence, such as Fouquet's miniatures of *The Martyrdom of St. Apollonia* and *The Rape of the Sabines*, which show spectators confined to tiered seats or booths erected along the perimeter of the round, with the central *platea* reserved for the actors.[22] Such outdoor round theatres, far

[21] F. E. Halliday, *The Legend of the Rood* (London, 1955), pp. 36–9.

[22] See Plate 4. The 'Rape of the Sabines' has been reproduced in Richard Hosley, 'Three Kinds of Outdoor Theatre Before Shakespeare', *Theatre Survey* XII (1971), pp. 1–33 and in Klaus G. Perls, *Jean Fouquet* (London, Paris and New York, 1940), Plate 253.

Southern's conjecture that spectators stood in pie-shaped wedges throughout the platea, kept in order by 'stytelers', is supported neither by the medieval pictorial evidence nor by the experience of modern productions. The recon-struction of the Cornish cycle by the Bristol University Drama Depart-from being outmoded relics of a distant past, were still being constructed in England during Burbage's lifetime. At least one of them, the 'game-place' recently discovered in the village of Walsham-le-Willows, Suffolk, was in use as a theatre in an area where Burbage is known to have acted before coming to London.[23] Allardyce Nicoll has cited stage-directions from a number of plays produced in the public playhouses between 1589 and 1602 calling for processional entrances at the 'ends' of the stage rather than through the tiring-house doors.[24] A number of other plays cited by Nicoll, dating from after 1599, require similar processional entrances but fail to specify entrance at the 'ends', suggesting the tentative conclusion that the practice of filling the yard with spectators may date from around the year 1600. It is tempting to identify the practice with the opening of the Globe.

Whatever the truth of this suggestion may be, it is clear that the Elizabethan theatre looked—in practice—a good deal more like its medieval forebears than we have usually imagined. Battlements, towers and castles of the sort indicated in 1 *Henry VI* are required in numerous plays written during the 1580s and 90s.[25] As a further sample in the Shakespearian canon we may mention the Flint Castle scene in *Richard II*. When Bolingbroke approaches the castle with his army, for instance, young Percy tells him that 'King Richaid lies / Within the limits of yon lime and stone'. That limestone castles had been a speciality of English scene-designers for at least a century we know

---

ment in Piran Round, Cornwall, revealed that the entire *platea* was needed to accommodate the action of the play. Overflow crowds were occasionally seated about the perimeter of the *platea*, below the tiered seats; if they had stood up they would have blocked the view of those sitting on the banks. This practice is shown in Fouquet's miniatures. Southern's 'stytelers' may have been the stage-managers, with their prompt-books and batons, shown by Fouquet standing in the middle of the Place, or the 'conveyors'—i.e. Kabuki-style stagehands—mentioned in the stage-directions of the Cornish *Creation of the World*.

[23] See Kenneth M. Dodd, 'Another Elizabethan Theatre in the Round'. *Shakespeare Quarterly* XXI (1970), pp. 125–56, with photographs.

[24] 'Passing Over the Stage', *Shakespeare Survey* XII (1959), pp. 47–55.

[25] Some non-Shakespearian plays requiring scenic architecture for battle and siege scenes are: Greene's *James IV* (1590), the anonymous *Siege of London* (c. 1594), Dekker's *Troilus and Cressida* (1599), the anonymous *Samson* (1602) and Middleton's *Family of Love* (c. 1602).

from the description of the 'mansion' prepared for Katherine of Aragon's royal entrance into London in 1501: 'batilments of tymber covered and leyed over with canvas empeynted like frestone and whight lyme, so that the semys of the stone were perceyved like as mortur or sement had ben betwene'.[26] As Shakespeare's scene continues, Bolingbroke commands Northumberland to 'go to the rude ribs of that ancient castle', whereupon King Richard enters 'on the Walls'. While they are talking there, Bolingbroke marches with his forces 'upon the grassy carpet of this plain', the strength of his army visible to Richard 'from his castle's tatter'd battlements' (III. 3 25–62). In Holinshed there is no mention of a 'plain'; was Shakespeare possibly thinking of De Witt's *planities* here? Wherever Bolingbroke is stationed, the castle remains an indispensable prop. The climax of the scene is Richard's descent from the battlements to the 'base-court', in full view of the audience. (The Folio gives no directions for an 'exit above' and re-entry 'below', as most modern editions do.) As he comes down, Shakespeare's verse makes a poetic symbol out of the piece of stage-carpentry—Henslowe's 'i payer of stayers for Fayeton'— that has made this dramatic moment possible:

> Down, down I come, like glist'ring Phaeton,
> Wanting the manage of unruly jades.

(III. 3. 178–9)

Precisely what the original performances of these and other plays with similar requirements were like we may never be able to reconstruct with certainty. Much further study is obviously necessary. But that they consisted of no more than 'two boards and a passion'—as most scholars continue to believe—is a myth that we may probably lay to rest. No playwright inheriting the sophisticated stagecraft of the Middle Ages would have condescended to write for such a stage, nor would he willingly have done without the scenic devices which it offered him. An open stage, yes; a naked stage, no!

[26] Quoted in Wickham, *EES*, Vol. I, p. 101 (my italics).

Index

[*This index excludes information given in the Preface, Notes and footnotes.*]

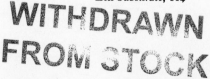